THE ELEMENTS OF ARGUMENTS

THE ELEMENTS OF ARGUMENTS

AN INTRODUCTION TO CRITICAL THINKING AND LOGIC

Philip Turetzky

broadview press

BROADVIEW PRESS – www.broadviewpress.com
Peterborough, Ontario, Canada

Founded in 1985, Broadview Press remains a wholly independent publishing house. Broadview's focus is on academic publishing; our titles are accessible to university and college students as well as scholars and general readers. With over 600 titles in print, Broadview has become a leading international publisher in the humanities, with world-wide distribution. Broadview is committed to environmentally responsible publishing and fair business practices.

The interior of this book is printed on 100% recycled paper.

Library and Archives Canada Cataloguing in Publication

Title: The elements of arguments : an introduction to critical thinking and logic / Philip Turetzky.
Names: Turetzky, Philip, 1949- author.
Description: Includes bibliographical references.
Identifiers: Canadiana 20190049235 | ISBN 9781554814077 (softcover)
Subjects: LCSH: Logic—Textbooks. | LCSH: Critical thinking—Textbooks. | LCGFT: Textbooks.
Classification: LCC BC71 .T87 2019 | DDC 160—dc23

Broadview Press handles its own distribution in North America:
PO Box 1243, Peterborough, Ontario K9J 7H5, Canada
555 Riverwalk Parkway, Tonawanda, NY 14150, USA
Tel: (705) 743-8990; Fax: (705) 743-8353
email: customerservice@broadviewpress.com

Distribution is handled by Eurospan Group in the UK, Europe, Central Asia, Middle East, Africa, India, Southeast Asia, Central America, South America, and the Caribbean. Distribution is handled by Footprint Books in Australia and New Zealand.

 Broadview Press acknowledges the financial support of the Government of Canada for our publishing activities.

Book Design by Em Dash Design

PRINTED IN CANADA

This book is dedicated to the memory of Ron G. Williams, Dan Lyons, and Leroy Meyer, from whom I learned so much about critical thinking and logic.

CONTENTS

___

INTRODUCTION FOR STUDENTS

"A great many people think they are thinking when they are merely rearranging their prejudices."—William James

We often come to judgments about and understanding of ourselves and the world we live in by means of habits, impulses, and instinct. However, while these grounds for judgment may sometimes guide us correctly, they often lead us into unforeseen difficulties and outright disastrous situations. Such difficulties often occur when our well-being depends on knowing what is true and what is false. We are fortunate that we can also turn to our ability to reason, to analyze and evaluate arguments: reasoning gives us more reliable methods for sorting out what is true from what is false, and so for arriving at judgments that are more likely to be true.

Most people reason well some of the time, but without sufficiently reflective thought about how to reason, they often go astray. Critical thinking studies ways to nurture our reasoning powers to make them more reliable by becoming more self-consciously clear and reflective about how to use these powers. Hence, critical thinking aims explicitly and overtly at analyzing and evaluating arguments in order to sort out what is true from what is false. Critical thinking examines patterns and methods of reasoning in order to discover which are successful at arriving at true judgments. In doing so, it applies the principles and concepts of logic to propositions that appear in our daily discourse. Logic is an evaluative discipline that seeks methods and principles for distinguishing good reasoning from bad reasoning. It does so, primarily, by discovering the ways in which the truth or falsity of some propositions depends solely upon the truth or falsity of other propositions. Logic develops formal models of these patterns of dependency, which can then be applied to everyday problems.

This text will systematically present the basic concepts and skills of logic and critical thinking with the aim of training students to become aware of and proficient in these basic concepts and skills. This will require that students learn many basic definitions and principles, which involve a high level of rigor in their presentation and application. Consequently, students should understand the definitions with precision and be able to apply the principles rigorously. However, simply remembering these definitions and principles will not be enough. Critical thinking is a skill, and like any skill it is acquired and developed only through continual practice and use. The materials presented here will be useful to students only if they practice the skills and develop the ability to apply them to reasoning and problems encountered in their studies and in daily life.

There is a wealth of material written on logic and critical thinking. Most texts on these topics cover more or less the same materials, although they may do so with different approaches and different emphases. A quick glance at any of these texts will show that there is much more to even the basic principles than can be covered in a one-semester course. Although some of the material in these texts is difficult and technical, much can be understood by, and be useful to, anyone who is willing to put forth some concentrated work and practice. This text aims only at presenting some basic principles and skills, but it can be supplemented with other materials. It is worthwhile to skim through some of these other materials, especially to find more exercises on which to practice. Here is a short list of some of the many available logic and critical thinking texts and websites:

Alec Fisher, *The Logic of Real Arguments*, 2nd ed., Cambridge University Press, 2004.

Arthur K. Bierman and Robin N. Assali, *The Critical Thinking Handbook*, Prentice Hall, 1995.

Patrick J. Hurley, *A Concise Introduction to Logic*, 10th ed., Wadsworth, 2008.

Irving M. Copi, Carl Cohen, and Kenneth McMahon, *Introduction to Logic*, 14th ed., Prentice Hall, 2011.

http://www.earlham.edu/~peters/courses/logsys/lshome.htm.

On critical media literacy, see http://gcml.org/the-global-critical-media-literacy-educators-resource-guide/.

I am grateful to the many people who have helped improve this text. My former teaching assistants, Danielle Hampton and Matt Solak, did so much hard work for our students and made many useful suggestions. Several of my colleagues and friends have read all or part of the text and suggested many improvements. These include Fred Johnson, Dan Lyons, Robert W. Jordan, Mike McCulloch, Rick McKita, Adrian W. Moore, David Newman, Linda Rollin, Lee Speer, Garrett Thomson, Tom Trelogan, Paul Trembath, Suzanne Unger, and Ron G. Williams. I am especially grateful to Dr. Michael LeBossiere for his kind and generous permission to use the valuable materials on and examples of informal fallacies to be found on the Nizkor website. Finally, I would like to thank the many students who have taken my course, made many helpful suggestions, and found so many flaws in the text. Any remaining errors are my own responsibility.

INTRODUCTION FOR INSTRUCTORS

This is a pedagogical text. It arose out of decades of teaching from the standard logic and critical thinking textbooks and finding that such texts did not address significant problems and confusions—those that were common among the students in those classes and those that appeared among students in other philosophy courses, even when such students had taken more than one class in logic and critical thinking. The book began as a series of handouts used to supplement the standard texts, but it soon grew into enough material to be used as a text in itself. Over many years of teaching the course, the material has been revised and developed in response to practical problems in teaching, student criticisms, and suggestions from many colleagues, including several teaching assistants.

The book seeks to be both an introduction to critical thinking skills and some basic elements of logic, and a practical set of tools for students to use in their studies. As a result, it does not follow the traditional approaches to teaching basic critical thinking and logic in that it is primarily a text in critical thinking and not primarily one designed to teach formal logic. While it covers the basics of propositional logic, unlike other books it uses that formal system in the service of clarifying issues in critical thinking. While in later chapters the formal elements are covered to some extent on their own, they are elaborated mainly in order to explicate the informal concepts and practices of critical thinking. So, for example, many of the informal fallacies are explicated in terms of formal structures of propositional logic. Rather than being thrown together in a single chapter, the fallacies are distributed among the chapters according to three criteria: (1) their fallacious character depends on the premises of these fallacious types of argument supporting their conclusions; (2) their fallacious character depends on the truth of the premises; or (3) their fallacious character depends on the meaning of sentences. Three additional fallacies—circular reasoning, the straw man fallacy, and hasty generalization fallacies—are discussed in the last two chapters in order to put them, respectively, in the context of chains of arguments and of extracting arguments from everyday texts. Moreover, other elements of the formal structures of propositional logic are useful in explicating elements of critical thinking. So, for example, because truth tables are useful in explicating modal concepts, this use was a consideration in focusing on propositional rather than categorical logic (although there is an appendix to Chapter III listing the forms of the valid categorical syllogisms).

Critical thinking, as understood in this book, includes logic—formal and informal—but in addition all rigorous methods for reliably arriving at true propositions. Hence the book contains a minimalist account of the values true and false. Such an account is not part of logic, which is concerned only with the preservation of truth in arguments. The account of truth and falsity given here is minimal in the sense that it includes all schemas of the form "It is true *that* P if and only if P," where *that* P is a proposition which may be expressed in some language and P picks out the state of affairs which the proposition purports to describe. This account is stated less formally in the text by distinguishing the state of affairs picked out by the proposition "P" from the proposition "P." While this account is close to deflationary accounts such as those given by Horwich,[1] it is not meant to be a philosophically adequate account of truth and falsity, but rather, in keeping with the pedagogical purposes of the book, is meant to help students avoid common confusions by distinguishing the language with which we talk about the world from the world about which we talk. Moreover, this account of truth and falsity is not intended to rise to the level of a correspondence theory of truth, since it proposes no detailed articulation of states of affairs in accord with the articulation of propositions.

In addition to this minimal approach to truth values, since the book is intended merely as an introductory book, it unavoidably runs roughshod over many other philosophical issues. It takes the laws of bivalence and excluded middle as unproblematic. It operates with a distinction between sentences and propositions. It presupposes a germinal truth-conditional account of

---

1 See Paul Horwich, *Truth*, Basil Blackwell, 1990.

meaning. All of these are much-debated philosophical positions, and the only justification for taking them as unproblematic in this context is pedagogical, since they are useful in helping students clear up many prevalent confusions.

Many years of teaching have made it clear that these confusions have become barriers to coming to think clearly for a great many students. In particular—and the confusion that motivated the first handouts that evolved into this book—is the confusion between propositions and propositional attitudes. This confusion seems to be so prevalent and so detrimental to clear thinking that the distinction generates the greatest difficulties for students (far more than any of the formal aspects of propositional logic), and constantly having to confront it eventually led to what is now Chapter II of the book. Little of this material is discussed, or discussed very clearly, in critical thinking books now available, including the important distinctions between critical thinking and logic, on the one hand, and psychology and rhetoric, on the other.

In using the book in classes, the study questions and problems that appear at the end of each part of each chapter have proven to be invaluable. They are structured to pick up each of the significant points in those parts, can usually be correlated with particular parts of the text, and have provided a means for conducting classes. The procedure has been to have students write out answers to the study questions and problems before the class period in which the issues covered by the questions are discussed, and then to ask students to read out their answers in class (having written answers helps shy students have something to say so they can participate in class discussions). The instructor may then give feedback to help students improve their answers. It must be emphasized that close reading and clear writing are, themselves, critical thinking skills, ones that are not learned once and for all but that can be continually developed and improved (a point to which I can testify in that I continued to improve the text with every class). Hence the usefulness of having students write out answers to the study questions and problems. Such written work makes the course part of the writing curriculum, which helps improve students' ability to write on the level of structuring sentences and connecting one sentence with another (as, for example, in arguments). Finally, it has proved useful to encourage students to rewrite their study questions after having gone over them in class, and then to give written exams that consist simply of a selection of a half dozen or so of the most important study questions and problems. Again the suggestion is that students rewrite their answers to the study questions and problems as a way of preparing for these exams, which helps them develop a better understanding of the point of rewriting in their written work more generally.

In addition, the book includes some simple guidelines for the crucial critical thinking skill of making and respecting distinctions. Too often, students have the habit of looking for similarities that lead them to vague and overly general answers; while such answers may be true, because of their vagueness and generality they miss the point or fail to show an understanding of the issues with which the students are grappling. The simple formula for making and respecting distinctions, given in Chapter I and continued throughout the book, is useful for overcoming this habit and helps to justify and explain the need to acquire and use the specialized vocabulary developed throughout the book.

This is an unusual book in that it is not intended to cover all the issues that have been or might be of interest in beginning logic and critical thinking courses, nor just to cover procedures of formal logic and to discuss some fallacies. It is intended to provide a single coherent and interconnected introductory course of study, with the practical intent of addressing the problems and difficulties that contemporary students have in thinking critically. I hope that it may prove as useful and effective for other instructors as it has been in classes I have taught over the last couple of decades.

Chapter I

BASIC DEFINITIONS AND STRUCTURE OF THE TEXT

Part I: Arguments

For our purposes, the central concept of logic is that of an **argument**. In the sense the term is used in critical thinking and logic, an argument is not a quarrel or fight between people, but rather consists of propositions, including both a number of **premises** and one **conclusion**. Premises give reasons that are supposed to support the truth of a single proposition, the conclusion. Arguments can be presented by a single person and even presented anonymously; that is, they and their content and their evaluations are independent of who, if anyone, presents them. To argue for a conclusion is to present reasons for that conclusion to be true; to argue from one or more premises is to present them as reasons for thinking that the conclusion being argued for is true. An argument thus consists of the whole, including the reasons, the premises, the conclusion those reasons are supposed to support, and the **relationship of support** that is supposed to hold between the premises and the conclusion.

An example of an argument is the following:

Example 1:   When it snows, the road gets slippery, and it has been snowing all night. So, the road will be slippery.

This argument gives reasons that are supposed to support the proposition that the road will be slippery. Those reasons are both that it has been snowing all night and that when it snows, the road gets slippery. We can make this clear by rewriting the argument in what we shall call premises and conclusion form (see below) as follows:

(1) When it snows, the road gets slippery, and it has been snowing all night.

Therefore, (2) the road will be slippery.

Where (1) is the reason or premise and (2) is the conclusion which is supposed to be supported by (1).

We define argument rigorously as follows.

DEFINITION OF ARGUMENT:
Something is an argument if and only if it is a set of propositions such that the truth of one (called "the conclusion") is supposed to be supported by the truth of the others (called "the premises").[1]

This definition is complex and in need of clarification. Accordingly, we will divide up the material covered by this text in a way that corresponds to the separate elements of this definition.

First, arguments consist of **propositions**. The term "proposition" is used here in a specific sense that requires considerable clarification. Chapter II will explore what, for the purposes of logic and critical thinking, a proposition is and how propositions are to be distinguished from other seemingly similar things. Chapter II will also sort out some typical confusions about the nature of propositions and will examine some common errors in reasoning that arise because of these confusions. Having sorted out these confusions, we will then be able to see in greater depth why logic and critical thinking skills are important.

Chapter III will continue the exploration of propositions begun in Chapter II by identifying several important types of propositions and showing some logically important ways in which complex propositions can be constructed from simpler propositions. Chapter III will also consider some common errors that arise out of misunderstanding these types of complex propositions.

---

1 We shall always write definitions in the form "Something is a T if and only if it fits the defining characteristics D," where T is the term to be defined, D is a sentence stating the defining characteristics, and the phrase "if and only if" expresses the claim that the defining characteristics D give a definition for the term T. The reason for this way of expressing definitions will be discussed and clarified in Chapter III.

Second, arguments consist of **sets of propositions**. Even though some arguments may be expressed in a single sentence, arguments must always contain more than one proposition. If an argument is expressed in a single sentence, that sentence is always complex and expresses a relationship between at least two propositions. That every argument includes at least one premise and exactly one conclusion demonstrates this point. The conclusion of an argument is the proposition being argued for; that is, the conclusion is that proposition whose truth the truth of the other propositions, the premises, are supposed to support.[2]

DEFINITION OF CONCLUSION:
A proposition is the conclusion of an argument if and only if it functions in that argument as the proposition whose truth is supposed to be supported by the argument's premises.

For example, the following sentence contains an argument.

Example 2:   Sue will get the promotion because she is the best qualified for the job, and whoever is best qualified for the job will get the promotion.

Although this argument is expressed in a single sentence, it contains the proposition that expresses the conclusion

Sue will get the promotion

and the complex proposition that expresses the premise,

She is the best qualified for the job, and whoever is best qualified for the job will get the promotion.

The complex premise in Example 2 can be divided into two separate premises, since the two propositions that compose the premise are connected with "... and ..." or what we shall call logical conjunction (see Chapter III) as follows:

(1) Sue is the best qualified for the job.
(2) Whoever is best qualified for the job will get the promotion.

---

2 Sometimes people will say that since the premises argue for the conclusion, the premises are the argument for the conclusion. However, for our purposes we will always count the combination of premises and conclusion and the support relationship that is supposed to hold between the premises and the conclusion as an argument, never the premises alone.

Notice that these propositions can each be expressed in separate complete sentences. A sentence is a grammatical structure belonging to a particular language and forming a complete unit, while a proposition is the meaning or content that may be expressed in a sentence (we will define "proposition" more rigorously in Chapter II).

By convention we count the number of arguments by counting the number of conclusions, for each argument has exactly one conclusion.

The premises are the other propositions in the argument: those propositions whose truth is supposed to give support to the truth of the conclusion. Arguments can have any number of premises.

DEFINITION OF PREMISE:
A proposition is a premise of an argument if and only if it functions in that argument as a proposition whose truth is supposed to give support to the truth of the argument's conclusion.

For example, the following sentence contains an argument.

Example 3:   I won't miss any of the course work, because if I go to class, then I won't miss any of the course work, and I do go to class.

Although this argument is expressed in a single sentence, it contains a complex proposition that expresses its premise,

If I go to class, then I won't miss any of the course work, and I do go to class,

and the proposition that expresses the conclusion,

I won't miss any of the course work.

The premise in Example 3 can be divided into two separate premises, since the two propositions that compose the premise are connected with "... and ..." (see Chapter III) as follows:

(1) If I go to class, then I won't miss any of the course work.
(2) I do go to class.

While premise (1) is complex, since it contains the two propositions "I go to class" and "I won't miss any of the course work," this premise cannot be broken up and separated into its parts as with the propositions connected with "... and...." We shall see why this is in Chapter III.

What makes a proposition count as a premise or as a conclusion is how the proposition **functions** as part of an argument. A proposition need not be part of any argument at all, in which case we simply call it a proposition, but when a proposition is part of an argument, then it should instead be called a premise or a conclusion depending on how it functions in that argument.

Since each argument alleges that there is a connection between the truth of its premises and the truth of its conclusion, it is important to study how the truth or falsity of one claim may depend solely upon the truth or falsity of another. Such dependencies are called **logical relations**. Chapter IV explores various types of logical relations, as well as some important consequences that follow from the fact that the truth or falsity of some propositions depends solely on the truth or falsity of others.

The connection between the premises and the conclusion of an argument is supposed to be one of **support**. As the definition states, the truth of an argument's conclusion is supposed to be supported by the truth of its premises. This aspect of arguments is both the most important and the most challenging. It is crucial to notice that the definition of argument does not say that the premises of an argument *do* support its conclusion; it only says that the premises of an argument are *supposed* to support its conclusion. The reason for this is that not all arguments are good arguments. In a good argument the premises do support the conclusion. But bad arguments still count as arguments; they still make the claim that their premises support their conclusion, even though their premises may actually fail to do so. So in giving a definition of argument we are careful to say that the premises are *supposed* to support the conclusion, so that our definition includes all arguments regardless of whether they are good arguments or bad ones.

However, good arguments differ in definite and distinguishable ways from bad arguments. **The primary tasks of logic and critical thinking are to discover, explain, and apply methods for determining of any argument whether it is good or bad.** These three tasks are related to one another. The study of logic and critical thinking seeks to provide explicit **methods** for identifying which arguments are good and which are bad. Most people reason well some of the time, but because they seldom reflect explicitly on how they are reasoning, they often develop bad habits and consequently fall into error and confusion without noticing that they do so. Part of the difficulty is that we are usually and for the most part concerned with what we are reasoning about, the specific subject matter, rather than with how and how well we are reasoning about that subject matter. Studying logic and critical thinking helps us become more aware of these pitfalls and urges us to take a reflective step back so as to explicitly examine how—that is, by what methods—we are reasoning, rather than what we are reasoning about.[3] So studying logic and critical thinking provides us with explicit methods that we may **apply** to actual arguments to sort out which arguments are good and which are bad. However, in order to use such methods, we must develop and **discover** which methods work reliably. This is what logicians—people who study logic—do: they seek to discover methods that work reliably to sort out which arguments are good and which are bad. We are fortunate to be able to draw on over 2,000 years of such studies. Finally, if we are to have methods that reliably sort out which arguments are good and which are bad, then we must be able to **explain** why those methods work, so as to justify the reliability of those methods and understand their power, scope, and limits.

Chapter V will identify some important types of arguments, explain the standards for evaluating them, and develop some methods for testing some types of arguments to see if they meet these standards of evaluation.

The types of arguments investigated in Chapter V will be presented through formal models designed to be clear and simple and to make the standards for evaluating arguments easier to grasp. However, such clarity and simplicity necessitate a certain amount of abstraction and simplification. When we confront arguments in our everyday lives, they are seldom presented in these neat and rigorous forms. First, we are ordinarily confronted with and produce arguments that are expressed in a disjointed and fragmentary way; they are not expressed in rigorous or formal language. In addition, the arguments we ordinarily come across or produce ourselves tend to be mixed in with other things we do and say, and they appear in the context of other activities and other concerns (many things that are said or written are neither arguments nor parts of arguments). This means that to apply the insights and methods of logic to ordinary arguments requires that we develop skills in reading, interpreting, and translating between ordinary discourse and the more formal models we explore in Chapter V. The task of Chapter VI is to provide some tips and rules of thumb for applying the methods and insights developed in previous chapters to arguments as they appear in ordinary discourse.

This text is organized as we have just outlined. We will concentrate on and emphasize the elements of arguments in the indicated order:

---

3 Throughout this book, we will focus exclusively on how examples of reasoning work and will never be concerned about what is actually true or false with regard to any subject matter (see Chapter II).

Chapter II: propositions
Chapter III: constructing complex propositions from simple propositions
Chapter IV: sets of propositions; logical relations between propositions
Chapter V: the support relation, forms of arguments, and methods for
evaluating the support relation claimed by arguments
Chapter VI: arguments in ordinary discourse

However, in following this path we will often have to anticipate some matters
and consider them in a more or less intuitive way until we are able to explore
them more explicitly and in detail. We will rely, to some degree, on a common-
sense grasp of the elements until we can refine and explore them more rigorously
in the order we have specified. In this respect, arguments are both most important and exemplary. Arguments are central to logic and critical thinking. So
although we will not study arguments and their evaluation rigorously and
precisely until Chapter V, we will be discussing, illustrating, and using arguments from the very beginning and in every chapter. While each chapter will
emphasize some particular elements, the elements of critical thinking and
logic are so closely connected and bound up with one another that we will be
operating with all of them throughout the text. It is a key feature of logic and
critical thought that critical thinking connects propositions of various types
in logical relations such that the truth or falsity of some propositions depends
solely on the truth or falsity of others. This means that while in this text we
are approaching logic and critical thinking primarily through arguments, it
would be possible to approach the subject through other logical relations,
such as logical inconsistency (see Chapter IV). It also suggests that the more
connections that can be made between the different elements of arguments and
the more directions from which we can approach the central issues, the easier
it will be to understand the material, which will seem less and less a matter
of memorizing what may at first seem a large amount of material and more
and more a matter of coming to certain central issues from various different
perspectives and emphases.

Finally, it is important to emphasize that everyone to some degree practices
and has developed some reasoning skills. Had people not learned to do this, they
would have had great difficulties in getting on with even the ordinary affairs of
life. The simple fact that people have learned to use a natural language (such
as English) shows that they have to some degree learned some reasoning skills,
since no one could acquire or use a language without developing some skills
in reasoning. However, despite having developed some skill in reasoning, few
people take the time and effort to reflect on and develop these skills. This text
is designed to help its readers attain both a reflective and a self-conscious grasp

of the basic elements of critical thinking and logic so as to develop and improve these skills. The text will distinguish and make explicit different elements and procedures involved in thinking critically. The text will also provide, and give rigorous definitions of, a vocabulary designed to enable students to explicitly reflect on the elements and procedures involved in thinking critically, and to make and respect clear distinctions so as to avoid confusions. Learning to make such distinctions and to use this specialized vocabulary will provide tools to enable students to improve their reasoning skills.

Study Questions and Problems

Respond to each of the following questions and problems clearly and precisely.

1) Define and give an example of each of the following (give both a paraphrase in your own words and the formal definition as given in the text):
    (a) argument
    (b) premise
    (c) conclusion

2) What is the smallest number of propositions that can make up an argument? Why?

3) Explain the differences between sentences and propositions.

4) What is the smallest number of sentences that can express an argument? Why?

5) By what criterion do we count arguments?

6) What kind of connections do logic and critical thinking explore?

7) Why is it important that we say that an argument only supposes that its premises support its conclusion? In other words, why must the definition of argument include the word "supposes" or some equivalent term?

8) What are the primary tasks of logic and critical thinking?

9) State the two main differences between arguments that arise in everyday concerns and the simplified formal models of arguments that will be developed throughout most of this text.

Part II: Some Types of Arguments and Standards of Evaluation

"Query: Whether any man hath a right to judge, that will not be at the pains to distinguish?"—George Berkeley

Other than careful reading and clear writing, which are themselves critical thinking skills, the most basic of all critical thinking skills are the skills involved in making distinctions and in respecting those distinctions once they have been made. To make a distinction between two sorts of things, one must say what the one sort of thing is, what the other sort of thing is, and what difference makes the difference between those things. We will usually do this by giving explicit and rigorous definitions[4] of the terms designating each of the two sorts of things, and then stating the crucial difference between them. In order to respect a distinction once it has been made, the usual practice is to mark each distinct sort of thing with a different word or phrase and when one later discusses things of that sort to use this specialized vocabulary to mark the specific sort of thing about which one is speaking or writing so as not to confuse it with other similar sorts of things (see also Part II (B) of Chapter II). Part II of this chapter (and much of the remainder of this book) will make many important distinctions and mark the different sorts of things distinguished with special vocabulary. This vocabulary will be used thereafter and will be one of the means by which we will be able to reflect on and discuss the practices of thinking clearly and critically, and sorting out good from bad arguments (and thereby sorting out which propositions are true and which are false).

As we have already said, logic and critical thinking seek to evaluate arguments to determine how good they are in supporting the truth of their conclusions. To accomplish this task of evaluation, we must establish some **standards of evaluation** that will serve to distinguish good arguments from bad ones, or, at least, to distinguish better arguments from worse ones.

---

4 While we will try to give explicit and rigorous definitions, this is not always necessary in making distinctions so long as the sorts of things distinguished and the crucial difference between them are identified. The definitions we give will be real definitions (see Chapter III, Part IV (E)), hence the need to select words to mark those definitions.

Arguments are good when the truth of their premises supports the truth of their conclusions with good reasons. There are two separate and independent considerations that must be taken into account when judging whether the premises of an argument give good reasons in support of its conclusion. The most obvious consideration is whether all of the premises are themselves actually true. For the most part, an argument will not be a good argument unless it has all actually true premises.[5] However, while the question whether the premises of an argument are all actually true is important, it is neither decisive nor the primary question to consider. The premises of an argument may all actually be true and the argument may still be a bad argument. In addition to having all actually true premises, in a good argument the premises would have to support the conclusion. Whether the premises of an argument support its conclusion is more important in assessing reasoning than whether the premises are all actually true (why this is so will be clarified in more detail in Chapter V). Support is a **relationship** between the premises and the conclusion of an argument, such that the truth of the premises together give good reasons for the truth of the conclusion. **Whether the premises of an argument support its conclusion is an issue completely separate from and independent of whether those premises are actually true or false.** This point is crucially important to any reasoning and so must be emphasized.

This means that the premises of an argument may all actually be false, yet those premises may still give good support for the conclusion of that argument. It also means that the premises of an argument may all actually be true and the argument may still be a bad argument, because it may be that even though the premises of the argument are all actually true, they do not support the conclusion. It also means that the premises of an argument may not support its conclusion even though the conclusion is actually true; bad arguments may have actually true conclusions.

The two considerations—whether the premises of an argument support its conclusion and whether the premises of an argument are all actually true—are independent of one another for two reasons:

1. It is possible to have a conclusive answer to the question whether the premises of an argument support its conclusion and have no answer to whether the premises of that argument are all actually true, and
2. It is possible to have a conclusive answer to the question whether the premises of an argument are all actually true and have no answer to whether the premises of that argument support its conclusion.

---

5 We will consider exceptions to this in Chapter V.

So, for example, the following arguments each contain all actually false premises and an actually false conclusion, yet the premises do support the conclusion:

Example 4a: (1) All scientists are now alive.
                  (2) William Shakespeare is a scientist.

                  Therefore, (3) William Shakespeare is now alive.

Example 4b: (1) If Don is in London, then Don is in Colorado.
                  (2) If Don is in Colorado, then Don is in China.

                  Therefore, (3) if Don is in London, then Don is in China.

After all, if it were true that all scientists are now alive and it were also true that William Shakespeare is a scientist, then William Shakespeare would have to be alive. It would be impossible for premises (1) and (2) to be true and the conclusion (3) to be false. Of course, all three of the propositions that make up this argument actually happen to be false, but despite that, the premises *do* support the conclusion. Similarly, with respect to Example 4b, while all of the propositions actually happen to be false, if premises (1) and (2) were true, then the conclusion (3) would have to be true.

The following argument contains all actually true premises and an actually true conclusion, but the premises do not support the conclusion:

Example 5:   (1) If Colorado State University were located in Laramie, then it would be in Wyoming.
                  (2) Colorado State University is not located in Laramie.

                  Therefore, (3) Colorado State University is not in Wyoming.

While every proposition in this argument is actually true, the premises do not support the conclusion. The premises do not support the conclusion because, were Colorado State University located in some other place in Wyoming, say in Cheyenne, then the conclusion would be false while the premises would still be true. So, it is **possible** for the premises to be true and the conclusion false, and that possibility suffices to show that the premises do not support the conclusion. The actual truth of the premises does not even make it more likely that the conclusion be true than that it be false, since Laramie is only a small part of Wyoming.

(A) STANDARDS FOR EVALUATING ARGUMENTS

That the question whether the premises of an argument support its conclusion is separate from and independent of the question whether those premises are actually true or false requires that there be at least two different and independent standards by which we evaluate arguments. This means that an argument is only a good argument, strictly speaking, if it can meet both of these separate and independent standards. Testing to see if an argument meets these standards will give answers to the following two questions:

(1) Do the premises support the conclusion?
(2) Are the premises all actually true?

From the point of view of logic, and for the purposes of this book, question (1) is of the utmost importance. Logic is concerned primarily with how the truth or falsity of propositions fit together, that is, how the truth and falsity of some propositions depend upon the truth and falsity of other propositions. The claim that the premises of an argument support its conclusion is just this sort of question; specifically, in the case of an argument (there are such dependencies that are not necessarily parts of arguments), it is a question of whether the truth of the conclusion depends on the truth of the premises. It is, therefore, a central concern of logic to make the relationship of support clear and precise and to devise general methods for testing whether the premises of any given argument support its conclusion. This text will focus on and emphasize the study of whether the premises of arguments support their conclusions.

The premises of an argument may support its conclusion in two different ways. The truth of the premises may make it impossible for the conclusion to be false. In such cases, if the premises were true, then the conclusion *would have to be* true. On the other hand, the truth of the premises may only make the conclusion more likely to be true than to be false. In such cases, if the premises were true, then the conclusion would be *more likely to be true than to be false*. These different kinds of support divide arguments into two groups: deductive and non-deductive arguments. **Deductive arguments** claim to support their conclusions with necessity; that is, they claim that if the premises were all true, then the conclusion would have to be true. **Non-deductive arguments** only claim to support their conclusions with sufficiently high probability; that is, they claim that if the premises were all true, then the conclusion would be more likely to be true than to be false. In this book we will focus primarily on deductive arguments.

DEFINITION OF DEDUCTIVE ARGUMENT:

An argument is deductive if and only if it supposes that if the premises of the argument were true, then its conclusion would have to be true.

We need to take note of three important points about this definition.

First, in a deductive argument the premises are supposed to support its conclusion with *necessity*—that is, the definition states that *if* the premises were true then the conclusion *would have to be* true. The definition does *not* say merely that if the premises are true then the conclusion *is* true; that is, it does *not* say that the conclusion *is* true if the premises are. It claims or *supposes* that the conclusion *must be* true if the premises are true (of course, this claim will actually be true only if the argument is valid; see below). Another way of expressing this claim is that a deductive argument supposes that it is *impossible* for the premises to be true and the conclusion false.

Second, as in the definition for argument, we only say that a deductive argument *supposes* that if the premises of the argument were true, then the conclusion would have to be true. We say this for the same reason as before, because not all deductive arguments are good ones. An argument may be put forward as a deductive argument and yet be a bad deductive argument, because it is *possible* for the premises to be true and the conclusion false. The point here is that there is a clear distinction between deductive arguments and good (i.e., valid; see below) deductive arguments such that while every valid deductive argument is a deductive argument, not every deductive argument is a valid one. In other words, some deductive arguments are bad—that is, invalid—arguments.

Third, and moreover, the definition says nothing at all about whether any of the premises are actually true or false. The definition says that a deductive argument supposes that *if the* premises were true, then the conclusion would have to be true. The word "if" indicates that whether an argument is deductive is completely separate from and independent of whether the premises are actually true or not. Only the nature of the support relation between the premises and the conclusion is relevant to determining whether an argument is deductive, while the actual truth or falsity of the premises is not relevant.

We should also point out that we are here making a distinction between types of arguments. As given above in the definition of argument, deductive arguments do not include all arguments in general. Deductive arguments are only one type of argument. So in accord with the procedure for making clear distinctions, we have said what the one sort of thing is—arguments in general—and what the other sort of thing is—deductive arguments. But to complete the distinction we must point out that the difference that makes the difference between arguments in general and specifically deductive arguments is that while all arguments make the claim that their premises support their conclusion, deductive arguments claim that a specific sort of support relationship holds between their premises and their conclusion: they claim that the support relationship is one of necessity such that if the premises were true, then the conclusion *would have to be* true. (From this point forward, whenever we make a distinction, we will take the definitions to specify the sorts of things we are distinguishing and simply add, in each case, a statement of the crucial difference that makes the difference between the distinct things.)

An example of a deductive argument is the following:

Example 6:   Only citizens of Utah are eligible for Colorado driver's licenses. Vanessa is not a citizen of Utah, so she must not be eligible for a Colorado driver's license.

Let us write this in a more transparent form. We write the argument listing each premise and the conclusion separately, one sentence to a line. We next number each premise in the argument consecutively. And then we write the conclusion last, writing the word "Therefore" before the number of the conclusion. We draw a line between the premises and the conclusion, to emphasize their different functions. When we rewrite arguments in this way, it is called writing the argument in **premises and conclusion form**. Here is Example 6, written in premises and conclusion form.

Example 6a: (1) Only citizens of Utah are eligible for Colorado driver's licenses.
(2) Vanessa is not a citizen of Utah.

Therefore, (3) Vanessa is not eligible for a Colorado driver's license.

Notice that even though the first premise is false, the argument is still a deductive argument. Here the word "must" has not been included as part of the conclusion (even though it appears in the original text). This is because the necessity indicated by the word "must" is the **necessity** claimed by the **relationship of support** that is supposed to hold between the premises and the conclusion of a deductive argument; it tells us how the premises are supposed to support the conclusion—that is, the word "must" tells us that this is a deductive argument. Notice that *it is the relationship between the premises and the conclusion that is supposed to be necessary*. The argument makes the claim that if the premises were true, then the conclusion *would have to be* true. (It is worth noting here that this is importantly different from the claim that the conclusion itself is a necessary truth, which in this case and usually is not true.) The word "so" has also been replaced with the standard term "Therefore." To summarize: when we write an argument in premises and conclusion form, we do not include words that indicate which propositions are conclusions and which are premises (we will return to this point in Chapter VI), nor do we include any words that indicate how the premises are supposed to support the conclusion.

The procedure for writing an argument in premises and conclusion form, then, is as follows:

(1) Write the premises and conclusion of the argument as separate propositions. (This may involve breaking up sentences into separate propositions. If so, make sure that each proposition is expressed in a grammatically complete sentence. This may also require some paraphrasing and adjustments in the grammar of the original sentences.)

(2) Write the premises out, one premise to a line.

(3) Write the conclusion last on a separate line.

(4) Number the premises and conclusion consecutively. (The highest number, on the last line, will then be the number assigned to the conclusion.)

(5) Write the word "Therefore" before the conclusion (before the number of the conclusion).

(6) Draw a horizontal line above the conclusion and below the last of the premises.

(B) STANDARDS FOR EVALUATING DEDUCTIVE ARGUMENTS

As noted above, arguments must be evaluated by two separate and indepen- *(valid)* dent criteria: whether the premises support the conclusion, and whether the *(good/sound)* premises are all actually true. Since this is so, deductive arguments will have to be evaluated in two stages. First, we must determine whether a deductive argument gives the support it claims to give; that is, we must determine whether it is true that the relation of deductive support holds, whether if the premises of the argument were true, then its conclusion would have to be true. Hence, we must evaluate deductive arguments according to whether it is impossible for the premises to be true and the conclusion false. This standard of evaluation is called **validity**, and a deductive argument that meets this standard is called a **valid deductive argument.**[6]

T-T-F

> DEFINITION OF VALID DEDUCTIVE ARGUMENT:
> A deductive argument is valid if and only if it is impossible for the premises to be true and the conclusion false; that is, if the premises of the argument were true, then the conclusion would have to be true.

A deductive argument is an argument that is *supposed* to be valid—it *supposes* that if the premises are true then the conclusion must be true. However, when a deductive argument is valid we no longer merely *suppose* that if the premises are true then the conclusion must be true. This is the difference that makes the difference between a deductive argument and a *valid* deductive argument. For a valid deductive argument, *it is true that* if the premises were true, then the conclusion must be true. Consider the following examples of valid deductive arguments.

Example 7:   (1) If the rent is late, then we will be evicted.

(2) The rent is late.

Therefore, (3) we will be evicted.

Example 7 is a straightforward valid deductive argument. It would be impossible for both its premises to be true and its conclusion to be false.

Example 8:   (1) All students are intelligent people.

(2) All intelligent people get good grades.

Therefore, (3) all students get good grades.

Example 8 is also a valid deductive argument. In this case, however, at least one of the premises must be false, since the conclusion is actually false. However, the argument is still a valid deductive argument, because if it were the case that the premises were actually true, then the conclusion would have to be true. It would be **impossible** for both the premises to be true and the conclusion false.

---

6 Notice that the word "valid" is used in a special technical sense. In ordinary conversation, people seldom use the word "valid" in our technical sense. When Celeste says, "Tim's point of view is valid," she does not mean the word valid in our technical sense; she means something like that Tim's point of view is worthy of serious consideration. Unfortunately, people sometimes use the word "valid" to mean true, but as the two evaluative considerations noted above (and considerations to be discussed in later chapters) show, truth and validity mark distinct and independent concepts.

If the conclusion is false, then at least some students do not get good grades. If some students do not get good grades, then it must either be false that all intelligent people get good grades or be false that all students are intelligent people. Both premises could be false. Now consider the following example:

Example 9:   (1) Pierre is a bachelor.
_____
Therefore, (2) Pierre is unmarried.

Example 9 has only one premise. However, it is still a valid deductive argument. It would be impossible for the conclusion to be false and the premise true: if the conclusion were false, then it would be false that Pierre is unmarried. But part of the meaning of "bachelor" is to be unmarried, so it is impossible for Pierre both to be married and to be a bachelor. If the conclusion is false, then so must the premise be. It would be impossible for the premise to be true and the conclusion false.

If a deductive argument is not valid, we call it **invalid**.

DEFINITION OF INVALID DEDUCTIVE ARGUMENT:
A deductive argument is invalid if and only if it is possible for the premises to be true and the conclusion false.

Notice that it only needs to be *possible* that the premises be true and the conclusion false for a deductive argument to be invalid. So the difference that makes the difference between valid deductive arguments and invalid deductive arguments is that while both are deductive arguments, in the case of a valid deductive argument it is *impossible* for the premises to be true and the conclusion false, while in the case of invalid deductive arguments it is *possible* for the premises to be true and the conclusion false.

This means that the actual truth or falsity of the premises is irrelevant to whether a deductive argument is valid or invalid. This point is a consequence of the independence of the two separate evaluative considerations. Because the standard of validity is concerned only with the support relation, it does not matter whether the premises are actually true or actually false. Likewise, it does not matter whether the premises of an invalid deductive argument are actually true or actually false. Consider the following examples:

Example 10:   (1) If the rent is late, then we will be evicted.
(2) The rent is not late.
_____
Therefore, (3) We will not be evicted.

Example 10 is an invalid deductive argument, because it is possible for the premises to be true and the conclusion false. It could be both true that if the rent is late, then we will be evicted, and true that the rent is not late, and still be false that we will not be evicted. For we may have done something else that would get us evicted. For example, if we wantonly destroy the major appliances in the apartment, we may be evicted for that even though our rent is on time.

Example 11:   (1) If an animal is a dinosaur, then it is an egg layer.
(2) If an animal is a reptile, then it is an egg layer.

Therefore, (3) If an animal is a dinosaur, then it is a reptile.

Example 11 is an invalid deductive argument, because it is possible that the premises be true and the conclusion false. While it may be true that all dinosaurs are reptiles, this argument does not support that conclusion. It could both be true that all dinosaurs are egg layers and that all reptiles are egg layers, and still be false that all dinosaurs are reptiles. Suppose that (as some paleontologists claim) dinosaurs were birds. In that case, they would be egg layers (since birds are egg layers) and it would still be true that reptiles are egg layers, but dinosaurs would not be reptiles. The possibility that dinosaurs are birds shows that it is possible that the argument may have true premises and a false conclusion. Therefore, Example 11 is an invalid deductive argument.

Moreover, we can show that a deductive argument is invalid by showing that it has the same form or structure (see Chapter V) as another argument that is clearly invalid, since that other argument actually has true premises and a false conclusion.[7] Hence, that Example 11 is invalid can be shown by giving an argument with the same form, but which **actually** has true premises and a false conclusion, such as the following:

Example 12:   (1) If an animal is a man, then it is normally a two-eyed creature.
(2) If an animal is a snake, then it is normally a two-eyed creature.

Therefore, (3) If an animal is a man, then it is a snake.

This shows that the original argument is invalid because the validity and invalidity of deductive arguments depends on their form or structure, not on what the argument is about (see Chapter V).

---

7 If an argument actually has true premises and a false conclusion, then it is possible for the argument to have true premises and a false conclusion, for everything actual must be possible.

NOTES ON TERMINOLOGY:

(1)   When a deductive argument is valid, we may also say that the conclusion **follows from** the premises (this does not mean the same as follows after—what is at issue is support, not order of presentation), or that the premises **entail** the conclusion, or that the conclusion is a **logical consequence** of the premises (see Chapter IV).

(2)   So long as we remember that the standard of validity applies only to deductive arguments, we may refer to valid deductive arguments simply as **valid arguments**. Likewise we may also simply refer to invalid deductive arguments simply as **invalid arguments**.

According to the standard of validity, no valid argument can have a false conclusion if all its premises are actually true. Hence, while it is possible for a valid argument to have a false conclusion, if a valid argument has a false conclusion then one or more of its premises must also be false.

In the example we gave of a deductive argument:

Example 6b: (1) Only citizens of Utah are eligible for Colorado driver's licenses.

(2) Vanessa is not a citizen of Utah.

Therefore, (3) Vanessa is not eligible for a Colorado driver's license.

The argument is valid because if it were true that only citizens of Utah are eligible for Colorado driver's licenses, as claimed by premise (1), and if it were true that Vanessa is not a citizen of Utah, as claimed by premise (2), then it would have to be true that she would not be eligible for a Colorado driver's license, as stated in the conclusion (3). It is impossible for the conclusion to be false and the premises true. However, the first premise is not actually true. Citizens of Colorado are eligible for Colorado driver's licenses, while citizens of Utah are not eligible. So while this argument is valid, it is still not a good argument because one of its premises is actually false. This argument fails to meet the second criterion for a good argument, namely that all of the premises actually be true.

A deductive argument that meets both of the criteria for a good argument is called a **sound deductive argument**.

DEFINITION OF SOUND DEDUCTIVE ARGUMENT:

A deductive argument is sound if and only if both it is valid (i.e., if its premises were true, then its conclusion would have to be true) and all its premises are actually true.

Notice that for a deductive argument to be sound it has to be *both* valid *and* have all its premises actually be true. The difference that makes the difference between a sound deductive argument and an invalid deductive argument is that a sound deductive argument must be valid. More to the point, the difference that makes the difference between a sound deductive argument and a valid deductive argument is that in addition to being valid, in a sound deductive argument all of its premises must actually be true.

It follows from the definition of valid argument that a sound argument cannot have a false conclusion. The conclusion of a sound deductive argument will have to be true, since if its premises were true, then its conclusion would have to be true, and all of its premises are actually true. <u>Sound deductive</u> <u>arguments are the strongest arguments possible</u> because a sound deductive argument <u>guarantees</u> that its conclusion is true. We can put this point in the form of an argument from the definition of sound deductive argument for the conclusion that if a deductive argument is sound, then its conclusion must be true, as follows:

> (1) If the premises are all actually true, then the conclusion must be true
> (this is the definition of a valid deductive argument, and by the definition of sound
> deductive argument, every sound deductive argument is valid).
> (2) The premises of the argument are all actually true
> (this is also true by the definition of sound deductive argument).
>
> ---
> Therefore, (3) the conclusion must be true.

Consider the following examples.

Example 13:   (1) Either three multiplied by pi is ten, or greater than ten, or three multiplied by pi is less than ten.
    (2) Three multiplied by pi is not ten nor greater than ten.

Therefore, (3) three multiplied by pi is less than ten.

In Example 13, it would be impossible for the premises to be true and the conclusion false. For if it were false that three multiplied by pi were less than ten, then either premise (1) would be false and there would be another alternative besides the three mentioned, or premise (2) would be false and three multiplied by pi would be either equal to or greater than ten. In either case, the argument would not have true premises and a false conclusion. However, both premises (1) and (2) are actually true. There is no other alternative to the product being either ten or larger or less than ten, and the product is approximately 9.4247..., which is neither ten nor larger than ten.

Example 14:   (1) If an animal is a marsupial, then it is a mammal.

(2) If an animal is a mammal, then it suckles its young.

Therefore, (3) if an animal is a marsupial, then it suckles its young.

Again it would be impossible for the premises to be true and the conclusion false. For were the conclusion false, then either premise (1) would be false and there would be some marsupials that were not mammals, or premise (2) would be false and there would be mammals that do not suckle their young. In either case, the argument would not have true premises and a false conclusion. Moreover, both premises (1) and (2) are actually true. Marsupials are a subclass of mammals (mammals with pouches), and it is part of the nature of mammals that they suckle their young.

Both Examples 13 and 14 are sound deductive arguments. They guarantee that their conclusions are true. If a deductive argument is not sound we call it **unsound**.

DEFINITION OF UNSOUND DEDUCTIVE ARGUMENT:

A deductive argument is unsound if and only if it is either invalid or has at least one actually false premise.

If an argument is invalid it is automatically unsound; that is, every invalid argument also must be an unsound argument. So we do not need to have a special term for invalid arguments with false premises. An argument is unsound if it fails to meet either one of the two criteria for a good argument—namely, if it either is invalid or has at least one false premise. So the difference that makes the difference between unsound arguments and valid arguments is that an argument may be valid and still be unsound if it has at least one false premise. Moreover, Example 5 (above) is an example of an unsound argument because it is invalid (even though all the premises and the conclusion of that argument happen to be actually true). Examples 4a and 4b (above) are also examples of unsound arguments because, while they are valid, they have at least one false premise. Of course, any argument that is both invalid and has at least one false premise is also unsound.

NOTE ON TERMINOLOGY:

So long as we remember that the standard of soundness applies only to deductive arguments, we may refer to sound deductive arguments simply as **sound arguments**. Likewise we may also simply refer to unsound deductive arguments as **unsound arguments**.

(C) NON-DEDUCTIVE ARGUMENTS AND THEIR STANDARDS OF EVALUATION

kinds

In addition to deductive arguments, there are various types of non-deductive arguments. These include arguments by enumeration of cases, arguments by the accumulation of evidence, statistical arguments, and probabilistic arguments. While there are significant differences between these various types of non-deductive arguments, we will follow custom and call them all **inductive arguments**. In all these types of argument, the support relationship is weaker than deductive necessity. In each type, it is *supposed* that if the premises of the argument were true, then its conclusion would be more likely to be true than false. Hence, the primary difference that makes the difference between inductive arguments and deductive arguments is whether the support relation that is supposed to hold between the premises and the conclusion of the argument is one of likelihood or probability (in inductive arguments), making the claim that if the premises were true then the conclusion would be more likely to be true than to be false, or one of necessity (in deductive arguments), making the claim that if the premises were true then the conclusion would have to be true.

Notice that the difference between deductive and inductive arguments concerns the way in which the premises are supposed to support the conclusion.[8] The truth or falsity of the premises and conclusion that make up an argument is irrelevant to whether that argument is deductive or inductive.

DEFINITION OF INDUCTIVE ARGUMENT:
An argument is inductive if and only if its conclusion is supposed to be made more likely to be true than to be false, given the truth of its premises; that is, inductive arguments suppose that if their premises were true, then their conclusion would be more likely to be true than to be false.

The conclusions of inductive arguments are supposed to follow with high probability: the conclusion is supposed to be *more likely to be true than to be false* if the premises are true. This means that, unlike valid deductive arguments, even in the strongest of inductive arguments it is *possible* for the conclusion of these arguments to be false even if the premises are true. While inductive arguments claim to provide good reason that their conclusions are true, **inductive**

---

8 The difference between deductive and inductive arguments is sometimes characterized as being concerned with the generality or particularity of the premises and conclusion, but this is not true. There are deductive and inductive arguments with premises and conclusions that are general as well as both deductive and inductive arguments with premises and conclusions that are particular.

arguments—unlike deductive arguments—can be neither valid nor invalid, sound nor unsound. It makes no sense to apply these terms to inductive arguments. Only deductive arguments can be valid or invalid, sound or unsound. Moreover, inductive arguments can be better or worse. How good the support that the truth of the premises of inductive arguments gives for the truth of their conclusions is a matter of degree: the more likely the truth of the conclusion, given the truth of the premises, the stronger the inductive argument is; the less likely the truth of the conclusion given the truth of the premises, the weaker the inductive argument is. However, as we have seen, even the strongest inductive arguments can still have true premises and a false conclusion.

Suppose we are observing the color of swans and find that each of 1,000 swans we observe is white, this yields the following inductive argument, with 1,000 premises, by simple enumeration of instances.

(1) Swan #1 is white.
(2) Swan #2 is white.
.
.
.
(1,000) Swan #1,000 is white.

Therefore, (1,001) all swans are white.

This is an inductive argument from the enumeration of instances, and how strong it is will depend on whether the sample of swans we observe is representative of the population of swans. So if we are observing swans on only one lake, the argument will be much weaker than if we were to observe swans all over the world (in fact, were we to observe swans in certain places, we could eventually observe a black swan). So if we are observing swans on only one lake, the conclusion is too general to be supported by the premises. However, we could substitute a different argument with the conclusion "All swans in the area of this lake are white," and we would have a much stronger inductive argument by simple enumeration. However, that is a different argument than the one given above, and since it is still inductive, it still leaves open the possibility that there are swans in the area of this lake that are not white.

The following is an example of an inductive argument from the accumulation of evidence:

Example 15:   Since Dotty had a tennis racquet in her hand, was coming from the tennis courts dressed in a tennis outfit, was perspiring heavily, and was complaining about having lost, it is likely that she has been playing tennis.

Let us write this in premises and conclusion form.

(1) Dotty had a tennis racquet in her hand.
(2) Dotty was coming from the tennis courts.
(3) Dotty was dressed in a tennis outfit.
(4) Dotty was perspiring heavily.
(5) Dotty was complaining about having lost.

Therefore, (6) Dotty has been playing tennis.

This is an argument that accumulates evidence that makes it likely to be true that Dotty has been playing tennis. However, this evidence is not conclusive because it is still possible that all the propositions (1)–(5) be true and the conclusion still be false. Dotty may, for example, have been auditioning for a job modeling tennis equipment, in which case all the premises might be true and the conclusion false. However, this alternative is not nearly as likely as the conclusion of the argument. The evidence may well make the actual conclusion more likely to be true than to be false. Notice that the phrase "it is likely that" is neither a part of the premises nor of the conclusion. This phrase applies to the *relationship* of support that is supposed to hold between the premises and the conclusion; it indicates how the premises are supposed to support the conclusion—that is, the phrase "it is likely that" tells us that this is an inductive argument.

Other sorts of non-deductive arguments include statistical and probabilistic arguments. Here are two examples. The first is a **statistical argument** and the second a **probabilistic argument**.

Example 16:   (1) Sixty-seven percent of smokers contract some form of lung disease.

(2) Trevor smokes two packs of cigarettes a day.

Therefore, (3) Trevor will contract some form of lung disease.

Example 17:   (1) There are 49 white marbles in jar A.

(2) There are 51 blue marbles in jar A.

(3) The white marbles are thoroughly mixed with the blue marbles.

Therefore, (4) the first marble picked randomly out of the jar will be blue.

Example 16 applies the statistical distribution of a property (contracting lung disease) over a population (smokers) to a member of that population (Trevor).

Its conclusion is likely to be true if the premises are true, but it is still possible that the conclusion be false even if the premises were true. Trevor, for example, may die in a car accident and never contract any form of lung disease.

Example 17 draws its conclusion from the chances that one event will occur rather than another. Its conclusion is just barely more likely to be true than to be false, because the chances of picking a blue marble are slightly better than 1 out of 2; that is, there is a 51% chance that the first marble picked will be blue. So it is still possible that its conclusion will turn out false, since the first marble picked randomly out of the jar could turn out to be white.

Like deductive arguments, inductive arguments must be evaluated by the two separate and independent criteria: whether the premises support the conclusion and whether the premises are all actually true. So inductive arguments will also have to be evaluated in two stages. As with deductive arguments, inductive arguments only **suppose** that the premises support the conclusion. So, first, we must determine whether the premises of an inductive argument do support its conclusion. This is more complicated with inductive arguments, because inductive support is a matter of degree. The question is how likely is it that the conclusion is true, *if* the premises were true. So we must determine how strong the support is that the premises give to the conclusion. Although there may be different degrees of strength or weakness for inductive arguments, there is still a sharp distinction between strong inductive arguments and weak ones. This is the point in saying that the standard by which to judge inductive support is whether if the premises were true, then the conclusion would be *more likely to be true than to be false*. When the chances that the conclusion of an inductive argument are true are the same as the chances that the conclusion of that argument are false, then this would be the same as the chances that any random proposition, by itself, be true or false, that is, regardless of whether it is the conclusion of an argument. In such a case, the premises of the argument would give no more support to the conclusion than random guessing whether the conclusion is true, no more support than deciding on the truth or falsity of the conclusion by flipping a coin. Since the point of having an argument, and so of having premises that are supposed to support the conclusion, is to give us reason, more reason than a mere guess or chance, for the conclusion to be true, an inductive argument will be strong if and only if its premises give more support to its conclusion than mere chance—than merely flipping a coin to decide whether the conclusion is true or false.

The standard for evaluating inductive arguments is that of inductive strength or inductive weakness.

DEFINITION OF STRONG INDUCTIVE ARGUMENT:

coin flip

An inductive argument is strong if and only if the argument is such that if the premises of the argument were true, then the conclusion would be more likely to be true than to be false.

Since inductive strength is a matter of degree, the more likely the truth of the premises would make the truth of the conclusion (were the premises true), the stronger the inductive argument. The difference that makes the difference between any inductive argument and a strong inductive argument is that while every inductive argument makes the *claim* that if its premises were true, then its conclusion would be more likely to be true than to be false, in a strong inductive argument *that claims* it is true that if the premises were true then the conclusion would be more likely to be true than to be false. So Example 17 (above) is an example of a **strong inductive argument**. It is not a very strong inductive argument, of course, because the premises do not make the conclusion very much more likely to be true than to be false. But if the premises of an inductive argument make the conclusion more likely to be true than chance (more likely than it would be as an isolated proposition not supported by any premises at all, but with no more support than could be obtained from a random flip of a coin), then the argument is still a strong inductive argument. A similar but much stronger argument would be the following:

Example 18:   (1) There are 4 white marbles in jar A.

(2) There are 96 blue marbles in jar A.

(3) The white marbles are thoroughly mixed with the blue marbles.

Therefore, (4) the first marble picked randomly out of the jar will be blue.

In Example 18, the probability that the first marble picked randomly out of the jar will be blue is 96%, which is significantly greater than the 51% probability provided by the premises in Example 17.

If an inductive argument is not strong, then we call it a **weak inductive argument**.

DEFINITION OF WEAK INDUCTIVE ARGUMENT:

An inductive argument is weak if and only if the argument is such that if the premises of the argument were true, then the conclusion would be less likely (or no more likely) to be true than to be false.

The difference that makes the difference between any inductive argument and a weak inductive argument is that while every inductive argument makes the claim that if its premises were true, then its conclusion would be more likely to be true than to be false, in a weak inductive argument it is false that if the premises were true then the conclusion would be more likely to be true than to be false. So, the difference that makes the difference between a strong inductive argument and a weak inductive argument is that in a strong inductive argument the claim is true that if the premises were true then the conclusion would be more likely to be true than to be false, while in a weak inductive argument this claim is false.

Since inductive strength is a matter of degree, the less likely that the conclusion would be true if the premises were true, the weaker the inductive argument. We can again take as an example a probabilistic argument as follows.

Example 19: (1) There are 51 white marbles in jar A.
(2) There are 49 blue marbles in jar A.
(3) The white marbles are thoroughly mixed with the blue marbles.

Therefore, (4) the first marble picked randomly out of the jar will be blue.

Example 19 is a weak inductive argument because the premises give only a 49% probability that the first marble picked randomly out of the jar will be blue. This makes it less likely, given the truth of the premises, that the conclusion will be true than that the conclusion will be false. An inductive argument in which the chance was exactly 50% that its conclusion were true given the truth of its premises would still be a weak inductive argument, since the premises would give no more likelihood to the truth of the conclusion than chance. Again weakness of an inductive argument is a matter of degree. An example of a very weak inductive argument would be as follows.

Example 20: (1) There are 96 white marbles in jar A.
(2) There are 4 blue marbles in jar A.
(3) The white marbles are thoroughly mixed with the blue marbles.

Therefore, (4) the first marble picked randomly out of the jar will be blue.

In Example 20, the premises yield only a 4% probability that the conclusion will be true.

As we have seen, we must treat separately and independently the following questions:

(1) Do the premises of an inductive argument support its conclusion?

(2) Are all of the premises of the argument actually true?

In addition to the premises of an inductive argument giving strong support to its conclusion, a **good inductive argument** also needs to have all actually true premises. This is why the definitions of strong and weak inductive arguments say only that the premises *would* give inductive support to the conclusion *if* they *were* true. To have a good inductive argument, not only do the premises of that inductive argument have to give strong inductive support to its conclusion, but the premises must also all be actually true.

DEFINITION OF GOOD INDUCTIVE ARGUMENT:
An inductive argument is good if and only if both it is strong and its premises are all actually true.

For an inductive argument to be good it *both* has to be strong *and* all its premises must actually be true. The difference that makes the difference between a good inductive argument and a strong inductive argument is that while for both strong inductive arguments and good inductive arguments the claim is true that if its premises were true then its conclusion would be more likely to be true than to be false, in addition to being strong, good inductive arguments must also have all actually true premises. An example of a good inductive argument is the following:

Example 21:   (1) The sun has risen each day for all of recorded history.

Therefore, (2) the sun will rise tomorrow.

In Example 21, the truth of the premise (really the many thousands of premises condensed into and summarized by premise (1)) makes it likely that the conclusion will be true and the argument has an actually true premise.

If an inductive argument is good, that indicates that its conclusion is more likely to be true than to be false. This is because if its premises were true then its conclusion would be more likely to be true than to be false, and all of its premises are actually true. We can put this point in the form of an argument from the definition of good inductive argument for the conclusion that if an inductive argument is good, then its conclusion is more likely to be true than to be false, as follows:

> (1) If the premises are all actually true, then the conclusion is more likely to be true than to be false (this is the definition of a strong inductive argument, and by the definition of good inductive argument, every good inductive argument is strong).
>
> (2) The premises of the argument are all actually true (this is also true by the definition of strong inductive argument).
> _____
> Therefore, (3) the conclusion is more likely to be true than to be false.

If the premises of an inductive argument do not give strong inductive support to its conclusion, the argument is a **bad inductive argument**. In addition, if at least one of the premises of an inductive argument is actually false, then even if the premises of the argument give strong support to its conclusion, the argument is a bad inductive argument. Bad inductive arguments are still inductive arguments, since they still *claim* that if their premises were true their conclusions would be more likely to be true than to be false.

DEFINITION OF BAD INDUCTIVE ARGUMENT:
An inductive argument is bad if and only if it is weak or has at least one actually false premise.

If an argument is inductively weak, it is automatically a bad inductive argument. So we do not need to have a special term for bad inductive arguments with false premises. An inductive argument is bad if it fails to meet either one of the two criteria for a good argument, that is, if it either is weak or has at least one false premise. So the difference that makes the difference between bad inductive arguments and strong inductive arguments is that an argument may be strong and still be a bad inductive argument if it has at least one false premise. Examples 19 and 20 are examples of bad inductive arguments that are bad because the premises give weak support to the conclusion. The following is an example of an inductive argument that is bad because it has false premises, even though the many premises condensed into (1) give strong support to the conclusion.

Example 22: (1) The sun has been destroyed each day for all of recorded history.
_____
Therefore, (2) the sun will be destroyed tomorrow.

The premises in Example 22 give the same sort of evidence with the same strength as in Example 21, but in Example 22 the premises are actually false. Hence Example 22 is a bad inductive argument.

We can now give a more general definition of a **good argument**.

good arg.

DEFINITION OF GOOD ARGUMENT:
An argument is a good argument if and only if it is either a sound deductive argument or a good inductive argument.

This is a strict definition of good argument. Since validity and the strength of inductive arguments apply standards of evaluation, we also sometimes use the term "good argument" more loosely. In this looser sense we may call valid deductive arguments and strong inductive arguments good arguments. This indicates that these arguments employ good reasoning and succeed purely as a matter of logic even when they have actually false premises. (In Chapter V, we will see why the truth of the premises is not nearly as important as the validity of deductive arguments or the strength of inductive arguments.)

We can also give a more general definition of a **bad argument**.

DEFINITION OF BAD ARGUMENT:
An argument is a bad argument if and only if it is an argument such that either it has at least one actually false premise or, even were all its premises actually true, it is either an invalid deductive argument or a weak inductive argument.

Bad arguments may be bad in various ways and to various degrees. A bad argument may be an invalid deductive argument with all true premises, or a valid deductive argument with at least one false premise; or an invalid deductive argument with at least one false premise, or a weak inductive argument with all true premises, or a strong inductive argument with at least one false premise, or a weak inductive argument with at least one false premise.

Since good and bad arguments, strictly speaking, can be either deductive or inductive, we should include the term "inductive" when speaking specifically of a good or bad inductive argument and include the term "deductive" when speaking specifically of a good or bad deductive argument so as to be clear which standard of support is in question. To repeat and to emphasize the point, it is *never* proper to call an inductive argument valid or invalid, sound or unsound, or to call a deductive argument strong or weak.

When assessing arguments it is best to check whether the premises support the conclusion first, and then only if the premises do support

the conclusion to consider whether all the premises are actually true. *Structure before truth*
While this goes against many people's habits and inclinations, we will see that
proceeding in this order avoids many difficulties. This applies to both deductive
and inductive arguments (see Chapter V).

Deductive arguments can be understood with more clarity, simplicity,
and rigor. Since this is so, and since understanding the principles at work
in deductive argument makes understanding inductive arguments easier, in
what follows we will concentrate almost exclusively on deductive arguments.

We may conclude this chapter by giving the following graphic representation of the distinctions made so far. The chart below shows which
questions we ask and the distinctions that flow from answers to those
questions.

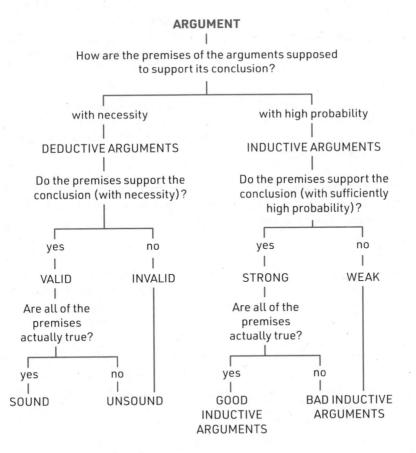

ARGUMENT

How are the premises of the arguments supposed
to support its conclusion?

with necessity   with high probability

DEDUCTIVE ARGUMENTS   INDUCTIVE ARGUMENTS

Do the premises support the   Do the premises support the
conclusion (with necessity)?   conclusion (with sufficiently
                                              high probability)?

yes   no   yes   no

VALID   INVALID   STRONG   WEAK

Are all of the   Are all of the
premises   premises
actually true?   actually true?

yes   no   yes   no

SOUND   UNSOUND   GOOD   BAD INDUCTIVE
                                             INDUCTIVE   ARGUMENTS
                                             ARGUMENTS

Study Questions and Problems

Respond to each of the following questions and problems clearly and precisely.

1) What are the elements of making a clear distinction? What does it mean to respect a distinction, and how do we usually accomplish this? Give an example (other than the examples given in the text).

2) What are the steps for putting an argument in premises and conclusion form? Give an example which puts an argument that is not in premises and conclusion form into that form.

3) What are the two separate and independent considerations that must be taken into account when judging whether the premises of an argument give good reasons in support of its conclusion? Explain why and what it means for these considerations to be independent of one another.

4) Give the definition of a deductive argument. Give both a paraphrase in your own words and the formal definition as given in the text. Give an example of a deductive argument (other than the examples given in the text).

5) Why must we say that a deductive argument only supposes that its premises support its conclusion? In other words, why must the definition of deductive argument include the word "supposes" or its equivalent?

6) Give the definition of a valid argument. Give both a paraphrase in your own words and the formal definition as given in the text. Give an example of a valid argument (other than the examples given in the text).

7) Give the definition of an invalid argument. Give both a paraphrase in your own words and the formal definition as given in the text. Give an example of an invalid argument (other than the examples given in the text).

8) If a deductive argument is valid, what does that indicate about the truth or falsity of that argument's premises? Why?

9) If a deductive argument is invalid, what does that indicate about the truth or falsity of its premises? Why?

10) If the conclusion of a valid argument is false, what does that indicate about the truth or falsity of that argument's premises? Why?

11) Using an example, explain how a deductive argument can have true premises and a true conclusion and still not be valid.

12) Using an example, explain how a deductive argument can have false premises and a false conclusion and still be valid.

13) Give the definition of a sound argument. Give both a paraphrase in your own words and the formal definition as given in the text. Give an example of a sound argument (other than the examples given in the text).

14) Give the definition of an unsound argument. Give both a paraphrase in your own words and the formal definition as given in the text. Give an example of an unsound argument (other than the examples given in the text).

15) If an argument is sound, what does that indicate about its validity? Why?

16) If an argument is sound, what does that indicate about the truth or falsity of its conclusion? Why?

17) Explain the difference between deductive and inductive arguments.

18) Give the definition of an inductive argument. Give both a paraphrase in your own words and the formal definition as given in the text. Give an example of an inductive argument (other than the examples given in the text).

19) Why must we say that an inductive argument only supposes that its premises support its conclusion? In other words, why must the definition of inductive argument include the word "supposes" or its equivalent?

20) Give the definition of a strong inductive argument. Give both a paraphrase in your own words and the formal definition as given in the text. Give an example of a strong inductive argument (other than the examples given in the text).

21) Give the definition of a weak inductive argument. Give both a paraphrase in your own words and the formal definition as given in the text. Give an example of a weak inductive argument (other than the examples given in the text).

22) What does the definition of strong inductive argument say about the actual truth of the argument's premises? Why?

23) If an inductive argument is weak, what does that indicate about the truth or falsity of its premises? Why?

24) Give a definition of a good inductive argument. Give both a paraphrase in your own words and the formal definition as given in the text. Give an example of a good inductive argument (other than the examples given in the text).

25) Give definitions of a bad inductive argument. Give both a paraphrase in your own words and the formal definition as given in the text. Give an example of a bad inductive argument (other than the examples given in the text).

26) If an argument is a good inductive argument, what does that indicate about its strength? Why?

27) If an argument is a good inductive argument, what does that indicate about the truth or falsity of its conclusion? Why?

Chapter II

PROPOSITIONS

- propositions, attitudes, states of affairs
- fact / opinion

Part I: Truth and Falsity of Propositions

In the last chapter we saw that an argument is a set of propositions such that the truth of one proposition, the conclusion, is supposed to be supported by the truth of the other propositions, the premises. Clearly an argument is composed of propositions. This means that for us to develop a clear and rigorous understanding of what an argument is, we must now clarify what a proposition is.

> DEFINITION OF PROPOSITION:
> A proposition is that aspect of language that can be true or false.

def. of prop.

It follows from this definition that a proposition is the meaning of a sentence, in the sense that the proposition expressed by a sentence is the possibility of that sentence expressing a truth or falsehood. We understand the meaning of a sentence insofar as we understand what matters would be like were the sentence true (regardless of whether matters are actually so arranged). We say that a proposition is an aspect of language, rather than a part, since propositions cannot be expressed except through some language or other and so propositions cannot be detached from their expressions in sentences. A proposition can always be expressed in a complete sentence in English (or some other language). For example, the following sentences all express propositions:

if this is true, how wd. things be?

sentences can express propositions

The first programmable computer was built in Cambridge.

Pigs cannot see color.

Berlin is the capital of France.

The first is true, the third false, and it may not be clear whether the second is true or false but nevertheless it is either true or false.

While propositions cannot be detached from sentences, propositions are not the same as sentences because the same meaning may be expressed in different words. So, the sentences "John hit the ball" and the sentence "The ball was hit by John" both express the same meaning, the same proposition—(that is, matters would be the same were each of these sentences to express a true proposition.)Also, the same meaning—the same proposition—may be expressed in sentences in different languages. So, for example, the English sentence "It is raining," the German sentence "Es regnet," and the French sentence "Il pleut" all express the same meaning. We shall say that these sentences all **express the same proposition.**

different languages, sentences; —same proposition

The defining aspect of propositions is that they *can be* true or false. We shall call these values true and false **truth values.** Propositions, then, are whatever can have a truth value. Consider the following chart:

(My) Father	hasn't	any reason	to become querulous	in that manner.
(My) Dad	doesn't have	any cause	to complain	like that.
(My) Daddy	doesn't got	no reason	to make a fuss	like he's doing.
(My) Pop	don't have		to gripe	
My old man	ain't got			

If we take one item from each column in order, we get an English sentence each time. That means there are 3,600 sentences that can be produced by this means.[1] While the sentences so constructed may present images of speakers with different social statuses, every sentence so constructed is an English sentence (no one but an English speaker says any of these). The point is that every one of these sentences has the same meaning—that is, every one expresses one and the same proposition: the states of affairs that would make any one of these sentences true or false are the same for every sentence.

meaning bound up w/ proposition

---

1   We have adapted this example from an unpublished lecture by linguist James Bostain. The total number of possible sentences arises from multiplying the number of items in each column. The word "My" in parentheses is optional, while the word "my" in the last line of the first column is not. This means that we count the optional words as if they were a column of four. So, the total number of possible sentences will be 4x5x5x3x4x3 = 3600.

We should never confuse truth values of propositions with the validity or invalidity of arguments. While we may sometimes use a word like "valid" loosely and say things like "What she said is valid," in this text we will use the term "valid" exclusively to apply to valid deductive arguments (see Chapter I). Confusing these very different values is so common that the difference is worth emphasizing as follows:

(1) **Arguments can never be true or false; only propositions can be true or false.**

(2) **Propositions can never be valid or invalid; only deductive arguments can be valid or invalid.**

Truth values apply only to single propositions. Each proposition has a truth value, but arguments do not have truth values since they are composed of several propositions standing in specific relationships with one another (relations between the premises and conclusion of each argument). Neither the whole set of propositions nor the relationships between them have a truth value. So no argument can be true or false; only individual propositions, whether parts of an argument or not, can be true or false. We may present this reasoning in the form of an argument as follows:

1) The values "valid" and "invalid" express **relationships** between the premises and conclusions of deductive arguments.

2) For there to be a relationship between the premises and conclusions of deductive arguments requires at least two propositions (because exactly one proposition must function as a conclusion and at least one proposition must function as a premise).

Therefore, (3) no single proposition by itself can express an argument, and consequently no proposition can be valid or invalid.

The values of validity and invalidity, on the other hand, apply only to the relationship between the members of the set of propositions that compose a deductive argument. We evaluate the validity relationship between the premises and conclusion of deductive arguments by determining whether if the premises of the argument were true, then its conclusion would have to be true. When the truth values of the individual propositions stand in this relation of necessity, the deductive argument will be valid. Similarly, the strength and weakness of inductive arguments designate relationships between the members of the set of propositions that compose inductive arguments. We evaluate the relationship between the premises and conclusion of inductive arguments by determining whether if the premises of the argument were true, then its conclusion would be more likely to be true than to be false. Since the soundness of a deductive argument implies that the argument is valid, and the goodness of an inductive argument implies that the argument is strong, these evaluations also, in part, concern the relationships among members of the set of propositions that compose the arguments. None of these evaluations concerns merely single propositions; they always concern sets of propositions and the relationships in which they stand. Hence, no single proposition nor any propositions that are not parts of arguments can be valid or invalid. We may present this reasoning in the form of an argument as follows:

> 1) Every argument consists of the assertion of a relationship between several different propositions.
>
> 2) Such relationships between propositions are not, themselves, propositions and cannot have truth values.
>
> ――――――――――――――――――――――――――――――――――
>
> Therefore, (3) arguments cannot have truth values.

The relationship between propositions and truth values, and so the definition of "proposition," is given by the first two **laws of logic**. A law of logic states a condition that is necessary before it is possible for anything to count as a proposition. To count as a proposition, something must be able to be either true or false, that is, be meaningful or make sense (whatever cannot be either true or false lacks meaning, strictly speaking, for, in this sense, the meaning of a sentence is the possibility of the sentence being true). This amounts to saying that a law of logic states a condition that is necessary before it is possible for a proposition to be meaningful rather than nonsense. Laws of logic establish what must be true before anything could count as meaningful.

DEFINITION OF LAW OF LOGIC:
A law of logic states a condition that must hold before any proposition could possibly have a truth value.

The laws of logic differ radically from the laws of nature such as Newton's laws of motion. Laws of nature express causal relations between events in the world: causal relations determine which events will or will not occur under certain conditions. We must engage in empirical scientific investigation of the natural world to discover the causal laws of nature. In order to investigate the natural world we must already have a meaningful language in which to express the methods, procedures, and results of those investigations. This means that we must already operate with the laws of logic before we could even begin to investigate nature. The laws of logic do not express causal laws governing nature; instead, the laws of logic govern what can *possibly* be true or false. Laws of logic are necessary rules governing our talk about anything whatsoever (including any talk about causal relations and laws of nature). We shall return to these issues later in this chapter and also in Chapter IV.

Laws of nature regulate causal relations between (contingent) actual events in the world. (Causal relations determine which events will or will not actually occur under certain conditions.)

Laws of logic are necessary conditions for the possibility of there being any proposition whatsoever. (Laws of logic are conditions for the possibility for any claim to be meaningful, i.e., for the truth or falsity of any possible proposition.)

There are four laws of logic. We will discuss the first and second laws here, and discuss the third and fourth laws in Chapter III. The first two laws of logic are the law of bivalence and the law of truth values.

1) **Law of bivalence: Each proposition is either true or false.**

2) **Law of truth values: No proposition is both true and false.**

Together these two laws define what a proposition is. The **law of bivalence** says that every proposition must have at least one truth value and that there are only two truth values: true and false. Notice that the law of bivalence does not rule out that a proposition could be both true and false (see Chapter III, Part III regarding inclusive disjunction); this is partly why we need the second law, the **law of truth values**. The law of truth values says that no proposition can have more than one truth value (given that there are only the two truth values, true and false). Taken together and as a consequence, the first two laws of logic imply that every proposition must have exactly one of the two truth values, true and false. We can represent this in a table where "P" is a variable that stands for any proposition, "T" stands for the truth value true, and "F" stands for the truth value false.

P
T
F

This diagram is called a truth table (the structure and use of truth tables will be clarified in Chapter III). Symbols for propositions appear above the line, while the rows below the line stand for the alternative possible truth values the proposition may have when circumstances differ. Each row stands for a different possible situation. So the first row represents the possible situation where the proposition P is true, and the second row represents the alternative possible situation where the proposition P is false. We shall find in later chapters that truth tables give us a useful way of representing the possible relations between the truth values of some propositions and the truth values of other propositions.

Study Questions and Problems

Respond to each of the following questions and problems clearly and precisely.

1) What is a proposition? *examples*

2) Explain why a proposition can never be valid or invalid, and why an argument can never be true or false. T/F

3) What is a law of logic?

4) Name and state the first two laws of logic.

5) What do the first two laws of logic imply about propositions?

6) Explain the difference between a (causal) law of nature and a law of logic.

Part II: Identifying Propositions

(A) TRUTH AND FALSITY: PROPOSITIONS ARE ALWAYS ABOUT SOMETHING

When we talk, we talk *about* ourselves and the world around us. This may seem obvious, but it is surprising how easily we may forget this and confuse those things we are talking about with our talk about those things; in other words, we tend to confuse language with the world. The distinction becomes clear if we consider the following sentence:

(1) The door is open.

Sentence (1) expresses a proposition about the position of a particular door. We may picture the relationship as follows:

The door is open.

[handwritten: either it's or it isn't]

↓

In this picture, the proposition says that the door is open, and the door is actually open. So, the proposition describes the arrangement of things in the world (about which we are talking) as it is. We shall call whatever a proposition claims to be talking about (for example, an arrangement of things) a state of affairs. So the open position of the door is the state of affairs that the proposition "The door is open" is talking about. We can summarize this in the following way:

[handwritten: def. State of affairs ✓]

- **A state of affairs is an arrangement of things in the world.**
  (The word "thing" here is intended to include anything about which there are truths. Hence, arrangements of things include arrangements of mathematical things like square roots, ethical and moral values, as well as things like physical objects in space.)

[handwritten: "thing"=any object]

- **Propositions are about states of affairs.**
  (Propositions purport to describe the states of affairs they are about.)

- **Propositions claim that things stand in a certain arrangement.**

  The following are examples of propositions (expressed in English sentences):

  The first programmable computer was built in Cambridge.
  Pigs cannot see color.
  Berlin is the capital of France.

As we saw above, the first is true, the third is false, and while we may not know whether the second is true or false, it must be one or the other; that is, either pigs actually do see color or they do not.

This gives us a way of understanding what the truth values, true and false, mean.

relation b/w TV + states of affairs [handwritten margin note]

DEFINITION OF A TRUE PROPOSITION:
A proposition is true if and only if the state of affairs the proposition purports to describe is as the proposition claims it to be.

DEFINITION OF A FALSE PROPOSITION:
A proposition is false if and only if the state of affairs the proposition purports to describe is not as the proposition claims it to be.

Thus, proposition (1) is true when the door is actually open (as depicted in the picture), and false when the door is not open. The ancient Greek philosopher Aristotle put the point this way: "To say of what is that it is not, or of what is not that it is, is false, while to say of what is that it is, and of what is not that it is not, is true."[2] "True" and "false" designate *relations* between propositions and states of affairs (represented by the arrow in the picture) such that a proposition is true or false *of* the state of affairs that the proposition purports to describe.[3]

(B) PROPOSITIONS AND ATTITUDES

Now contrast Proposition (1) with the following proposition:

"believes that" [handwritten margin note]

    (2) Lara believes that the door is open.

Proposition (2) is about Lara and her state of mind, that is, about her attitude toward the truth value of the proposition "The door is open." It is true when Lara believes the door is open and false when she does not believe the door is open. However, with proposition (2) the situation becomes more complex. This is because proposition (2) also contains another proposition within it—that is, proposition (2) contains proposition (1), "The door is open," as a part. But the truth or falsity of proposition (2) is completely independent of the truth or falsity of proposition (1). We can represent the independence of the truth and falsity of the two propositions in a truth table as follows:

---

2 Aristotle, *Metaphysics* IV, 7, 27 in *The Basic Works of Aristotle*, edited by Richard McKeon, Random House, 1941. The definitions of "true proposition" and "false proposition" used here need only be a minimal account of these concepts; in other words, the definition includes only the (indefinitely large) set of claims of the form "P" is true if and only if P, and does not entail any articulation of the state of affairs P.

3 In Chapter IV we will see that this account of truth and falsity applies specifically to contingent propositions.

Lara believes that the door is open.	The door is open.
T	T
T	F
F	T
F	F

This table shows the four possible ways in which the truth or falsity of the two propositions could combine, and the point that the truth values of the two propositions are independent of one another implies that all four possible combinations could occur. That is to say, it could be true that Lara believes that the door is open and be true that the door is open. It could be true that Lara believes that the door is open and yet be false that the door is open. It could be false that Lara believes that the door is open and be true that the door is open. Finally, it could be false that Lara believes that the door is open and also be false that the door is open. The rows in the truth table represent each of these possibilities (reading the horizontal rows from the top row down as each representing a pair of possible states of affairs). For any two propositions whose truth values are independent of each other, these four rows represent all the possible ways in which their truth values could be combined.

Even though the truth values of the two propositions are completely independent of each other, proposition (2) does express a connection between the two. Proposition (2) says that Lara has a certain attitude directed toward proposition (1), namely an attitude of belief that (1) is true. But since the truth values of the two propositions are independent of each other, she could have the same attitude toward other propositions and she could have different attitudes toward the same proposition. An **attitude** toward the truth value of a proposition gives the way in which a person is directed toward the truth value of the proposition (such attitudes are often called "propositional attitudes," since the attitudes in which we are interested here are attitudes directed, specifically, toward propositions and their truth values; we will simply call these attitudes). Notice that attitudes are directed toward the truth values of propositions; they are not directed toward the states of affairs, but the relation to the state of affairs must be mediated by the proposition and its truth value (we will see the importance of this mediation later in this chapter).

In the first case, Lara could also have an attitude of belief toward many other propositions. For example, each of the following propositions might be true:

Lara believes that the first programmable computer was built in Cambridge.
Lara believes that pigs cannot see color.
Lara believes that Berlin is the capital of France.

In each of these examples, it could be true that Lara has the appropriate belief regardless of whether the proposition her attitude is directed toward is true or false. So, for example, it could be true that Lara believes that Berlin is the capital of France, even though it is false that Berlin is the capital of France.

In the second case, Lara could have various different attitudes toward the same proposition (1). So, for example, each of the following propositions might be true:

> Lara *wonders* whether the door is open.
> Lara *doubts* that the door is open.
> Lara *wants* the door to be open.

Likewise, Lara could *order* that the door be open, or *ask* whether the door is open, or *promise* to open the door, or *threaten* to open the door, or *trust* that the door is open, or have many other attitudes toward the proposition that the door is open. Each of these attitudes would be directed toward the same proposition, and that proposition is about the same state of affairs, the position of the door. In each of these cases (and in many others), whether Lara has a particular attitude toward proposition (1) is completely independent of whether proposition (1) is true or false. So, for example, she may ask whether the door is open regardless of whether the door is actually open.

The result of these points is that we must be careful to distinguish propositions from two other things: from the states of affairs the propositions are about on the one hand, and from the person who expresses the proposition, together with that person's attitude toward the truth value of the proposition, on the other hand. We may represent the two distinctions in the following picture.

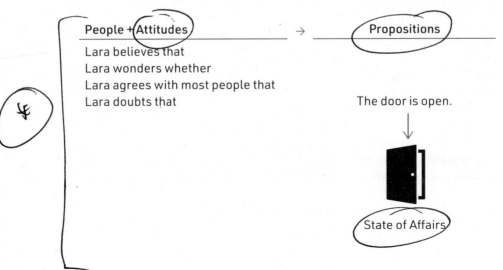

People + Attitudes   →   Propositions

Lara believes that
Lara wonders whether
Lara agrees with most people that
Lara doubts that   The door is open.

State of Affairs

A propositional attitude is a psychological state of a person that is directed toward a proposition and its truth value. So the difference that makes the difference between a propositional attitude and a proposition is that a propositional attitude is a psychological state of some person; it is an event in the world that is not itself a proposition but may be described by some proposition, while a proposition is an aspect of language. So the proposition "Lara hopes that the door is open" is a proposition that purports to *describe* Lara's psychological state of hoping, but her hoping—her attitude directed toward the proposition "The door is open"—is not itself a proposition.

attitudes are not props but can be desc. by a prop.

Moreover, it is clear that the truth or falsity of a proposition is independent of any person having any attitude directed toward the truth or falsity of that proposition. This can be seen by considering the case where one shakes a die in a cup and inverts the cup with the die in it on a table without removing the cup. No one can know which of the following propositions is true:

1) **The side of the die reading one is face up.**
2) **The side of the die reading two is face up.**
3) **The side of the die reading three is face up.**
4) **The side of the die reading four is face up.**
5) **The side of the die reading five is face up.**
6) **The side of the die reading six is face up.**
7) **No side of the die is face up.**

Proposition 7 is in the list to account for such extremely unlikely, but nevertheless real, possibilities as that the die could melt or crumble to dust. The point is that **one of these propositions must be true regardless of whether anyone believes or doubts that it is true or has any other attitude toward the proposition.**

(C) LOGIC AND PSYCHOLOGY

It is especially easy to confuse the content of what is said with who says it, that is, to confuse propositions with people and their attitudes directed toward those propositions' truth values. This confusion results in several misunderstandings about the nature and purpose of logic. In the first place, it results in confusing logic with psychology, something that unfortunately is quite common. However, these are very different enterprises. When we talk about what people think and why they think what they do, we may be talking about two very different things: psychological states or logical relations.

In the first case, in talking about what someone thinks, we would be talking about what psychological states someone is in and what has caused them to be in those states. So, for example, we may say that Meg believes that God exists because her parents raised her in a strict religious environment. This is about Meg and her attitude of belief, and it explains what caused her to have this attitude of belief, namely the circumstances of her upbringing. Notice that the relation between Meg's upbringing and her attitude is a **causal relation**; her upbringing is a series of social events that together cause her to have that particular attitude, that particular belief. This causal relationship explains certain (psychological) states as results of certain (social) events. Although we may sometimes loosely say that Meg's upbringing is the "reason" she believes God exists, this merely means that her upbringing plays a role in a causal explanation of her psychological state. In any case, such causal explanations concern what *actually* happens and what brings it about that it happens. In our example, the causal explanation is concerned with what beliefs Meg actually has and what earlier events and laws of nature brought it about that she have those beliefs. Psychological states include (among other things, such as feelings) people's propositional attitudes.

The discipline of psychology studies the psychological states of organisms; that is, it studies **events** in the **actual** world and seeks to discover the **causal relations** and laws that govern which actual events bring it about that organisms have the psychological states they actually have. Psychology, as a scientific discipline, is **descriptive** *and* **explanatory**: it describes actual psychological states and gives causal explanations for why they occur. Here the question "Why?" is asking what caused the event that someone is in a particular psychological state. Discovering and explaining psychological states can be done only by observing actual events, so psychology is an **empirical** discipline.

The second case, the case of **logical relations**, is fundamentally different. In the case of logical relations, no one's psychological states are relevant at all. Logical relations are relationships between the truth and falsity of propositions, regardless of who, if anyone, believes them to be true, doubts that they are true, or has any other attitude toward those propositions and their truth values. In the case of Meg's belief that God exists, logic would not be concerned with Meg or her psychological states or attitudes such as belief. Instead, the issue for critical thought is whether the proposition "God exists" (toward which Meg's attitude is directed) is true or false. To settle this issue, we would have to examine the arguments that give reasons that are supposed to support the truth of the proposition "God exists" and to determine whether those arguments are good or bad.

As a discipline, logic is *not* concerned with what thoughts we actually have, *or* with what causes us to have them. (Here the word "thought" refers to some sort of psychological event in the world, while in logic, insofar as we use the word "thought," it refers to thought contents, that is, to propositions, regardless of whether these thought contents enter into anyone's mind.) Logical relations are *not* psychological states at all, nor events at all, and as a consequence there is no genuine question about which prior events cause them, since only events have causes. *Logic, as a discipline, is not concerned with what actually happens nor with what* (cause) *brings about what actually happens*. Instead, logical relations are relations between the truth values of propositions.

Furthermore, as a discipline, logic is **evaluative**. Instead of focusing on how we actually think, as psychology does, logic focuses on how the contents of thought—propositions—can be connected so as to determine their truth values. The discipline of logic *evaluates arguments* that are supposed to give support to the truth of their conclusions. Among other things, the discipline of logic studies *relations between the truth values of propositions*: how the truth values of some propositions depend on the truth values of other propositions. Logic studies what would be good reasons (or bad reasons) for the truth of propositions. Here, "good reason" means a good argument in support of a conclusion, and "bad reason" means a bad argument claiming to support a conclusion. Here the question "Why?" is asking what reasons there are in support of the truth of some proposition. Logic studies the validity and invalidity of deductive arguments and the strength and weakness of inductive arguments. This also means that it studies what is *possible* and *necessary*—not which propositions are actually true nor is logic concerned with actual states of affairs—because it seeks to determine what possible relations the truth value of one proposition may have with the truth value of other propositions, and whether the truth or falsity of one proposition necessitates the truth or falsity of other propositions. Since the discipline of logic studies the possible and the necessary, it cannot arrive at its evaluations by empirical means. Hence logic, like mathematics, is an *a priori* discipline.

NOTE:
We have already seen the importance of logical possibility and necessity in, for example, the definitions of deductive argument and valid argument, and we will return to the concepts of possibility and necessity in later chapters, especially in Chapter IV.

We can then distinguish between the discipline of psychology and the discipline of logic by noting four differences that make the difference between the two areas of study in relation to the objects they study, the modality of the object of study, what is to be achieved by the study of their objects, and the form of justification of their claims to knowledge, as follows:

1) Object of study:

Psychology and other natural sciences study actual *events in the world* in order to discover causal laws, such that one type of event brings about another type of event.

Logic studies logical relations between *propositions and their truth values*, such that the truth values of some propositions depend upon the truth values of others.

2) Modality of the object of study:

Psychology and other natural sciences study the causal connections between events in the *actual* world.

Logic studies what propositions are *possibly* true or false and what propositions are *necessarily* true or false.

3) What is to be achieved by the study of their objects:

Psychology and other natural sciences are *descriptive* and *explanatory* sciences: they describe actual events in the world and explain, by means of causal laws of nature, why these events occur.

Logic is an *evaluative* science which evaluates arguments to see if they are good or bad and to thereby evaluate whether the conclusions of these arguments are true or false.

4) Form of justification of claims to knowledge:

Psychology and other natural sciences are *empirical* (empirical sciences seek to justify their claims by appeal to observation and sense experience).

Logic is an *a priori* science (*a priori* sciences seek to justify their claims independently of observation or experience).

So the discipline of logic studies logical relations between propositions, while the discipline of psychology studies causal relations that determine actual psychological states. The differences between the two disciplines may be derived from the differences between logical relations and causal relations, which are summarized as follows:

CAUSAL RELATIONS	LOGICAL RELATIONS
Causal relations connect *events* such that one type of event brings about another.	Logical relations connect truth values of *propositions* such that the truth values of some propositions determine the truth values of others.
Causal relations are relations that connect events in the *actual* world.	Logical relations concern what is *possibly* true and false and what is *necessarily* true and false.
Propositions about causal relations are *descriptive* and *explanatory*; they explain events in terms of causal laws.	Logical relations are *evaluative*; they evaluate arguments to see if they are good or bad in order to determine if the conclusions of the arguments are true or false.
Causal relations are known *empirically* (justified by appeal to experience and observation).	Logical relations are known *a priori* (justified independently of experience and observation).

D) FACTS AND OPINIONS

"Opinion is the inertia or failure of thought."
—Claire Colebrook

"Many years ago I realized how many false opinions I had been accepting as true ever since my childhood, and how doubtful everything I had based on them must be. I therefore decided that if I wanted to establish anything solid and lasting in the sciences, I must deliberately rid myself of all the opinions I had hitherto accepted, and begin building again from the foundations.... I shall apply myself earnestly and freely to the general overthrow of all my former opinions."
—René Descartes (1630)

Hobbes does this in politics

When someone expresses a proposition, especially a controversial one, someone else often may reply with the question "Is that a fact or is it an opinion?" This reply, while common, and even something asked as a matter of course, tends to lead people into various types of confusion. The reply assumes that there is a clear alternative, that there is some one sort of thing that alternatively could be either a fact or an opinion. However, once we reflect on what this supposed alternative amounts to, we will see that it is not clear at all that these are genuine alternatives; it is not clear that there is any one sort of thing that could alternate between being a fact and being an opinion in the way, for example, that a table could alternate between being gray or brown (or some other color). Nor is it clear how to locate such supposed alternatives in our picture of people with attitudes directed toward the truth values of propositions about the world (states of affairs). It is not clear whether we are speaking here of people and their attitudes, propositions, or states of affairs. *If there is no one thing that can alternate between being a fact and being an opinion, then the question "Is that a fact or is it an opinion?" does not really make any sense* (at least when the question is read literally; we will see that the question is not commonly taken literally). So the question "Is that a fact or is it an opinion?" is more like the question "Is that a square root or is it a carburetor?" than it is like the question "Is that gray or is it brown?," for in this latter question the same thing, for example, a table, may alternatively be gray or be brown, and the demonstrative "this" and the pronoun "it" in the question may refer to the same thing. On the contrary, in the case of the question "Is that a square root or is it a carburetor?," there is no *one* thing which might alternate between being a square root or being a carburetor; that is there is no one thing to which the demonstrative "this" and the pronoun "it" in the question may refer. Likewise, with respect to the question "Is that a fact or is it an opinion?," there is no one thing to which the demonstrative "this" and the pronoun "it" in the question may refer.

It is fairly clear that when we say that Lara's opinion is that the door is open, we mean that Lara believes that the proposition "The door is open" is true. To say something is someone's opinion is to say that that person believes some proposition to be true. In terms of our distinctions, to say something is someone's opinion primarily says something about a person, namely that the person's attitude toward some proposition is one of belief that the proposition is true. But, as we have seen, whether a person has some attitude (belief, doubt, wonder, etc.) toward some proposition is completely independent of whether that proposition is true or false. This point holds regardless of how many people share a belief. It does not matter how many people share the same attitude toward a proposition; their attitude still has no bearing on the truth or falsity of that proposition. That Lara agrees with most people that the door is open, for example, has no bearing on whether the proposition that the door is open is true. This is because that agreement has no bearing on the state of affairs, namely, the position of the door. All that matters for the truth or falsity of the proposition "The door is open" is the position of the door, that is, the state of affairs and whether the proposition describes that state of affairs as it is. Since truth and falsity are relationships between propositions and states of affairs, no one's attitude toward that proposition is relevant to whether the state of affairs (the door being open) is as the proposition ("The door is open") claims it is.[4]

It is less clear what is meant by the term "fact" in the supposed alternative "fact or opinion." In ordinary speech we use the word "fact" too loosely. In its most basic use, a fact is a particular kind of state of affairs (a contingent state of affairs; see Chapter IV); it is an arrangement of things about which we may talk (or not). In this sense, facts exist independently of whether any proposition is ever expressed about those facts. This also means that facts, in this basic sense, are independent of anyone's attitudes. Facts exist independently of whether anyone expresses propositions about them, believes propositions about them, doubts propositions about them, wonders whether propositions about them are true, or has any other attitude toward any propositions about them. So, for example, before there were any people, it was a fact (the actual state of affairs in the world) that the earth revolved on its axis. Had there never been any people or had no one ever said anything about this state of affairs, it still would have been a fact that the earth revolved on its axis. The revolution of the earth about its axis is a state of affairs, an arrangement of things in the world, that occurs regardless of people's attitudes or of whether any proposition is expressed about those states of affairs.

All too often, people also use the word "fact" to mean a true proposition about a state of affairs. But it is important to note that this use of "fact" must be understood as shorthand. If a proposition about a state of affairs is true, that is because the state of affairs is as the proposition says it is. So the fact (in the basic sense of a state of affairs) is correctly described by a proposition, and we may call the proposition a **statement of fact** because it correctly describes the state of affairs (the fact in the first, most basic, sense). People often shorten the phrase "statement of fact" and just talk about that proposition as if the true proposition were the fact. There is no harm in this shorthand, except when it leads us to confuse the proposition with the state of affairs the proposition is about. It is surprisingly easy to fall into this confusion. We must carefully separate language about the world from the world that language is about. As a result, and in order to avoid such confusions, either it is best to talk about true

---

4 This does not rule out that the states of affairs that make some statement true or false are subjective. What, for example, makes the statement "I like chocolate" true or false is my subjective state of liking chocolate. Such subjective states are themselves states of affairs in the world and propositions about such states are true or false depending on whether these subjective states are as the propositions claim them to be. Just because the state of affairs in these cases is subjective does not make the truth or falsity of propositions about such states of affairs subjective.

propositions and not call these facts, or, if one wants to use the term "fact," then it is best to talk about a statement of fact. Speaking of a true proposition or a statement of fact makes it clear that we are concerned with a proposition and its truth value and whether the proposition is true of a state of affairs, rather than being concerned solely with the state of affairs, as in the first, most basic, sense of the word "fact."

Notice that on neither of these first two uses of the term "fact" can facts be appropriately contrasted with opinions. Opinions, as we said, are attitudes people have toward propositions, but neither of these first two uses of "fact" is about a person or their attitudes toward any propositions. In the first sense, we are talking solely about states of affairs. In the second sense, we are talking about propositions and their truth values. So in the first sense, for example, we are talking about the position of the door. In the second sense, we are talking about the proposition "The door is open" and whether that proposition correctly describes the position of the door. No person's attitude determines or is relevant to either of these.

In asking the question "Is that a fact or is it an opinion?," people are most likely asking whether some person can be trusted when they assert that the proposition is true or whether instead they are merely guessing, posturing, or depending on hearsay, that is, whether they have or lack some sort of **justification** that the proposition is true. But to call this justification, or knowledge, "fact" blurs the very differences between states of affairs, propositions, and persons and their attitudes that we have been at such pains to distinguish. Knowledge is very complicated. While this is not the place to discuss the nature of knowledge in any detail (such matters are investigated by the branch of philosophy called **epistemology**), we can say that, for our purposes and in the appropriate sense, knowledge includes a person having a *justified* belief that some actually true proposition is true. Given this account, knowledge can be compared to opinion to the extent that it also involves some person's attitude of belief. However, in addition, to count as knowledge, that belief must be directed toward a true proposition, that is, a proposition that describes the state of affairs the proposition purports to describe as that state of affairs actually is. Moreover, to have knowledge, not only must a person believe a proposition that is actually true, but there must also be an adequate justification that the proposition is true. This means there must be good reasons that actually support the truth of the proposition they claim to know to be true, that is, a good argument for the truth of that proposition as its conclusion. It is important to notice in all this that knowledge concerns people and their attitudes, propositions, truth, states of affairs, and justifications (arguments).

Since knowledge involves all of these, it cannot help us get clear about how they are different. It simply leads to confusion if we fail to distinguish between knowledge and facts. We may have knowledge about a fact (in the most basic sense of a state of affairs), but that knowledge is not, itself, that fact, nor is knowledge the same as or comparable to an opinion.

One thing that these considerations show is that there is no one sort of thing that might be either a fact or an opinion nor alternate between being a fact or being an opinion. The word "fact" has been used to speak of several different sorts of things (states of affairs, true propositions, knowledge), none of which is merely an attitude toward a proposition in the way that an opinion is. What is important here is not the word "fact"; what is important is that we be clear about the distinctions we use that word to mark. What our discussion of the different uses of the term "fact" has shown is that there is no single distinction between facts and opinions. While the word is not important in itself, since its different uses lead to confusions, we should use the word "fact" only to refer to a (contingent) state of affairs, or better yet avoid the word "fact" altogether and instead use our technical term "state of affairs."

The confusions we have noticed arise because we forget that *our understanding of the world is mediated by language.* To communicate about or even to understand the states of affairs around us, we must be able to describe those states of affairs using language—that is, expressing propositions in sentences. An attitude such as belief, doubt, and the like is directed not toward states of affairs themselves but rather toward propositions and their truth values. So, for example, if Paulette doubts that the moon is made of green cheese, this is not an attitude toward the moon. It is an attitude toward the truth or falsity of the proposition "The moon is made of green cheese." What Paulette doubts is whether that proposition is true. When we fail to notice that propositions mediate between our attitudes and states of affairs, it leads us to ignore the function of propositions as bearers of truth values. *An attitude, even a propositional attitude, is neither true nor false*; it is the proposition toward which that attitude is directed that can be true or false. *States of affairs have no truth values* either; only a proposition about a state of affairs can have a truth value. In other words, it is nonsense to call a state of affairs true or false (so for example, the composition of the moon is not a part of language and so cannot be true or false). So if we ignore propositions, then we can no longer make sense of truth and falsity. But this is just what happens when someone asks "Is that a fact or is it an opinion?" As a consequence, that question makes no sense; it pretends to compare things of very different types—types that are not comparable. The state of affairs (for example, the composition of the moon)

attitudes → propositions → states of affairs

must be one that we are talking about using a proposition, and any attitude someone has must be directed toward a proposition and its truth value. Thus the question "Is that a fact or is it an opinion?" ignores propositions and their truth values and so leads to various types of confusion. The question poses an unreal alternative and has the consequence of obscuring the important notions of truth and falsehood.

To avoid confusion, the best policy is to avoid making a spurious single distinction between facts and opinion. Instead, we should always be careful to make two distinctions:

Make these distinctions instead

(1) the distinction between a proposition and the attitudes (and psychological states) of the person who expresses the proposition; and

(2) the distinction between a proposition and the state of affairs it claims to describe.

If we keep these two distinctions clear, we will then be able to get clear about more complicated things such as truth and knowledge. So instead of asking whether something is a fact or an opinion, we should keep separate and ask the following very different questions:

Ask these questions instead

(a) What is the state of affairs in question?   *SOA*
(b) What proposition is asserted about the state of affairs?
(c) Is the proposition asserted about the state of affairs true? *Prop.*
(d) Does the person believe that the proposition is true, or have some other attitude directed toward the proposition and its truth value? *att.*
(e) Has a justification that the proposition is true (an argument in support of the proposition) been provided?   *arg.*
(f) If a justification has been provided, is it a good argument for the truth of the proposition?

These are clear questions that avoid the confusions inherent in the spurious distinction between fact and opinion.

We may see the importance of avoiding such confusions by examining the consequences of holding onto the spurious dichotomy between fact and opinion. The prevalence with which people ask the question suggests that they do not usually take the question literally. Instead, when they ask "Is that a fact or is it an opinion?," they are asking, figuratively, whether they *What are they really asking?* may take the proposition to be true solely on the authority of the person who asserted it. The question assumes that we can acquire our beliefs only from someone who has the authority to decree that a proposition is true. In asking the question we are taking a passive attitude toward learning. We are seeking an authority to assure us of the truth of some claim. The only alternatives the question allows are better characterized as attitudes of dogmatism and skepticism. So that we may understand these attitudes, we will consider the two extremes: someone who is an extreme dogmatist and someone who is a extreme skeptic.

Extreme dogmatists are people who, by appealing to authority, seek to settle the truth of any proposition; a **dogmatist** is one who holds onto a claim regardless of any criticisms whatsoever. We shall discuss appeals to authority in detail later in this chapter. For the moment, it will be enough to note some of the consequences of the dogmatic attitude. Insofar as someone is dogmatic, that person bows to some authority and is unwilling to accept a claim as true or reject it as false unless it is certified by some authority (dogmatists may, of course, consider themselves to be the appropriate authority, claiming that a proposition is true just because they say or believe that it is true). Dogmatists are concerned primarily, then, with the person who asserts a proposition and whether that person has the status of an authority. Once someone's authority is established, dogmatists accept that person's claims (as "fact") without question and bow to their authority. Once dogmatists accept a claim, they will be unwilling to give it up, except, perhaps, in accord with the dictate of a greater authority. This means that dogmatists resist reason and will not be swayed by any arguments. This is because reasoning tests the truth values of propositions by appealing to standards that are independent of any person, while dogmatists accept claims or reject them solely on the command of an authority (including, too often, their own). Dogmatists may insist that their claims are "facts," but all they can do is insist and hang onto the proposition by the sheer force of their wills.

Skeptics, instead, are people who doubt the truth of propositions. The kind of extreme **skeptic** we are concerned with is someone who doubts that anyone knows the truth of a given proposition, and so he or she doubts that the proposition is true.[5] Such skeptics will say that the claim is "just someone's opinion," not a "fact." These skeptics reject the authority accepted by dogmatists. For this reason, the skeptic will often express their doubt as a challenge by saying accusingly "That's just your opinion." The word "just"

---

5 Not all skeptics are of this extreme sort. The kind of skeptic we are discussing here is more extreme than the kind of skeptic found in many philosophical works. The extreme skeptic we are discussing is neither like the ancient skeptics, who seek to get us to suspend judgment regarding any claim that can be doubted, nor like a philosopher such as David Hume who professes some skeptical views, doubting certain classes of claims.

in the accusation tends to belittle what has been said, without providing an argument against its truth (see the section on *ad hominem* fallacies later in this chapter). While these sorts of skeptics may seem more tolerant, less slavish, and freer than dogmatists, they are not. Like dogmatists, such skeptics are concerned primarily with the person who asserts a proposition and whether that person has the status of an authority. However, extreme skeptics reject propositions because they do not accept that this person, or perhaps that anyone, has the requisite authority. The dogmatist bows to authority, while the skeptic rejects it. However, both agree that the truth values of propositions should be settled by appealing to the authority of some person. Dogmatists believe they have found an authority, while skeptics believe they have not or cannot find one. Yet both look to obey someone's authority. Hence such skeptics are no more concerned with reason and argument than are dogmatists. These skeptics accept the dogmatists' standard that claims are to be accepted or rejected solely on the command of some person's authority, and so they are unable to test the truth values of propositions by the standards of reason, which are independent of any person. Skeptics may doubt claims as "mere opinions," but all they can do is insist and reject propositions by the sheer force of their wills.

We can now see why it is important to avoid making a single distinction between facts and opinion, and why we should not ask "Is that a fact or an opinion?" The question, as it is most commonly used, asks whether we should obey or disobey some person's authority. Whichever way we answer it, we assume that the way to settle disputes and sort out the truth values of propositions is to find out who to obey (the question impels us to commit the fallacy of complex question; see Chapter III, Part II). Both dogmatism and skepticism eliminate reason and argument and make us slaves to the authority of others. The question "Is that a fact or is it an opinion?" eliminates the possibility that we might apply our own reasoning abilities and discover the truth for ourselves. The question makes any genuine learning impossible.

We may summarize the difficulties with dogmatism and skepticism (of the extreme kinds that we are discussing) as follows:

(1) **Neither the dogmatist nor the skeptic is willing to consider any arguments; that is, both shun the use of reason.**

(2) **Both dogmatists and skeptics treat the truth values of propositions as if they could be settled only by appealing to authority.**

(3) **Both dogmatism and skepticism eliminate the possibility that we might apply our ability to reason and, by sorting out the good and bad arguments, figure out what is true for good reason.**

Study Questions and Problems

Respond to each of the following questions and problems clearly and precisely.

1) What is a state of affairs?

2) Using the distinction (make the distinction before using it) between propositions and states of affairs, explain what "true" and "false" mean. In what way are truth values relations?

3) Using an example, explain the distinction between a proposition and a person's attitude toward that proposition. (Hint: compare the truth values of propositions about people's attitudes towards propositions with the truth values of the propositions toward which they have those attitudes.)

4) What is the confusion involved in saying that an attitude is true or false?

5) Explain the four distinctions between the disciplines of logic and psychology in detail.

6) Using an example, explain why people's psychological states are irrelevant to considerations of logic.

7) What does it mean for someone to have an opinion? How do opinions differ from other propositional attitudes?

8) What are the different meanings of the word "fact"? Which meaning is most basic? Why?

9) In what circumstances should we say "true proposition" or "statement of fact" rather than "fact"? Why?

10) How does knowledge differ from a fact in the most basic sense?

11) Explain why (give the argument that) fact and opinion do not constitute genuine alternatives to one another.

12) What distinctions should we use instead of the bogus one between fact and opinion?

13) Instead of asking "Is that a fact or an opinion?" what questions should we ask instead? Why?

14) How does the question "Is that a fact or an opinion?" ignore propositions?

15) What are people usually asking when they ask the question "Is that a fact or an opinion?"? What confusions are involved in asking this question in this way?

16) What are dogmatism and skepticism?

17) Why does the question "Is that a fact or an opinion?" promote dogmatism and skepticism?

18) What is wrong with promoting dogmatism and skepticism?

Part III: Logic and Rhetoric

"For centuries we have been spoon-fed by our teachers, by our authorities, by our books, our saints. We say, 'Tell me all about it—What lies beyond the hills and mountains and the earth?' And we are satisfied with their descriptions, which means that we live on words and our life is shallow and empty. We are second-hand people. We have lived on what we have been told.... We are the result of all kinds of influences and there is nothing new in us, nothing that we have discovered for ourselves...."
—Jiddu Krishnamurti

"He who will not reason is a bigot, he who cannot reason is a fool, and he who does not reason is a slave."
—Henry Louis Vivian Derozio

A) THE IMPORTANCE OF LOGIC AND CRITICAL THINKING

Now that we have seen that propositions must be distinguished from people and their various attitudes directed toward those propositions, we can also separate different **aims** that we may have in speaking and writing, along with the corresponding standards for evaluating such talk. If the aim in speaking or writing is to persuade someone to believe something, the speaker or writer wants them to believe and often thereby to do something the speaker or writer wants them to do, then that speech or writing is called **rhetoric**. Rhetoric is the art of persuasion, and a person who uses rhetorical speech seeks to influence people by affecting their attitudes and actions.

> ### DEFINITION OF RHETORIC:
> A use of language is a form of rhetoric if and only if it seeks to persuade someone to believe something the speaker or writer wants them to believe and thereby to do something the speaker or writer wants them to do.

So rhetoric concerns people and their attitudes and is not, in itself, concerned with the truth or falsity of propositions. It is possible to persuade someone to believe some proposition or to act on that belief, regardless of whether the proposition is true or false and regardless of whether the arguments for that proposition are good or bad. As we have seen, whether someone believes or acts on a proposition is entirely independent of whether that proposition is true or false.

> ### DEFINITION OF RHETORICALLY EFFECTIVE ARGUMENT:
> An argument is rhetorically effective if and only if it typically succeeds in persuading its audience of the truth of its conclusion.

It is possible for a rhetorically effective argument to be a bad argument, and it is also possible for good arguments to fail to be rhetorically effective.

Rhetoric requires an asymmetric relationship between the person using rhetoric to persuade (the rhetorician or speaker) and the people to be persuaded (the audience). This means that *rhetoric is concerned with someone having power over someone else by causing them to believe and thereby to act in certain ways.* How persuasion takes place is irrelevant to achieving the aim of the rhetorical use of language. Rhetorical speech or writing tries to affect people psychologically. It relies on an understanding of what causal forces affect people psychologically. At its crudest, rhetoric may be reduced to simple force or brainwashing. For if such methods lead the audience to come to believe and thereby to act as the rhetorician wants them to believe and act, then the rhetoric is successful. In a more sophisticated vein, rhetoric uses the style, poise, and demeanor of the rhetorician to flatter, force, trick, or seduce the audience into believing and thereby into doing what the rhetorician wants. Note that this does not necessarily mean that the rhetorician wants the audience to believe what he or she believes. The rhetorician may want the audience to believe some proposition to be true that the rhetorician does not believe to be true. The most obvious, but far from the only, examples of rhetorical speech and writing include political propaganda, and marketing and advertising. Politicians or advertisers may or may not believe what they say but will still use rhetoric when trying to get their audience to believe what they say and thereby to get them to vote a certain way or buy a certain product—that is, to do what they want the audience to do.

Insofar as rhetorical argument is concerned with gaining power over others, it is concerned with who has won and who has lost a dispute (an argument in the sense of a fight, not in the sense of argument we have used in this text). Commentators in the contemporary media, for example, largely concern themselves with whether speech is rhetorically effective. They seldom focus on whether an argument is a good argument by the standards of logic and critical thought. This means they are not concerned with whether the reasons (premises) given provide good support for the conclusions drawn, nor with whether those reasons (premises) are true. Hence, they are not concerned primarily with the validity or invalidity or the strength or weakness of the argument, with the truth or falsity of the argument's premises, or even with the truth or falsity of the argument's conclusion.

Logic and critical thinking aim at arriving at true conclusions by means of argument (in our sense of the term) and are concerned with how well those conclusions are supported. Logic and critical thinking seek to evaluate the goodness of arguments and thereby the truth values of the conclusions of those arguments completely independently of people and their propositional attitudes. Since the truth and falsity of propositions and the evaluation of their support are independent of people and their attitudes, arguments can be critically evaluated independently of rhetorical aims. Whether anyone, the rhetorician or the audience, believes a proposition or acts on that belief is entirely irrelevant to its critical evaluation. For critical evaluation there is no asymmetry like that between rhetorician and audience. Anyone may critically evaluate an argument regardless of who, if anyone, puts it forward.

Hence it is even possible to examine and evaluate arguments that no one actually uses; in other words, arguments may be contemplated and evaluated purely hypothetically (this is often done in scientific investigations). For critical evaluation, what propositions are expressed, what truth values they have, and how they are logically related to one another are what is important, regardless of who, if anyone, expresses the propositions. Propositions are true or false depending on their relation to the states of affairs they are about, not because of any relation to people and their attitudes. Logic tests whether the reasons that are supposed to support a conclusion give good support for the truth of that conclusion and thereby whether that conclusion is true. Logic and critical thinking focus on whether arguments are strong or weak, or good or bad inductive arguments, or valid or invalid, or sound or unsound deductive arguments.

Consequently, logic and critical thinking are not concerned with the causes of people's beliefs and attitudes but instead with justifications (arguments) for the truth of propositions functioning as conclusions. This shows why logic and critical thinking are important. First, if we are interested in reliably knowing the truth, then we must reason well. Moreover, much of who we are and who we will become is due to our beliefs and values. Much of the importance of our beliefs is how they are manifested in our actions. Whenever someone tries to get someone else to believe something or do something by means of getting them to believe some proposition to be true, they are in effect claiming that the propositions they are expressing are true. It is all too easy to arrive at our beliefs and values because of what other people have told us. Logic and critical thinking give us ways to determine whether what we have been told is true or false—ways that are not matters of arbitrary decision, instinct, impulse, habit, tradition, or peer pressure. *If we do not take care to think for ourselves, someone else will surely think for us.* And if we are to reliably decide for ourselves what to believe and thereby what to do, and we want true beliefs, then we must be aware both of how our reasoning can go astray and of what it is to reason well.

In his dialogue *Meno*, Plato has his character Socrates distinguish between knowledge and true opinion by comparing true opinions to the statues of Daedalus.[6] These statues were supposed to be so lifelike that if one failed to keep them chained down they would run away. These, Socrates says, are like true opinions that run away if they are not chained down with good arguments. What this myth means is that even when the proposition toward

---

6 See *Meno*, lines 97a–98a.

which an opinion is directed happens to be true, that opinion does not by itself count as knowledge. A person has knowledge only if they can also justify with good reasoning that the proposition constituting the content of their opinion is true. If a person has an opinion such that the truth of its content (the proposition) is not justified by good arguments, then they only have their force of will to help them to hold onto their belief when confronted with the force of rhetoric. The point of rhetoric is to force people to hold the opinions that the rhetorician wants them to hold. And the techniques of rhetoric are specifically designed to overpower or subvert people's force of will. When subjected to rhetorical force, the claims (whether true or false) tend to run away like the statues of Daedalus if they are not chained down with good arguments. Good arguments allow us to hold onto true opinions (thus turning them into knowledge) because they seek to give adequate support to the truth of their conclusions by means of their relationship to the truth of their premises. The evaluation of arguments does not depend on the strength of will with which someone holds a belief. When confronted with rhetorical force, the person with knowledge (the person who has a good argument in support of a proposition constituting the content of their belief) can *check whether the argument meets our two independent standards for evaluating arguments: whether the rhetorician has shown either that the conclusion of the argument is not supported by the premises or that one or more of the premises are false.* If the rhetorician has not shown either of these, then the person who holds the belief for good reason need not fall prey to rhetorical tricks. The person with good reasons is thereby able to resist force (and not merely oppose rhetorical force with the force of the person's will). Reason thus enables us to resist force. *If we abandon reason, then all we are left with is force.* Without reason, we give in to the tyranny of whoever has the most power. We become unwitting or even willing slaves. Logic and critical thinking, then, are important because they give us the means to resist tyranny and despotism and the dogmatism they seek to impose.

The following chart summarizes the differences between the rhetorical use of language and the practice of thinking critically:

	RHETORIC	CRITICAL THINKING
AIM	Rhetoric aims at persuasion. It seeks to win power over others.	Critical thinking aims at good reasoning and true conclusions. It seeks to understand states of affairs by means of evaluating arguments in support of the truth of conclusions about those states of affairs.
CONTENT	People and their attitudes (who says something) is what is important for rhetoric, regardless of the truth or falsity of what is said.	What a proposition says, regardless of who says it, is what is important for critical thinking. The truth value of a proposition and how well it is supported by good reasons both matter for critical thought.
	(a) Truth is treated as if it were relative to who says something. So "is true" is (mistakenly) equated with "is believed to be true."	(a) Truth can be discovered through good reasoning. Truth is not relative to the person who expresses a proposition, but to the states of affairs the proposition is about and the reasons given to support the truth of the proposition.
	(b) Two *people* are necessary for rhetoric to take place. Rhetoric requires someone to do the persuading and someone to be persuaded. It is an essentially adversarial activity.	(b) Only one *position* is necessary for critical thinking. So anyone may contemplate a position and improve it by evaluating the arguments. Critical thinking is an essentially cooperative activity.
	(c) Rhetoric does not differentiate between a person and a position. Positions mistakenly seem to be owned by people (like objects). People get identified with their beliefs and opinions, so criticisms of positions get mistaken for attacks on the people who hold them.	(c) Positions may be held hypothetically— that is, one may evaluate positions no one actually believes. Whether anyone believes a position is irrelevant to the truth of the propositions it contains or to the goodness of the arguments that are supposed to support it.
FORM	Rhetoric proceeds by assertion of the opinions the rhetorician wants the audience to believe and act on, and by attacking any alternative opinions the audience may have. The rhetorician attacks other opinions and defends those that he or she asserts.	Critical thinking proceeds by evaluating the arguments in support of the truth of the proposition under consideration (for example, a proposition one is inclined to believe oneself). Critical thinking puts the truth of this proposition seriously in question.
MEANS	Rhetoric uses appealing forms of speech, flattery of the audience, and tricks (informal fallacies) to *cause* the audience to believe and do what the rhetorician wants. Rhetoric tries to find the weakest version of an opponent's arguments and attack it.	Critical thinking tries to find the strongest version of a position and *evaluates* this for logical adequacy—that is, do the premises of the arguments support their conclusions and are those premises all actually true?

(B) PERSUASIVE LANGUAGE

In 1946, George Orwell wrote an essay entitled "Politics and the English Language." In this essay, Orwell developed some ideas about the exploitation of language for propaganda purposes that two years later he would depict in his novel *Nineteen Eighty-Four* through the fictional language Newspeak.[7]

Orwell noted that words can be used to mislead and conceal rather than clarify. So, for example, certain concepts may be presented as good and others as bad through the use of euphemisms, weasel words, overstatements, understatements, and stereotypes. These uses of language can be thought of as **vocabulary propaganda** rather than **content propaganda**. The former seeks to deceive us regarding meaning—which propositions are expressed by sentences—while the latter seeks to deceive us regarding the truth or falsity of propositions.

> DEFINITION OF CONTENT PROPAGANDA:
> A use of rhetoric is an instance of content propaganda if and only if it tries to deceive us that false propositions are true and that true propositions are false.

> DEFINITION OF VOCABULARY PROPAGANDA:
> A use of rhetoric is an instance of vocabulary propaganda if and only if it tries to deceive us by distorting the meanings of words or phrases so as to make it unclear which propositions sentences are expressing.

The difference that makes the difference between content propaganda and vocabulary propaganda is the difference between truth and meaning: content propaganda seeks to deceive us regarding the truth values of propositions, while vocabulary propaganda seeks to deceive us regarding the meanings of sentences. We may depict the distinction between the expression of meaning in the sentence and the representation of the state of affairs by a true proposition in the following:

---

7 Orwell wrote of what he called "doublethink": "The power of holding two contradictory beliefs in one's mind simultaneously, and accepting both of them.... To tell deliberate lies while genuinely believing in them, to forget any fact that has become inconvenient, and then, when it becomes necessary again, to draw it back from oblivion for just so long as it is needed, to deny the existence of objective reality and all the while to take account of the reality which one denies ..." (*Nineteen Eighty-Four* [Harmondsworth: Penguin, 2008], 223). "Politics and the English Language" is widely available online.

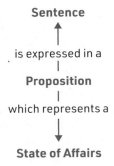

Sentence

is expressed in a

Proposition

which represents a

State of Affairs

As we have seen, a proposition is true insofar as the state of affairs the proposition is about is as the proposition says it is; this means that the proposition describes the state of affairs as it is. A proposition is false insofar as the state of affairs the proposition is about is *not* as the proposition says it is; this means that the proposition does not describe the state of affairs as it is. We have also seen that propositions are meanings that may be expressed in sentences and that the same proposition may be expressed in various different sentences and different propositions may be expressed in the same sentence. So **questions of meaning** are questions about which propositions are expressed in which sentences, while **questions of truth** are questions about whether the state of affairs is represented by the proposition as the state of affairs is (regardless of how the proposition is expressed).

We tend to be more on guard against content propaganda's deceptions regarding the truth values of propositions, where information is presented selectively and often with some sort of bias, because we are usually focused on the states of affairs that the propositions are about rather than how the propositions are expressed in sentences. Content propaganda misinforms us about issues, but vocabulary propaganda is much more subtle and effective because it interferes with our ability to think or talk about issues in such a way that we could come to understand them. Vocabulary propaganda tries to deceive us by distorting the meanings of words or phrases. So when it is successful, vocabulary propaganda interferes with our abilities to think and talk clearly about issues because it distorts the meanings of sentences containing such distorted words or phrases; that is, it tries to deceive us regarding which propositions sentences express. Hence, while content propaganda tries to mislead us about the truth values of propositions, vocabulary propaganda distorts the meanings of sentences.

Let us try to make this point more clearly. Language is the medium through which we describe, understand, and communicate about the world and ourselves.

When vocabulary propaganda distorts the meaning of what is said, it makes it difficult to have a clear vision of the world and ourselves. It is as if we are seeing the world through rose-colored glasses, and we act as if the things we see were really rose-colored rather than tinted by our distorting lenses. Likewise, we tend to attribute the distortions of vocabulary propaganda to the world and ourselves rather than to the distorted language through which we understand that world and ourselves, a tendency that may blind us to distortions in our own vision. As we noticed when discussing the spuriousness of the dichotomy between fact and opinion, we have the bad habit of not noticing that *propositions mediate between our attitudes and states of affairs.* We mistakenly operate as if language were transparent and unproblematic—that is, we tend to look through the language to the states of affairs the language is about without reflecting on the adequacy of the language we are using. If the language is vague, confused, or distorted, so will be our vision of what *possible* states of affairs there can be in the world. Vocabulary propaganda, therefore, is more difficult to detect because it is difficult for us to pause and *reflect* on the language we use to describe and understand the world and ourselves. Our practical interest usually concerns the states of affairs, rather than the medium of language through which we understand those states of affairs. When we are duped by content propaganda, we fail to sufficiently grasp the states of affairs through the medium of language; but when we are duped by vocabulary propaganda, we do not merely fail to clearly grasp the states of affairs but we also fail to sufficiently reflect on the language—the medium—through which we are able to articulate and thereby understand even the possibility that matters can stand one way rather than another, that is, even the possibility of the states of affairs.

We may defend against content propaganda by insisting that important claims be defended by good arguments. And so these arguments must be subjected to the evaluative standards that apply to all arguments. This means that we can defend against content propaganda by carefully analyzing arguments to determine if they meet the evaluative standards that must be applied in answering these two independent questions:

(1) **Do the premises support the conclusion?**

(2) **Are the premises all actually true?**

We may defend against vocabulary propaganda in two ways: first, by making clear distinctions, that is, by making explicit, for genuine and relevant differences, what one sort of thing is, what the other sort of thing is, and what difference makes the difference between them; and second, by carefully reading the texts we encounter (whether in writing or speech) so that we reflect on the language used and not merely the subject matter the language is about, checking whether the language presented to us observes rules of good writing. These rules can be found in style manuals[8] and those recommended in the set of rules offered by George Orwell (listed below).

Impoverishing and distorting language may make it impossible to entertain certain thoughts. As Orwell puts it in "Politics and the English Language," "... the English language ... becomes ugly and inaccurate because our thoughts are foolish, but the slovenliness of our language makes it easier for us to have foolish thoughts." In *Nineteen Eighty-Four*, the fictional language Newspeak had a limited vocabulary that was designed to restrict what people could think or express. If someone only has words for a limited set of alternatives, then they will find it extremely difficult to think about other options. So, for example, someone whose vocabulary contained words for only two political affiliations, say "liberal" and "conservative," would be unlikely to be able to think about options that did not fall within the scope of those affiliations. As a result, that person's actions would be restricted since they would not be aware that there were alternative possibilities on which they might act. In the novel, the central character, Winston Smith, is told, "Don't you see that the whole aim of Newspeak is to narrow the range of thought?... Has it ever occurred to you, Winston, that by the year 2050, at the very latest, not a single human being will be alive who could understand such a conversation as we are having now?" (55).[9]

As Orwell pointed out, vocabulary propaganda makes language erratic and capricious. He writes of some of the qualities common to poor writing,

> The writer either has a meaning and cannot express it, or he inadvertently says something else, or he is almost indifferent as to whether his words mean anything or not. This mixture of vagueness and sheer incompetence is the most marked characteristic of modern English prose, and especially of any kind of political writing. As soon as certain topics are raised, the concrete melts into the abstract and no one seems able to think of turns of speech that are not hackneyed: prose consists less and less of *words* chosen for the sake of their meaning, and more and more of *phrases* tacked together like the sections of a prefabricated hen-house. (italics in original)

---

8 For classic examples, see William Strunk Jr. and E.B. White, *The Elements of Style*, 4th ed., Macmillan, 1999, or the more thorough treatment in R.W. Burchfield, *Fowler's Modern English Usage*, Oxford UP, 2004.

9 George Orwell, *Nineteen Eighty-Four*, Secker & Warburg, 1949. Part 1. Chapter 5.

He then lists several types of rhetorical tricks commonly used to avoid the work necessary for clear writing and thinking. Among these are the use of clichés, dead metaphors, and imagery that has lost its force; the use of complicated verb phrases instead of simple verbs; the use of pretentious language; and the use of words that have lost their meaning and retain only their emotional tone. Let us consider these one at a time.

Clichés and Imagery That Has Lost Its Force

The use of clichés and worn-out imagery and metaphors makes it easy to write. A cliché is a phrase that is overused, predictable, and unoriginal and that betrays a failure to think about the subject matter in a fresh and attentive way. An example of a cliché is the phrase "as different as apples and oranges." This is so overused and well worn that people use it without thinking it through. The notion is that it applies to things that are not comparable, but of course apples and oranges can be compared: they are both kinds of fruit and may be compared in terms of their sweetness, their juiciness, their ripeness, and so on. Compare this cliché with the example used earlier to illustrate things that cannot be compared: they were as different as square roots and carburetors. This is not a cliché, is more vivid and unexpected, and contrasts things that are not genuinely comparable.

A metaphor is the transfer of vocabulary, associations, and commonplaces about one subject matter (the secondary subject matter) to emphasize, suppress, and reorganize another subject matter (the primary subject matter). So when we say that a politician "runs" for office, we emphasize the effort and competitive aspects of the politician's activity, de-emphasize the politician's need to cooperate with others, and reorganize political activity around seeking office rather than around governing. A metaphor fades insofar as we lose awareness of the transfer and thereby lose awareness of the secondary subject matter. When this loss of awareness is complete, the metaphor is dead. So, in our example, we still retain some awareness of the secondary subject matter of running a race, but in even in the case of running a race, used literally, we have completely lost the prior transfer from the whey of goat's milk, which was called "the run" and we now apply the word run to traveling swiftly by foot. Some further examples of faded or dead metaphors include "toe the line," "have an axe to grind," "swan song," "play into the hands of," and many others.

Such clichés, worn-out imagery, and faded metaphors too often get used to avoid thinking clearly enough about the primary subject matter to invent vivid and appropriate phrases and imagery. As a result, people often use them without understanding their meaning. Metaphoric transfer also contributes to a form of vocabulary propaganda, framing an issue in a particular way. Every word comes with the related vocabulary, associations, and commonplaces that form a network through which an issue—a primary subject—can come to be viewed. As with metaphors, this network serves to emphasize, suppress, and reorganize that primary subject and at the same time tends to exclude other ways of understanding the issue. Instead of using faded metaphors or frames continually repeated in the media, we should avoid and eliminate clichés, stock phrases, and habitual or worn-out metaphors and instead take the time to think clearly enough about the state of affairs we are discussing to invent vivid and appropriate imagery.

The Use of Complicated Verb Phrases Instead of Simple Verbs

Good writing and clear thinking require us to pick out and use appropriate verbs and nouns. Deception, imprecision, and obscure writing often result when we use complicated phrases instead of simple verbs. Examples include using "render inoperative" instead of "break," "militate against" instead of "stop," "make contact with" instead of "call" or "write," and so on. These complicated phrases make sentences unnecessarily wordy and euphemistic and tend to soften our language and obscure what could be said, often to greater effect, in simple, direct language. An especially important example of this sort of vagueness and obscurity is the use of the passive voice instead of the active. An example is the sentence "Mistakes were made." Because this sentence has its verb in passive voice, it hides the fact that someone made the mistakes, and as a result it diverts attention from whoever is responsible. Passive voice has its place in writing, but not when its use deliberately obscures agency.

Pretentious Words, Foreign Loanwords, and Jargon

Pretentious words, foreign loanwords, and jargon are often used to make simple or biased sentences seem objective, scientific, or impartial. So the use of nouns such as "individual" instead of "person," verbs such as "liquidate" instead of "kill," and adjectives such as "epoch-making" or "inexorable" and "veritable" may be used euphemistically to make terrible practices seem praiseworthy. Euphemisms are ways of softening the language so as to talk about bad things as if they were good things or even as if they were neutral, thereby obscuring the values those things have. Similarly, talking about good things as if they were neutral or bad things distorts their values; these are sometimes called dysphemisms ("euphemism" literally means "sounding good"; "dysphemism" means "sounding bad").

Foreign expressions such as "status quo" or "Weltanschauung" seek to produce a rhetorical atmosphere of cultural refinement. But they may obscure the straightforward content of what is said. Of course, there are also legitimate uses for such words and phrases; they seldom become part of the language if there is no legitimate use for them. So, for example, among specialists in a certain field of study, specialized vocabulary is useful shorthand. But when the same language is used in addressing a general audience, it tends to obscure the subject matter and confuse and even belittle the audience. It is important to select the language appropriate for the purposes for which it is used. As good critical thinkers, we aim at good reasoning, clarity, precision, and truth. In trying to achieve these ends, we should avoid unnecessarily obscure jargon and technical language.

Vague, Ambiguous, and Meaningless Words and Phrases

Finally, words that sound fine or impressive but get used without any clear meaning or without sorting out which of their various meanings is intended may be used to dishonestly mislead or obscure what is said. So, for example, a newspaper may report an action against an enemy, with no mention that the same people were faithful allies as recently as yesterday's edition. This omission tends to make the history of the conflict invisible. When the application of terms like "enemy" and "ally" shift from day to day, and the history of their application is lost, such terms lose meaning. They tend to retain only an emotional coloring of approval or disapproval. When a word like "reform" is used to designate any change at all, it becomes a way of encouraging people to support a proposal without critically examining it to find out if it will be a genuine improvement rather than merely a change (perhaps for the worse). Other examples of commonly used words that often get abused by neglecting to specify their meanings include "democracy," "freedom," "patriotic," "realistic," and "justice."

Loaded or emotive terms may mislead by attaching value or moral goodness to believing a proposition. Consider the following examples:

(1) Right-thinking Americans will agree with me that we should have another free vote on capital punishment.

(2) A reasonable person would agree that our income estimate is too low.

(3) Senator Jones claims that the new tax rate will reduce the deficit.

(4) The proposal is likely to be resisted by the bureaucrats in Congress.

(5) A company denied that it was laying off 500 people, saying, "We're managing our staff resources."

In (1), the phrase "right-thinking Americans" insinuates that anyone who disagrees with the proposition would be wrong-thinking and perhaps unpatriotic. Similarly, in (2), the word "reasonable" makes it seem as though disagreeing with the proposition would make someone unreasonable. In (3), an emphasis on the word "claims" may suggest that what Jones says is false. And in (4), the word "bureaucrats" is loaded with negative associations of needless complexity, red tape, and pettiness. Compare (4) to the sentence "The proposal is likely to be rejected by members of Congress." The phrase "members of Congress" is more precise and avoids unwarranted negative associations. This example shows that to counteract such misleading language, one needs to identify the prejudicial terms used and substitute a more appropriate word or phrase. Notice that we say that "more appropriate" terms be substituted; this is not the same as saying "neutral" terms. Neutral language can distort as much as positive or negative language. In (5), for example, the phrase "managing our staff resources" sounds like a neutral term but is a distorting euphemism for firing people. Here the use of a neutral term distorts our view of what is actually a bad situation. Similarly, if the company says that it is "rightsizing," when this means it is firing employees, this hides the bad thing happening to the employees by turning it into an allegedly good thing happening to the company. Firing employees may also be obscured by the use of other vague terms such as "repositioning" and "release of resources."

Such misleading language may or may not accompany good reasoning, but emotionally charged and biased language, while it may influence us psychologically, gives no reason for either accepting a proposition as true or rejecting a proposition as false. Misleading language often persuades, but it also obscures the issues and distracts us from critically assessing the truth values of propositions presented in such language and from clearly understanding which aspects of the subject matter are important. Misleading language, then, is not, by itself, bad reasoning. However, it can promote bad reasoning by distorting the language and terms of discussion; when reasoning uses distorted language it will inherit the biases and distortions of the language in which it expresses the arguments. In cases of misleading language, we are all too easily led to accept the terms of debate given in statements made; that is, we too easily overlook important differences and distinctions that can be marked by a richer and clearer vocabulary. This can distort our understanding of the states of affairs at issue and lead us to be deceived by just the kind of vocabulary propaganda that Orwell warned against.

In order to write well—clearly, concisely, and accurately—it is important to rewrite several times. Each rewrite should improve both the structure of our sentences and the choice of vocabulary. It may even be said that the greater part of good writing is rewriting. Orwell offered a few rules to follow to help us avoid misleading language:

(i)   Never use a metaphor, simile or other figure of speech which you are used to seeing in print [or are used to hearing in the media].

(ii) Never use a long word where a short one will do.

(iii) If it is possible to cut a word out, always cut it out.

(iv) Never use the passive voice where you can use the active voice.

(v)   Never use a foreign phrase, a scientific word or a jargon word if you can think of an everyday English equivalent.

(vi) Break any of these rules sooner than say anything outright barbarous.

We have discussed rule (i) above, but here it is expanded to include all media and not merely the print medium that was still dominant when Orwell was writing. Rule (ii) is meant to rule out unnecessarily complicated phrases that obscure rather than illuminate the subject matter. It should be noted that in English the short words tend to be of Anglo-Saxon origin and the longer words tend to be of Latinate origin; this has had political repercussions in British English regarding class divisions. Rule (iii), ironically enough, is a violation of rule (iii) itself. Strunk and White, in *The Elements of Style*, give a much more elegant version of this rule: "Eliminate unnecessary words." This formulation is admirably short, and it is worth noting that this is partly due to the use of a substantive verb, here the verb "eliminate." We discussed rules (iv) and (v) above. The last rule (vi), is meant to turn our attention to the states of affairs we are talking about and to consider them seriously and honestly. It embodies an ethics of speech that values both honest straightforward speech as well as acting ethically. The rules written for operating the ovens in the Nazi death camps were models of clear, precise German; perhaps they should not have been.

These rules help us avoid both vocabulary propaganda and the sort of self-deception that arises from insufficient care in choosing how to express propositions in language. In addition, we may resist the force of vocabulary propaganda by making clear distinctions and respecting them once they have been made; in other words, as we saw in Chapter I, to make a distinction between two sorts of things, one must say what the one sort of thing is, what the other sort of thing is, and what difference makes the difference between those things. In order to respect a distinction once it has been made, mark each distinct sort of thing with an appropriate word or phrase and when later discussing things of that sort use this same vocabulary to mark the specific sort of thing about which one is speaking or writing so as not to confuse it with other similar sorts of things. Making clear distinctions and respecting them expands our vocabulary so as to avoid blurring significant differences and thereby falling prey to vocabulary propaganda.

Study Questions and Problems

Respond to each of the following questions and problems clearly and precisely.

1) What is rhetoric?

2) Define rhetorically effective argument.

3) Compare and contrast the aim of rhetoric with the aim of logic and critical thinking.

4) Compare and contrast the content of rhetoric with the content of logic and critical thinking.

5) Compare and contrast the form of rhetoric with the form of logic and critical thinking.

6) Compare and contrast the means of rhetoric with the means of logic and critical thinking.

7) Why are logic and critical thinking important?

8) How do logic and critical thinking help us resist force?

9) Distinguish between content propaganda and vocabulary propaganda.

10) What makes vocabulary propaganda especially deceptive (and more deceptive than content propaganda)?
    (a) Explain how logic and critical thinking help us to resist the rhetorical force of content propaganda *and*
    (b) how logic and critical thinking help us to resist the rhetorical force of vocabulary propaganda.

11) Explain and give an example of each of the following (try to find examples different from those in the text):
    (a) clichés or dead imagery;
    (b) complicated verb phrases substituted for simple verbs;
    (c) pretentious words, foreign loanwords, and jargon;
    (d) vague, ambiguous, and meaningless words and phrases.

12) State and explain Orwell's six rules to help avoid misleading language.

Part IV: Informal Fallacies

Another kind of difficulty arises when the arguments used to give reasons in support of some conclusion do not support those conclusions. Any case where the premises of an argument do not support its conclusion is called a **fallacy**, and the reasoning is called **fallacious**. When the fallacy is not due to mistakes in the structure of the arguments and especially when the fallacy is due to rhetorical elements rather than content or formal elements of the argument, we call the fallacy an **informal fallacy**. Such fallacies are informal in that their errors arise from some source other than the argument's form.[10] These fallacies are often found in what we have called content propaganda, but they can also appear in our own thinking, leading us astray regarding which propositions are true and which are false.

It is impossible to list all the ways in which people can go wrong in reasoning. At best, we can identify a few common and typical types of errors. We can, however, show what goes wrong in these sorts of cases, why even very intelligent

---

10 We will say more about the form of an argument in Chapter V.

people are tempted to fall into such errors, and what to do to counteract such arguments when we find them or are tempted to make such errors ourselves. Here we will examine some general types of informal fallacy that arise from confusing people and their attitudes (who says something) with propositions (what is said). Since people and their attitudes have no bearing on the truth values of propositions, these fallacies are fallacies of irrelevance. We will consider four types of such fallacies: (1) appeals to motives or emotions in place of support, (2) appeals to authority, (3) arguments against the person rather than against what is said (*ad hominem* arguments), and (4) arguments that treat truth values as if they were subjective or relative to persons and their attitudes.

(A) APPEALS TO MOTIVES OR EMOTION IN PLACE OF SUPPORT

The first kind of informal fallacy arises when we appeal to some person's emotions or motivations in place of rational support. This sort of fallacy may often be effective rhetoric, in that appeals to emotion and motivation have powerful psychological effects on people and affect their attitudes toward propositions, regardless of whether there are good arguments in support of those propositions or of whether the propositions are actually true or false. Instead of good arguments, the appeal to emotion uses various means of producing strong emotions in the audience. People commit the **fallacy of appeal to emotion** when they come to accept a proposition as true or reject it as false because they are induced to or come to feel good or feel bad about that proposition. In attempting to get people to buy products or support certain candidates or proposals, advertising and political rhetoric commonly commit this sort of fallacy. Critical thinking can be difficult and time consuming, while people are often more readily motivated by their emotions than by reason. Hence, fallacies of appeal to emotion are widely used and too often effective.

We should note that there is nothing wrong with inspiring people to action by arousing their emotions, so long as such inspiration is not confused with support for the truth of propositions. Hence, **there is nothing inherently incompatible between being emotionally engaged and being rational;** one can be both. Attempts to affect the psychological state of an audience by arousing their emotions, associating certain emotions with a proposition, or influencing the audience's motives for believing a proposition to be true are, at worst, attempts to manipulate and control people and, at best, ways of giving them prudential reasons to accept a proposition or to act in a certain way. A **prudential reason** to accept a proposition is a reason to accept it as true because of fear of harm, or a hope of a benefit that may be an effect of holding the proposition to be true: a factor other than the proposition's actual truth value (remember the difference not only between propositional attitudes and propositions but also between reasons and causes in this context). Prudential reasons are relevant to people and their attitudes but not to the truth or falsity of propositions. For example, it might be prudent to say what a bully tells us to say in order to avoid a beating. But this gives no support for the truth of the proposition that the bully wants us to say is true.

When speakers attempt to incite people to action by evoking an emotion, it may not be evident what proposition they are trying to get their audience to act on. Should someone try to incite people to acts of violence by provoking anger or hatred among them, the proposition implicit in provoking the emotion might be something like "You should participate in these acts of violence." Here the anger or hatred might motivate people to act, regardless of whether this proposition were true. Similarly, a beer advertisement might show happy, beautiful, scantily clad people at play, in an attempt to evoke pleasurable excitement and to get the audience to accept something similar to the proposition "You should buy this beer," regardless of its truth value.

Specific fallacies that appeal to emotion and motivation include the following:

Appeal to Fear

In this fallacy, also known as the appeal to force, or scare tactics, the speaker tells the audience that unpleasant consequences will follow if they do not accept some proposition. At best it might be prudent to accept the proposition, but the threat gives no support for its truth.

> **Example 23:**   You had better agree that the new company policy is the best policy for the company to adopt, if you expect to keep your job.

This is a threat, yet it contains an implicit argument. We can reconstruct this argument by noticing that the threat to the worker's job is supposed to give the worker reason to agree to the new company policy. We can paraphrase the argument in premises and conclusion form as follows:

> (1) If, you disagree with the new company policy, then you will lose your job.
>
> Therefore (2), the new company policy is the best policy for the company to adopt.

If the person cares about keeping their job, then it might be prudent to go along with company policy regardless of whether it is true that it is the best policy for the company to adopt. But the threat to this person's job gives no support for the truth of any propositions concerning company policy that would make it appropriate to agree with them. Notice that the actual propositions concerning the content of policy are not given in the argument. Whether the new company policy is best for the company would depend on which policies the company could adopt—that is, what actual policies are proposed—and what the consequences of adopting various policies would be for the company. This suggests that the truth of the premise of the argument is irrelevant to the content of the propositions expressing the policy; in other words, the truth of the premise is irrelevant to the truth of the conclusion. To argue against this fallacy, we should identify the threat and the proposition it is supposed to support, note that a threat bears on people's psychological states or attitudes and not on the truth or falsity of the proposition the threat is supposed to support, and so argue that the threat is irrelevant to the truth value of the proposition.

Appeal to Pity (or Sympathy)

In this fallacy, the speaker tries to get the audience to accept a proposition because the speaker deserves the audience's pity or sympathy.

Example 24:   The board of directors should accept our recommendations for improving company labor policies. We spent the last three months working overtime on them.

We can paraphrase this example as an argument by noticing that the second proposition is supposed to give the board of directors a reason to accept the recommendations. In premises and conclusion form the argument can be paraphrased as follows:

(1) We spent the last three months working overtime on our recommendations for improving company labor policies.

Therefore, (2) the board of directors should accept our recommendations for improving company labor policies.

While the speakers may deserve our sympathy or pity for having worked so hard, that gives no support for whether it is true that the board should accept the recommendations. Whether the recommendations should be accepted depends on what they are and whether it is true that they state improvements in company labor policies. Notice that this particular argument does not give the content of the recommendations; it only says that they are about labor policies but does not state the actual policies. This suggests that the truth of the premise of the argument is irrelevant to the propositional content of the policies and thereby that the truth of the premise is irrelevant to the truth of the conclusion. To argue against this fallacy, we should identify the proposition and the appeal to sympathy and argue that whether the speaker deserves our sympathy or pity has nothing to do with the truth value of the claim.

The fallacy of appeal to pity is committed only if the pity evoked is supposed to serve as support for some conclusion. Feelings of pity or sympathy may accompany good arguments, but the pity or sympathy those arguments evoke is irrelevant to whether the arguments are good. Consider the following example:

> **Example 25:**   Professor: "You missed the midterm, Richard."
> Richard: "I know. I think you should let me take a makeup test."
> Professor: "Why?"
> Richard: "I was hit by a truck on the way to the midterm. Since I had to go to the emergency room with a broken leg, I think I am entitled to a makeup."
> Professor: "I'm sorry about the leg, Richard. Of course you can make it up."

While Richard's situation evokes and deserves sympathy, his argument is a good one because his injury is a legitimate excuse for him missing the test. The reason the professor is justified in letting him make up the test is that his injury is a genuinely good excuse, not because the professor feels sympathy for Richard (even though the professor may, indeed should, feel sympathy for him). It should also be noted that this example shows that emotion and reason are compatible and that they are not inherently in conflict. Being rational does not require being unemotional or suppressing our emotions; it is perfectly appropriate to have even strong emotions accompanying good reason. Fallacies and confusions arise only when we confuse these very different things: we get fallacies of appealing to emotion only when we confuse even appropriate feelings we may have directed toward some propositions with any reasons at all for thinking that those propositions are true or false.

Appeal to Flattery (or Vanity)

In this fallacy, the speaker tries to get a proposition accepted by flattering the audience.

Example 26: You sure are a great manager. You care so much about the lives of the people you manage. Surely, you will let me have tomorrow off work so I can attend my softball game.

The first claim in this example is an attempt to flatter the manager, which is supposed to support the implicit claim in the second sentence that the employee should get the day off to play softball. We can paraphrase this in premises and conclusion form as follows:

(1) You sure are a great manager; you care so much about the lives of the people you manage.

(2) I have a softball game scheduled for tomorrow.

Therefore, (3) I should get tomorrow off work.

The employee is trying to get the manager to act on the proposition that he be given the day off. He is trying to do this by flattering the manager and appealing to her vanity. But whether the employee's flattery makes the manager feel good is irrelevant to whether it's true that the employee should get the day off work; in other words, the truth of the premise is irrelevant to the truth of the conclusion. Whether the employee deserves the day off depends on issues concerning the conditions of employment regarding time at work. This fallacy is common in politics and advertising, where flattery may disarm the audience far more effectively than threats. To argue against this fallacy, we should identify the flattery and the conclusion and argue that whether the audience is admirable (in the flattering respect) is irrelevant to the truth value of the conclusion.

flattery
→
threats

Appealing to Other Emotions

Fallacies appealing to other emotions and motivation (such as spite, anger, guilt, indignation, devotion, hope, etc.) besides the ones we have examined can be constructed in a parallel manner. They will include premises that are designed to arouse the emotions of the audience and a conclusion that the speaker tries to get the audience to accept without taking relevant considerations into account. In all these cases, the emotions the audience comes to feel are strictly irrelevant to whether the conclusion is actually true; the truth values of the premises are irrelevant to the truth value of the conclusion. The truth value of the conclusion depends on its subject matter and on whether it describes that subject matter as it is, not on whether people feel good or bad about the proposition.

(B) APPEAL TO AUTHORITY

Appeals to emotion are fallacies in which the premises, which are supposed to support some conclusion, are completely irrelevant to the conclusion's truth value because these fallacies concern the people involved rather than the propositions themselves. This sort of diversionary tactic is common and leads to other types of informal fallacy that do not appeal to emotions in place of support but still dwell on people and their attitudes rather than on propositions, albeit in different forms. The two most important general forms of such fallacies are appeals to authority and attacking the person (*ad hominem* arguments). While both forms dwell on people and their attitudes rather than on propositions and arguments, these fallacies differ from appeals to emotion in that their premises are *about* people and their propositional attitudes rather than their premises being designed to have *effects* on people's attitudes as in the appeals to emotion. In this section we will discuss the **fallacy of appeal to authority**, with *ad hominem* arguments following in the next section.

The general form of the appeal to authority is:

(1) **Some person (who is taken to be an authority) says that P is true.**

Therefore, (2) P is true.

Here the premise is about the person who is taken to be an authority and what proposition that person claims to be true, while the conclusion is just the claim that the proposition is true. But since the truth or falsity of a proposition is independent of whether any person claims it to be true or false—that is, independent of any propositional attitudes—premises of this form are irrelevant to the truth or falsity of their conclusions.

Nevertheless, we often have to rely on authorities as sources of information. No one person can investigate every proposition to see if it is true, since such investigations require time, resources, and effort. So we divide the labor: certain people become expert about one subject matter and other people become expert about other subject matters. Those of us without a high level of expertise about some particular subject matter, then, rely on the competence of the experts to sort out which propositions are true and which are false about that subject matter. If done carefully and in appropriate circumstances, such appeals to the authority of experts are both legitimate and necessary. But when they are made dogmatically or without due consideration of the purpose that such appeals serve, they become fallacies. In order to distinguish between legitimate and illegitimate appeals to authority, we may test them by seeing if they meet certain standards. For an appeal to authority to be legitimate, it must meet *all* six of the following standards.[11] If an appeal to authority fails to meet one or more of these standards, then it is illegitimate.

Standards for a Legitimate and Illegitimate Appeals to Authority

(1) The person cited as an authority actually has sufficient expertise in the subject matter in question.

(2) The proposition justified by appealing to the expertise of the person cited as an authority is a proposition about matters within that person's area of expertise.

(3) There is agreement—for good reason—among the experts in that area about the truth or falsity of the proposition in question.

(4) The area of expertise is a legitimate area or discipline.

(5) The person cited as an authority is not significantly biased.

(6) The person cited as the relevant authority is identified.

We should also add that it should not be the case that the person cited as an authority was making a joke, drunk, or was otherwise not being serious when she or he expressed the proposition in question.

Since we often have to rely on authorities, many people develop a tendency to believe them without due caution. Hence, people often commit the fallacy of an illegitimate appeal to authority. To argue against this fallacy, we should show that the argument fails to meet one or more of the six standards. Let us examine each of these standards.

(1) The person cited as an authority actually has sufficient expertise in the subject matter in question.

The appeal to authority obviously gives no support to any proposition that is asserted by a person who lacks sufficient expertise in the subject matter the proposition is about. The point of the appeal to authority is that the person

---

11 These standards are variations derived and adapted, in part, from the standards given by the Nizkor Project at http://www.nizkor.org/features/fallacies/. Copyright 1995 Michael C. Labossiere.

appealed to as an authority has put in the time, effort, and resources required to have worked out, with good reasoning (see standard (3) below), what is true and false in their area of expertise. So no authority is legitimate if they have failed to gain sufficient expertise in the subject matter the proposition is about.

Factors relevant to determining whether a person has sufficient expertise in areas of academic study (such as engineering, history, sociology, etc.) include formal education, academic performance, publications, membership in professional societies, papers presented, awards won, and so on. However, these are only relevant factors; they are far from conclusive. Since many people may have expertise without academic credentials, and since academic credentials do not guarantee that a person has expertise, we must make good judgments about when and with regard to which propositions we should trust such indicators. This is a general point about the standards for a legitimate appeal to authority, namely that there is no substitute for caution and, through reflection and practice, developing good judgment about the application of these standards.

Moreover, we must make good judgments about which subject matters call for expertise in areas of academic study. There are many subject areas where expertise is not acquired through formal study but through long practice and experience. So, for example, practice and experience with making clothes can give someone expertise in tailoring. Also, people may be reliable authorities simply because they have the requisite skills. For example, one need only be able to use a particular tool to be a reliable expert who is able to teach someone how to use that tool. This means that whether someone counts as an expert is relative to the knowledge and skills of both the person claiming expertise and those appealing to that person's alleged expertise.

In making good judgments about who counts as a reliable authority, we should be careful to sort out whether the person's expertise is genuine. This may be a matter of some debate. We will have to determine what sort of education and experience a supposed expert has and whether that education and experience are sufficient to count that person as a reliable authority in the matter in question.

(2) The proposition justified by appeal to the expertise of the person cited as an authority is a proposition about matters within that person's area of expertise.

We have already noted that we need to rely on authorities because no one person can investigate every proposition to see if it is true or false. We must depend on a cognitive division of labor. Hence, although a person may be a genuine authority regarding one subject matter, that expertise has no bearing on propositions about any other subject matter. For to count as a genuine authority, the person has to have put in the requisite time, effort, and resources to have acquired expertise in a specific subject matter, and having done so does not mean that the person has done so with respect to any other subject matter. As a result, it is illegitimate to appeal to that person's authority regarding any proposition not specifically about that person's area of expertise. So, for example, it might be appropriate to appeal to what Albert Einstein said about matters of physics but not to what he said about architecture or about government. It is important, therefore, to determine what subject matter a proposition is about and to check to see whether the person cited as an authority is an authority concerning that subject matter.

Mistakes of this sort are, unfortunately, quite common. Advertising, for example, often violates this standard by using famous actors and sports figures to endorse products. Even though popular actors and great basketball players may be counted as experts on acting or basketball, they are no more qualified than anyone else to assess the merits of insurance companies, shaving cream, clothing, or political positions, and thus they do not count as appropriate authorities.

(3) There is agreement—*for good reason*—among the experts in that area about the truth or falsity of the proposition in question.

Even regarding propositions expressed by an expert about that expert's proper area of authority, it is only legitimate to appeal to that authority regarding matters that are well established in that field. This displays how weak an argument even a legitimate appeal to authority is. **When we appeal to authority, we rely on the authorities to whom we appeal to have good arguments to support their conclusions.** We depend on the experts because they have the training and resources and have taken the time to do careful investigations into the subject matter and to evaluate the relevant arguments so as to determine the truth or falsity of the propositions in question. So **the appeal to authority is only as good as the arguments the experts have accepted for the truth of their conclusions.** Hence, appeals to authority are weak arguments because they do not themselves give good arguments in support of conclusions, but rather they suppose—perhaps wrongly—that the authority cited does have good arguments in support of the truth of the conclusions in question. The appeal to authority says that some people, the alleged experts, have good arguments but does not actually give the arguments, instead merely gesturing indirectly at those arguments. This point lies at the core of the appeal to authority.

Since the appeal to authority defers the evaluation of the arguments to the experts, it is legitimate only when the disputes among those experts are fairly well settled and have been settled by good arguments. In disputes among the experts in a field, these experts cannot settle their differences by appealing to authority themselves. They have to evaluate the arguments about the subject matter and sort out which are the better and which the worse arguments. When the experts on a given subject are in dispute among themselves, appealing to the propositions affirmed by one expert may be countered by appealing to contrary propositions affirmed by another expert. In cases of this sort, the issues cannot be rationally settled by appeals to the experts, so the appeal to authority is useless. We should not accept these unsettled propositions on the basis of authority but instead should look to the actual arguments about the issues in contention.

For example, economists differ significantly about how to explain increases in inflation. Some attribute such increases to greater utilization of the productive capacities of a society, while others deny this and cite some other factor, such as increases in the money supply. As another example, experts in psychology and psychiatry often disagree about whether certain defendants in criminal cases are legally sane and competent to stand trial. In such matters, it is fruitless to appeal to authority. Instead, we must look at the actual arguments about inflation or about legal competence to stand trial. However, when we consult a table of square roots to find that the square root of 58 is 7.616..., there is every reason to accept this figure, since the matter is not one about which mathematicians, the appropriate experts, disagree. The experts agree on this because they have a good argument for its truth—namely, that well-established and reliable calculations give this result. This is the crux of legitimate appeals to authority: their legitimacy depends on the justifications given by the authorities. We are relying on the authorities having worked out what is true by assessing the arguments and coming to agree that the claim in question is true for good reasons. So, in appealing to authority, we are really appealing to the arguments the experts have worked out and successfully evaluated. We are not really appealing to the person and that person's propositional attitudes at all. And again, the appeal to authority can be no better than the arguments the experts have worked out.

Finally, we must beware of treating disagreements between experts by throwing up our hands and saying, "Well, then, it's just a matter of opinion" (see the discussion of extreme skepticism in Part II (D) above). This response mistakenly treats the appeal to authority as if it were the only way of settling disputes, as if when appealing to authority fails we are left with a completely arbitrary decision. Such a response forgets that the appeal to authority always depends on the authorities weighing actual arguments about the specific subject matter. Instead of giving up hope of settling the dispute, we must turn to the actual arguments and make a rational assessment of their merits; that is, when the appeal to authority is in doubt and it is important for us to determine the truth of the propositions about which we are appealing, we should abandon appealing to the authority of this or that person and examine the arguments about the subject matter itself. It is often surprising how far we can get, even regarding specialized fields of study, by simply thinking things through and reasoning matters out for ourselves.

In most subject areas there is some degree of disagreement; very little is settled to everyone's complete satisfaction. We have to exercise good judgment about how much agreement is significant enough to justify an appeal to authority. When in doubt, or when the issue is significantly important, we should investigate the matter ourselves. The more important the issue, the less we should rely on authorities and the more we should seek to work out the best arguments about the subject matter.

(4) The area of expertise is a legitimate area or discipline.

Not every subject matter counts as a legitimate area of expertise. Sometimes we know very little about a subject matter, or sometimes knowledge about some subject matter is so common that no one has any better claim to knowledge about it than anyone else. And sometimes it is questionable whether an area in which someone claims expertise counts as a legitimate subject matter at all. Obviously, propositions asserted about these supposed subject matters will not be reliable. For example, it is not clear whether there are any such things as psychic phenomena (pre-cognition, telepathy, or telekinesis, etc.). There are reasons to suppose that there are no such phenomena, and if this is the case, since there is no real content to the subject matter and no truths to be discovered, there can be no genuine expertise. If such phenomena do exist, we know very little about them or how to study them, in which case there can be no legitimate appeal to authority in these matters because there is no established body of knowledge. To be a legitimate authority, a person must have mastery over a genuine field of knowledge, one that takes time, resources, and study to master.

It is sometimes difficult, however, to determine which subjects are legitimate fields of study and expertise. Various natural sciences have had to struggle for acceptance as legitimate areas of study. For example, geology came to be a legitimate area of study only when the age of the Earth proved to be tremendously greater than had been previously thought (it had been thought that the Earth was only a few thousand years old). Only a very old Earth (billions of years old, as it turned out) could undergo the large-scale changes worthy of systematic scientific study. Whenever a field of study is not widely accepted as legitimate, we must avoid arguing by appealing to authority until the discipline has established itself as a genuine field of knowledge, a field in which there is sufficient knowledge to warrant specialized study and training. In such cases, once again we need to examine and assess the actual arguments about the subject matter.

(5) The person cited as an authority is not significantly biased.

When we appeal to the authority of an expert, we rely on the expert cited to give us the best judgment possible given the state of knowledge about the subject matter. However, since experts are as liable to biases and prejudices as any other person, we should be careful to assess any evidence that an authority may be biased in some way that would affect their reliability. Even were the proposition supported by the appeal to authority true, the expert's bias would make the already weak appeal to authority argument weaker still. This is because the expert's bias gives us reason to suspect that he or she has neither considered the arguments with due care nor evaluated the arguments solely according to the standards of good reasoning and the already known truths about the field of study. There are, however, various ways of controlling for such biases and prejudices. For example, in testing new drugs for effectiveness, double-blind studies are conducted. This is necessary in order to compensate for bias that may be produced by the placebo effect, the tendency for people to feel better when given something they are told is medication for some condition they have, even when the medication is not actually effective. So, in studying the effectiveness of new drugs, researchers give some of the test subjects the real medication and give others a sugar pill, a placebo. The researchers do not tell the test subjects who is getting the real medication and who the sugar pill (or even that some of them are getting a sugar pill). Moreover, since those giving the pills to the test subjects may inadvertently give away who is getting the real medication and who the placebo, those giving out the pills are not told which pill is which. Such double-blind experiments are used to eliminate even inadvertent biases.

Of course, no one is completely free of biases, so we must be prepared to accept some degree of bias in any expert testimony. But we must assess the degree and significance of people's biases when appealing to their authority. Again, we have to exercise good judgment about whether some expert's bias is of a degree significant enough to undermine their authority. For example, if researchers were paid by fossil-fuel companies to research the effects on the climate of burning fossil fuels, we may be suspicious that their economic tie to the interests of those companies might be biasing their results; and even if they are personally honest, such biasing factors may still affect them. Such suspicion does not automatically rule out their expertise as biased. It does, however, caution us to look for evidence that might show the effects of bias in their results. In evaluating situations of this sort we must rely on good judgment. As always, the more important it is that we arrive at the truth, the less we should rely on appealing to authority and the more we should turn to examining the actual arguments about the subject matter. (Compare these points with the section on *ad hominem* circumstantial arguments below.)

(6) The person cited as an authority in question is identified.

When we appeal to authority, we rely on the authority having evaluated the arguments carefully and in detail. If the authorities have done this, we should always be able to check what they have said and done. Since the appeal to authority always depends on the authorities having good arguments in support of the conclusions we accept on the basis of their authority, the authorities must have actually produced the arguments that settle these matters among the experts. This means that when we appeal to an authority, it must be open to us and our audience to examine the actual arguments the authorities have accepted. We can examine these arguments only if the authority is identified. When the authority is not named or identified, it is impossible for us or our audience to be in a position to examine and evaluate the arguments, or to tell if our source is actually an expert in the appropriate field. Hence, appealing to an anonymous authority is fallacious.

> **Example 27:**   A government official said today that the new gun law will lower the rate of gun violence.

Since the government official is not named, it is impossible to check if he or she actually expressed the proposition that the new gun law will lower the rate of gun violence, and hence to determine whether the law will lower that rate. Because we do not know the source of the information, we have no way to evaluate its reliability.

The appeal to anonymous authority is all too common. Often, the person making the argument will say things like "they say...," or "the experts say...," or "scientists believe that...," or "I read in the paper that...," or "I saw on TV...," or "I have a book that says...," or some similar introductory phrase. In such cases the person is often hoping that the audience will simply accept the unidentified source as a legitimate authority and dogmatically believe the proposition in question. However, such appeals are not legitimate, since they allow us neither to trace the appeal back to their sources in the arguments that the experts have worked out so that we might examine the arguments themselves, nor to evaluate the expertise of the source.

A variation on the appeal to anonymous authority is acceptance of hearsay or rumor. Any appeal to hearsay or to rumor depends on second- or third-hand sources. Since the source of a rumor is seldom known, it is impossible to sort out whether its source is reliable. The only way to evaluate whether a rumor is reliable is to investigate the truth or falsity of the proposition the rumor circulates. In this case, one has abandoned the rumor as an authority. In criminal courts, appeals to hearsay are not admissible as evidence; one is allowed to testify to what one actually has witnessed, but one is not allowed to testify to the truth of a claim that one has heard others make. Such a claim would be merely hearsay, and whoever made the claim would neither be able to testify nor be subject to cross-examination bearing on the truth of that testimony.

Examples of Legitimate and Illegitimate Appeals to Authority

Example 28:   A person goes to a skilled doctor specializing in respiratory diseases and the doctor examines him and tells him that he has a bronchial infection.

We can rewrite this legitimate appeal to authority in premises and conclusion form as follows:

(1) A doctor specializing in respiratory diseases examined the person and says that the person has a bronchial infection.

Therefore, (2) the person has a bronchial infection.

In this example, the patient has good reason to accept the doctor's conclusion. The doctor is a legitimate authority on illnesses and specifically on respiratory diseases, and bronchial infections are forms of respiratory disease. The doctor has examined the patient, and her assertion that the patient has a bronchial infection is in her area of expertise. There is wide agreement among experts on respiratory diseases about the symptoms of a bronchial infection. The study of respiratory diseases is a well-established area of medicine. In the example, there is no reason to expect deception or significant bias on the part of the doctor. And, of course, the doctor is not an anonymous source.

Recall that an appeal to authority becomes a fallacy when it violates one or more of the six standards. Should any one of the six standards be violated, the appeal to authority is not legitimate and does not give any support to the proposition in question.

Example 29: Noted psychologist Dr. Sidney Frane recommends that you buy Glowlight light bulbs.

bad.

We can rewrite this illegitimate claim to authority in premises and conclusion form by filling in the implicit but unstated conclusion as follows:

(1) Noted psychologist Dr. Sidney Frane recommends that you buy Glowlight light bulbs.

Therefore, (2) you should buy Glowlight light bulbs.

This argument violates several of the standards for a legitimate appeal to authority. It violates standard (1) because there is no reason to accept that Dr. Frane has any expertise about light bulbs. We have been given no such reason because the argument violates standard (2): Dr. Frane's expertise is in psychology, not light bulbs. Moreover, it is not clear whether quality of light bulbs is a legitimate area of expertise; after all, general knowledge may be sufficient to make the need for special expertise superfluous (see the next section), so the argument may also violate standard (4). But even if there is such an area of expertise, the argument may also violate standard (3). To determine this we would have to find out whether legitimate light-bulb experts, if there are any, generally agree with Dr. Frane's recommendation, and whether they agree with him for good reasons.

Appeal to Most People as an Authority—Appeals to Popularity

So far we have considered appeals to the authority of particular persons or experts. However, people often appeal to the authority of what most people believe, do, or approve of. These sorts of appeals are *always* fallacies. Most people collectively have no special expertise. And, more importantly, if there are propositions that most people know to be true, then anyone will be able to give the arguments that support those propositions and the appeal to authority will be superfluous. It is important to recall that the only reason we are ever justified in appealing to authority is when we must divide the intellectual labor because it takes time, effort, and resources to work out what is true and what is false in areas in which there is a considerable body of knowledge. Appeals to the authority of most people do not by their nature divide the intellectual labor, nor do they appeal to any specialized expertise, and so they are never legitimate.

While these appeals to the alleged authority of most people may generally be called **appeals to popularity**, there are several different more specific types of such appeals. Appeals to the authority of most people are differentiated by which attitudes most people are claimed to have toward the proposition in question. When someone appeals to what most people *believe*, the fallacy is called an **appeal to belief**. When someone appeals to what most people *do*, the fallacy is called an **appeal to common practice**. When someone appeals to what most people like or *approve of*, the fallacy is called an **appeal to approval**. These fallacies are distinct and should not be confused with one another; in particular, we should resist the temptation to reduce them all to appeals to belief.

Appeal to Belief

In this fallacy, the speaker appeals to the authority of what most people believe to be true. The fallacy concludes that some proposition **P** is true from the premise that most people believe that **P** is true, or concludes that **P** is false from the premise that most people believe that **P** is false. In premises and conclusion form, appeals to belief exhibit the following form:

(1) Most people believe that **P** is true.

Therefore, (2) **P** is true.

This pattern of reasoning is fallacious because, as we have seen above, the truth or falsity of a proposition is separate and independent from whether anyone, including most or even all people, believes or disbelieves that proposition. This separation and independence applies no matter how many people believe or disbelieve the proposition.

Example 30:   There must be some form of life after death. After all, most cultures have believed that there is some form of life after death.

We can paraphrase this as an argument in premises and conclusion form as follows:

(1) Most cultures have believed that there is some form of life after death.

Therefore, (2) there must be some form of life after death.

The argument in this example is fallacious because no matter how many people believe that there is some form of life after death, their belief is strictly irrelevant to the truth or falsity of the proposition that there is some form of life after death. It is perfectly possible that even all people believe that there is some form of life after death and it still be false that there is some form of life after death. Whether or not there is some form of life after death depends on the actual state of affairs in the universe, not on any person's or group of people's attitudes. Even if the conclusion is true, the premise gives no legitimate support for its truth.

Historical examples make this point, because we can find many instances where the overwhelming majority of people believed some proposition to be true, when it later turned out to be false. For example, for a long time most Europeans believed that the Earth stood unmoving in the center of the universe. This proposition turned out to be false. In general, to argue against a fallacy of this kind, we should show that although most people may believe the proposition in question, that is strictly irrelevant to whether the proposition is true or false.

We may be attracted to the appeal to most people as an authority because there are some very specific sorts of cases when the fact that many people accept a claim as true is an indication that it is true. For example, say you are visiting Colorado and you are told by several people that they believe that people older than 16 are eligible to have a driver's license. Barring reasons to doubt these people, the propositions they express give you reason to believe that anyone over 16 will need to obtain a driver's license in order to drive. However, in cases of this sort, the justification for believing these people is since they are from that state they are likely to know the truth—that is, they have the relevant expertise—and it is unlikely that they are being deceptive. We should not believe them because so many people believe the same thing; rather, we should believe them because they count as legitimate authorities and meet all six standards for an acceptable appeal to authority.

There are also very rare cases in which what people believe actually determines the truth of a proposition, namely when the proposition in question is about what most people believe. For example, the truth of claims about good manners and proper behavior might simply depend on what people believe to be good manners and proper behavior. Another example is the case of community standards, which are often taken to be merely those standards that most people accept. US courts, for instance, have failed to find universal standards of obscenity, so they have ruled that the only legal meaning of "obscenity" is whatever violates local community standards of obscenity. In this case, for the proposition "X is obscene" to be true just is for most people in that community to believe that X is obscene. Notice that the only reason for the relevance of what most people believe is that the content of the proposition in question is *about* what most people believe; in other words, what most people believe is the state of affairs the proposition is about. Such cases are atypical and relatively rare, and it is still prudent to question the justification of the proposition in question.

Appeal to Common Practice

This fallacy has much the same form as the appeal to belief, but instead of the speaker appealing to the authority of what most people believe, the speaker appeals to the authority of what most people *do* to justify the truth of the proposition that it is correct, moral, justifiable, or reasonable (i.e., okay) to do the same sort of action. The general form of such fallacies is as follows:

(1) Most people do some action **A**.

Therefore, (2) it is okay to do **A**.

This type of argument is fallacious because the truth or falsity of a proposition that it is correct, moral, justifiable, or reasonable to perform some action is separate and independent of whether anyone performs that action. This separation and independence applies no matter how many people perform that action. People do not always do what is correct, moral, justifiable, or reasonable; they often do incorrect, immoral, unjustifiable, or irrational actions. Therefore, it is perfectly possible for people to generally do incorrect, immoral, unjustifiable, or irrational actions. What people actually do lends no support to what is correct, moral, justifiable, or reasonable for them to do. It may well be true that before the Civil War many Americans kept slaves, but that does not make it true that the practices of forcing people into slavery and using them as slaves was the right thing to do.

> **Example 31:** I know some people say that cheating on your taxes is wrong. But, of course, everyone does it, so it's really okay.

We can paraphrase this as an argument in premises and conclusion form as follows:

(1) Everyone cheats on taxes.

Therefore, (2) it is okay to cheat on taxes.

Even if it were true that most people—or even, as claimed here, everyone— cheat on their taxes, that would not make it right to do so. The more people that cheat on taxes, the worse the situation becomes for the country and its finances. A bad action does not become better because many people do it. The more people do a bad thing, the worse the overall ethical situation becomes. To argue against this fallacy, we should identify the common practice (cheating on taxes in the example) and argue that just because something is regularly done is not sufficient to justify doing it. This fallacy also violates the principle that no conclusion about how things ought to be can be supported *solely* by premises about how things actually are. At least one premise in an argument for a conclusion about how things ought to be must also be about how things ought to be. ✓

practical premise → practical conclusion

For example, it is important to distinguish the fallacy of appeal to common practice from appeals to fair play. The **appeal to fair play** may be a good argument rather than a fallacy as long as it conforms to the **principle of relevant difference**. This principle states that **two cases (or two people) ought not to be treated or evaluated differently unless there is a relevant difference between them.** Without a relevant difference there can be no legitimate reason for treating cases differently. For example, it would not be rational to buy different-sized shoes for children whose feet were the same size. What counts as a relevant difference is specific to the case. For example, ✓ ability, experience, and level of performance would be relevant differences for determining what different employees will be paid; however, hair color, gender, and ethnic background would not be relevant differences, since they make no difference to job performance. So it would be justified for a woman to argue that she should get the same level of pay as a man who did the same job, demonstrated the same ability, had the same experience, and achieved the same level of performance. The argument from fair play is not an appeal to common practice because it is not arguing solely from premises about how things are to conclusions about how things ought to be. The principle of relevant difference serves as an evaluative premise about how things ought to be. The relevance of a difference that justifies treating cases differently acts as an assessment of the value of that difference. Consider the following argument:

Example 32:   (1) Joanne is a far better cook than Hugo is.

(2) We will hire either Joanne or Hugo for the job in the restaurant kitchen.

(3) For the purpose of hiring someone to work in a restaurant kitchen, differences in cooking ability are relevant differences. ← *what ought to be done*

Therefore, (4) (other things being equal) we should hire Joanne for the job in the restaurant kitchen instead of Hugo.

The conclusion, then, is not claimed to follow from premises that merely say how things are, since there is also a premise, (3), which is an evaluative premise telling us what ought to be done for the specific purpose at hand.

The principle of relevant difference also operates in relation to a type of fallacy called **special pleading**. In the fallacy of special pleading, the speaker applies standards, principles, and rules to others while taking herself (or those she has a special interest in) to be exempt, without providing adequate justification for the exemption. Adequate justification requires that there be a relevant difference between one's own case and that of others.

Example 33:   Jason and Marie are tennis partners. They have agreed on a time to meet and practice. They both have full days of work and barely make it to the tennis court at the arranged time. When they meet on the tennis court, they find that neither of them has brought any tennis balls. Jason tells Marie that she should have brought a can of balls since he did not have time to pick any up.

We can paraphrase this as an argument in premises and conclusion form as follows:

(1) I (Jason) had no time to pick up any tennis balls.

Therefore, (2) you (Marie) should have brought the tennis balls.

In this example, Jason has not cited a relevant difference, since Marie has also put in a full day of work and did not have time to pick up the tennis balls. Compare Example 33 with the situation where, when they became tennis partners, Marie promised Jason that she would always bring a can of tennis balls. In that case, Marie's prior commitment serves as a relevant difference and to that extent would justify Jason's claim. To argue against fallacies of special pleading, we should show that no relevant differences exist between the person pleading for special consideration and similar people. To do this clearly and explicitly, it is worth stating what would be a relevant difference in each case under consideration.

Appeal to Approval

This fallacy is similar to the appeal to belief and the appeal to common practice fallacies because it relies on the supposed authority of the majority of people. This fallacy, however, relies not on the authority of what most people believe, nor of what most people do, but instead on the authority of what most people *like* or *approve of* (such approval or liking is not the same as a belief or action). The appeal to approval aims at getting people to accept some proposition as true about the goodness or badness of an object because most people have a favorable attitude toward that object—they like that object or think it is a good thing of its kind. Often people are seduced into committing this fallacy because they confuse how things are—most people actually having a certain attitude—with how things ought to be—the object is a good thing of its sort. This fallacy, then, confuses propositions with people and their attitudes. The general form of such fallacies is as follows:

(1) Most people approve or like some object **O**.

Therefore, (2) **O** is a good object of that kind.

Here is an example of such an argument:

Example 34:   Most people really like the new Speedie smartphone, so it must be the best smartphone to buy.

We can paraphrase this as an argument in premises and conclusion form as follows:

(1) Most people really like the new Speedie smartphone.

Therefore, (2) the new Speedie smartphone is the best smartphone to buy.

In this example, the premise that most people like or approve of the Speedie smartphone is supposed to support the conclusion that it is true that the Speedie smartphone is the best smartphone to buy. However, whether the Speedie smartphone is the best smartphone to buy does not depend on whether people approve of it. What would matter is whether it performs the appropriate tasks well, and whether it does this depends on those tasks and the phone's performance compared to similar phones, not on anyone's attitude. A proposition's truth or falsity does not depend on whether people are favorably inclined toward that proposition, and the goodness or badness of an object does not depend on whether people are favorably inclined toward that object.

The appeal to approval, like the appeals to what the majority of people believe or do, is often psychologically persuasive because many people tend to have a psychological predisposition to conform to the majority. However, this psychological tendency offers no rational support for the truth or falsity of the propositions that the majority believe or the goodness or badness of the objects of which they approve. The appeal to approval is often used by advertisers when they try to sell commodities by claiming that most people use and like those commodities.

(C) ATTACKING THE PERSON: *AD HOMINEM* ARGUMENTS

While appeals to authority are supposed to support a proposition because of the merits of the person who asserts that proposition as an authority, **ad hominem arguments** are supposed to contest the truth of a proposition because of the flaws in character, circumstances, or actions of the person who asserts that proposition. *Ad hominem* is Latin for "to the man." *Ad hominem* arguments attack the person who asserts a proposition rather than considering the truth or falsity of the proposition itself. They are fallacious when the speaker treats the flaws in the character, circumstances, or actions of a person who asserts a proposition as if they undermined the truth of that proposition. To argue against *ad hominem* arguments, we should identify the attack and show that the character, circumstances, or actions of the person who asserts a proposition have nothing to do with the truth or falsity of that proposition.

There are several varieties of *ad hominem* arguments, which differ depending on how the person is attacked.

(1) Ad hominem (*Abusive*)

When the speaker uses abusive or derogatory remarks or language to attack a person rather than consider the truth value of the propositions that person asserts, we call the fallacy an **ad hominem abusive**.

> **Example 35:**   Jane says that drug use is morally wrong, but she is just a censorious prig, so we don't have to listen to her.

Noting that the claim that we do not have to listen to her serves to deny the content of what Jane has said, we can paraphrase this as an argument in premises and conclusion form as follows:

(1) Jane says that drug use is morally wrong.
(2) Jane is a censorious prig.

Therefore, (3) drug use is not morally wrong.

In the example, the speaker calls Jane a "censorious prig," which in this context is a term of abuse. Even if the abuse were warranted, it would not have any bearing on whether it is true that drug use is morally wrong. Jane's character is strictly irrelevant to the truth value of the proposition about the morality of drug use. No matter how objectionable, naïve, or repugnant a person may be, that person may still assert true propositions and give good arguments. To sort out the truth value of the proposition that drug use is morally wrong, we would have to examine whether drug use violates appropriate moral standards.

(2) Ad hominem (*Circumstantial*)

When the speaker rejects a proposition as false because of the special circumstances of a person, or because of what is in the interest of the person asserting the proposition, rather than considering the truth value of those propositions, we call the fallacy an **ad hominem circumstantial**. People sometimes have special circumstances that affect what it is in their interest to say. So, for example, when someone works for a particular company, they may be motivated to publicly assert propositions that serve the company's interests or that cast the company in a good light. Although a person's interests may motivate them to support a proposition, those interests have no bearing on the truth value of that proposition or the goodness of their arguments. So, for instance, we commit an *ad hominem* circumstantial fallacy when we claim that the proposition someone is expressing is false simply because it is in their interest that it be true. In general, someone's interests, or the interests of some group or organization to which that person belongs, have no bearing on the truth value of their claims. While people may be psychologically inclined to express, or be pressured into expressing, propositions that serve certain interests, those inclinations or pressures are strictly irrelevant to the truth values of the propositions expressed. Even if people have a vested interest in asserting certain propositions, the propositions they express can still be true and the arguments they give can still be good.

> **Example 36:** Of course the Member of Parliament from Faslane supports continuing the Trident Nuclear Submarine Program. After all, Faslane is where Her Majesty's Naval Base, Clyde, is and that is where the Trident Submarines are docked.

This argument is an enthymeme (see Chapter VI). Adding the unstated premise that the Member of Parliament (MP) has a vested interest in sustaining the naval base in Faslane, we can paraphrase this as an argument in premises and conclusion form as follows:

(1) Her Majesty's Naval Base, Clyde, where the Trident Submarines are docked, is in Faslane.

(2) It is in the interest of the Member of Parliament from Faslane to sustain Her Majesty's Naval Base, Clyde, in Faslane.

(3) The Member of Parliament from Faslane supports continuing the Trident Nuclear Submarine Program.

Therefore, (4) the Trident Nuclear Submarine Program should not be continued.

It may well be, because of the circumstance that the MP represents Faslane, that it is in his or her interest to assert the proposition that the Trident Nuclear Submarine Program should be continued. But, the fact that it is in the MP's interest has no bearing on the truth value of that proposition. Nothing in the premise about the MP's vested interest in the truth of the conclusion demonstrates that the conclusion is true. It may well be true that the Trident Nuclear Submarine Program should not be continued. But to sort out whether the proposition is true, we would have to examine the nature of the Trident Nuclear Submarine Program, its drawbacks, its efficacy with respect to the goals that the program is supposed to achieve, and whether those goals can or ought to be achieved by continuing the program. All of these considerations bear on the state of affairs the proposition is about. The MP's interests have no such bearing. Of course, the circumstances may actually bias the MP's assessment of the situation, but that does not give a reason to reject the proposition that the MP asserted as false either. Instead, what the possibility that the MP is biased does is give us a prudential reason to investigate the arguments carefully to determine whether the proposition is true or false.

Similarly, in the law courts, we are careful about whether a judge presides over cases in which she or he may have an interest; we expect a judge to recuse herself or himself from a case when there is a conflict of interest (often even when there is merely an appearance of a conflict of interest). This, however, is an act of prudence, to avoid even the appearance of impropriety, and does not suggest that the judge would not have made a correct decision in the case.

A variation on the *ad hominem* circumstantial fallacy occurs when the manner in which a proposition or the manner in which people present themselves biases the audience for or against the truth of what those people say. This type of fallacy is called a **fallacy of style over substance**, because the psychological effect of the style of presentation of the proposition or argument, or of the person who expresses the proposition has an effect on whether the audience accepts the proposition as true or the argument as good.

> **Example 37:**   (a) My professor dresses like a slob, so he must be wrong when he says that the social security system is secure.
>
> (b) Max argued so aggressively that the social security system is secure that I doubt that anything he said is true, or why would he have to act that way?

We can paraphrase Example 37a as an argument in premises and conclusion form as follows:

(1) My professor dresses like a slob.

(2) My professor says that the social security system is secure.

Therefore, (3) the social security system is not secure.

In Example 37a, the speaker supposes that the reliability of the professor's claims can be inferred from his manner of dress. But the professor's appearance has no relevance to the truth value of whatever propositions he may assert. It is perfectly possible for well-dressed people to speak falsely and for slovenly dressed people to speak the truth.

We can paraphrase **Example 37b** as an argument in premises and conclusion form as follows:

(1) Max argued aggressively that the social security system is secure.

Therefore, (2) the social security system is not secure.

In this example, the manner in which Max presents the propositions has no bearing on their truth values. That a proposition is presented aggressively, excitedly, reluctantly, calmly, or in any other manner is strictly irrelevant to whether it is true or false. Sometimes people will tell someone to speak rationally when all they mean is for the person to be calm. This confuses the demeanor of the speaker with the rationality of the arguments and propositions the speaker presents. It is perfectly possible to present true propositions and give good arguments in an agitated manner, and to present false propositions and bad arguments calmly and coolly. Such calm, cool presentation of false propositions is a common rhetorical technique designed to lull the audience into accepting false propositions.

(3) Ad hominem (*Tu quoque*)

Sometimes a person will say one thing and do another, or assert one proposition at one time and later assert another proposition that is inconsistent with the first. This may show that the person has changed his or her mind, or that the person does not practice what they preach, or that the person is hypocritical. What it does not do is show anything about the truth value of the propositions the person asserts. That a person changes their mind, does not practice what they preach, or is a hypocrite says something about that person, not about the truth or falsity of any proposition they may assert. If a speaker argues that what someone says is false because they do not do as they say, or because they earlier said something inconsistent with what they are saying now, then they have committed a version of the *ad hominem* fallacy called an ***ad hominem tu quoque***. The Latin phrase *tu quoque* means "you also," that is, "you are one too." That a person asserts a proposition and does not do what the proposition says they should do does not show whether they acted rightly and expressed a false proposition or acted wrongly and expressed a true proposition. Likewise, as we shall see in Chapter IV, the fact that two propositions are logically inconsistent shows only that one of the propositions must be false, but the logical inconsistency does not determine which of the two propositions is false.

> **Example 38:**   Peter: "Given the arguments I have presented, it is evident that it is morally wrong to use animals for food or clothing."
> Paul: "But you are wearing a leather jacket and have been eating a roast beef sandwich! You can't say that using animals for food and clothing is wrong!"

We can paraphrase Paul's claims as an argument in premises and conclusion form as follows:

> (1) Peter is using animals for food and clothing (he is wearing a leather jacket and is eating a roast beef sandwich).
> (2) Peter claims that it is morally wrong to use animals for food or clothing.
> _____
> Therefore, (3) it not morally wrong to use animals for food or clothing.

If Paul's argument is meant to show that the proposition that it is morally wrong to use animals for food or clothing is false, then he has committed an *ad hominem tu quoque* fallacy. Of course, Peter can say what he did and it can be true. In the example, Paul is arguing against Peter, against the person, rather than arguing that the proposition Peter asserted is false. To argue that the proposition is false, Paul would have to discuss the moral problems concerning the treatment of animals and the actual arguments Peter gave, not Peter's habits and actions. Peter may be hypocritical for eating beef and wearing leather while arguing for the immorality of using animals for food and clothing, but that is strictly irrelevant to whether the proposition that it is morally wrong to use animals for food or clothing is true or false. That proposition may be true, in which case Peter is acting immorally. But even if this were so, Peter's immorality is strictly irrelevant to the truth value of the proposition about what is moral with respect to using animals for food and clothing. Notice that the actual arguments Peter gave are never stated or evaluated. But to sort out the truth or falsity of the proposition that it is morally wrong to use animals for food or clothing would require examining such arguments concerning the morality of the use of animals.

Example 39:   Steffi: "The United States is not losing any jobs to other countries, because new jobs are opening up in computer software."
Regina: "What you are saying now must be wrong. Last month you complained that the United States is losing jobs."

Making Steffi's comments into explicit premises, we can paraphrase Regina's argument as an argument in premises and conclusion form as follows:

(1) Steffi said last month that the United States is losing jobs to other countries.
(2) Steffi now says that the United States is not losing jobs to other countries.

Therefore, (3) the United States is losing jobs to other countries.

In this example, the argument commits an *ad hominem tu quoque* fallacy. While the proposition "The United States is losing jobs to other countries" and the proposition "The United States is not losing jobs to other countries" cannot both be true (they are contradictory; see Chapter IV), the fact that Steffi asserted one of these propositions a month ago and the other now does not show that what she says now is false (nor does it show that what she said a month ago is false). That she has expressed inconsistent propositions shows something about Steffi (that she has changed her mind, or she is confused, or she is being insincere or deceitful). It does not show which proposition is false (although, given that the states of affairs are not different from one month to the next, one of them must be false). To show which one of the propositions is false, we would have to investigate the state of jobs in the United States and in the other countries. We would have to be concerned with the subject matter, not with the person who expressed the inconsistent propositions.

(4) Guilt by Association

When a speaker rejects a proposition as false because people the speaker dislikes accept that proposition as true, the speaker has committed a fallacy of **guilt by association**. As with all *ad hominem* arguments, arguments of this sort are fallacious because the truth values of propositions are independent of people and their attitudes toward the propositions and their truth values. This fallacy is common because, psychologically, people do not want to be associated with people they dislike. Hence it is often rhetorically effective to try to get someone to change their view by arguing that a proposition that person believes is also accepted as true by people that person dislikes. While this tactic too often influences people psychologically to change their views, it does not by itself justify changing one's views. After all, many terrible and repugnant people have believed that the Earth moves, and that $1 + 1 = 2$. That such people have believed these propositions to be true is strictly irrelevant to whether they are true.

> **Example 40:** Betty and Dan are discussing who they are going to vote for as the next chair of their committee. Betty is contemptuous of George and Frank.
> Betty: "I was thinking about voting for Jill. But, I finally decided to vote for John, who will do an excellent job. He has a lot of influence, and he is a fair and reasonable person."
> Dan: "You know, George and Frank are supporting him. They really like the idea of having John as the new committee chair. I never thought I'd see you side with those two jerks."
> Betty: "Well, maybe I will vote for Jill after all."

We can paraphrase the argument that Dan presents and Betty mistakenly accepts in premises and conclusion form as follows:

(1) George and Frank are objectionable people ("jerks" as Dan calls them).

(2) George and Frank are supporting John for committee chair.

_____

Therefore, (3) Betty should not support John for committee chair.

In this example, Betty is coerced into changing her mind about voting for John because Dan claims that George and Frank, people she dislikes, are going to vote for John. But even if it is true that George and Frank are going to vote for John, and even if it is true that George and Frank deserve Betty's contempt, those factors are strictly irrelevant to whether it is true that she should vote for John. While Dan also uses abusive language (calling them "jerks"—an *ad hominem* abusive fallacy) to further incite Betty's defection, the main fallacy here is still an *ad hominem* guilt by association fallacy. What matters for determining who to vote for is the likelihood that one person will do a better job than another. Betty herself has given relevant arguments in favor of voting for John, since being a fair and reasonable person and having influence are relevant to whether someone will be a good committee chair.

(5) Poisoning the Well

Since *ad hominem* fallacies attempt to persuade their audience not to accept propositions as true because of the objectionable character, circumstances, or actions of the person who asserts the propositions, the premises that deal with character, circumstances, or actions of persons have no logical connection with the truth or falsity of their conclusions. This means that *ad hominem* arguments depend on turning their audience against the person regardless of what propositions the person may assert. Hence, someone can argue against a person without specifying any content for the propositions that person may assert or any arguments that person might give. When someone tries to discredit what a person might assert by attacking the person's character, circumstances, or actions before they have said anything, they have committed the fallacy called **poisoning the well**. Poisoning the well fallacies have one of the other forms of *ad hominem* arguments, but what is distinctive about poisoning the well fallacies is that they are put forward as a pre-emptive attack. By presenting an unfavorable impression (whether true or false) of a person's character, circumstances, or actions before they have a chance to say anything, the speaker is trying to bias the audience against the person so that the audience becomes psychologically more likely to reject as false any propositions that person may assert. Of course, as in all arguments concerning the person rather than the propositions the person asserts, no unfavorable claims about a person (even if they are true) count as good reasons for rejecting as false the propositions that person might assert. Even terrible people can assert true propositions and give good arguments for them. The truth or falsity of the propositions a person asserts is separate and independent of any feature of the person who asserts those propositions.

> **Example 41:**   At a political party convention, a candidate introduces the next candidate as follows: "Before turning the stage over to my opponent, I ask you to remember that those who oppose my policies have no consideration for the welfare of the party."

We can paraphrase this as an argument in premises and conclusion form as follows:

(1) The next speaker, who opposes my policies, has no consideration for the welfare of the party.

Therefore, (2) whatever he has to say should be rejected.

In this example, by saying that the person about to speak is an opponent and that people who oppose the speaker's policies have no consideration for the welfare of the party, the speaker hopes to bias the audience to reject as false any propositions the speaker's opponent may assert even before that person begins to speak. Even if it were true that the person about to speak has no consideration for the welfare of the party, that would be strictly irrelevant to whether what that person will actually say is true or false, or whether the arguments that person will present are good or bad. Even a person who has no consideration for the welfare of the party can assert true propositions and give good arguments about party policies. Since the person who is about to speak has not actually said anything, it is impossible to evaluate any claims or arguments she might give.

(D) THE SUBJECTIVIST FALLACY (OR RELATIVIST FALLACY)

We have been discussing informal fallacies that confuse the truth values of propositions (and the arguments that try to support those propositions) with persons and their attitudes. We conclude our discussion by considering the **subjectivist (or relativist) fallacy**. This fallacy embodies confusions about both of the distinctions that have been made regarding the nature of propositions. However, people usually commit the subjectivist fallacy because they have confused people and their attitudes with the truth or falsity of propositions. Also, if rarely, people commit the subjectivist fallacy because they have confused the truth values of propositions with the states of affairs that propositions are about.

Someone commits the subjectivist fallacy when they affirm the truth of a proposition by claiming that that proposition may not be true for other people but is true for the speaker, or by rejecting a proposition as false by claiming that the proposition may be true for other people but is not true for the speaker. This is called the subjectivist fallacy because it assumes that truth values are somehow subjective, as if truth values were determined by people's subjective states—in other words, that one and the same proposition could be true for one person and false for another person.

This fallacy is also called the relativist fallacy because it assumes that truth values are relative to persons. (Similar assumptions that truth values are relative to times, cultures, places, etc., commit similar fallacies.) The assumption that truth values are relative to the person clearly confuses the proposition with people and their attitudes. As we have seen, truth and falsity are relations between propositions and the states of affairs that those propositions are about. Truth values, like propositions, are completely separate and independent of persons and their attitudes. So it is utterly meaningless to say that some proposition is true for some person or false for some person. (Nonsense phrases of the form "true for so-and-so" characteristically mark the subjectivist or relativist fallacy.)

Example 42:   Zara: "People who eat too much fast food tend to be unhealthy."
Yuval: "That may be true for you, but it is not true for me."

We can paraphrase Yuval's assertion as an argument in premises and conclusion form as follows:

> (1) It may be true for you (Zara) that people tend to be unhealthy when they eat too much fast food, but it is not true for me (Yuval) that people tend to be unhealthy when they eat too much fast food.
>
> ---
>
> Therefore, (2) people do not tend to be unhealthy when they eat too much fast food.

It is strictly *meaningless* for Yuval to say that the proposition that people who eat too much fast food tend to be unhealthy is either true or false for him. If the proposition is true, that is because it describes the state of affairs regarding the health of people who eat too much fast food just as that state of affairs is. If the proposition is false, that is because it does not describe that state of affairs as it is.

Most often when people say that some proposition is "true for me," they really mean that they believe that proposition, and that they believe it passionately (or, often, they dogmatically hold the proposition to be true). But, of course, the fact that someone believes a proposition to be true or false is completely independent of that proposition's actual truth value. So saying that the proposition is "true for me" confuses the person who says something with what they have said.

For example, it is confused and misleading to claim that it was true for Europeans in the Middle Ages that the Earth was flat, while it is true for us today that the Earth is round. Were this actually the case, then it would follow that the Earth changed shape when people changed their view, which is absurd (it would be pertinent to ask "When did the earth change shape?"). Instead, we should simply say that they believed that the Earth was flat and we do not agree with them. This way of speaking makes it clearer that we are talking about people and their attitudes, not about the truth values of propositions toward which those attitudes are directed.

People often tend to fall back on the phrase "true for me" during discussions about politics, ethics, or morality because these matters are difficult, many are unsettled, and many involve serious commitments that may differ from group to group or from person to person. But "true for me" is no more appropriate in these matters than in the case of the shape of the Earth. If it is true that plagiarism is wrong, then it is just true. Likewise, if it is true that we ought to have national health insurance, then that is just true. (Similarly, if these are false, then they are just false.) There is nothing special about the propositions "Plagiarism is wrong" and "We ought to have national health insurance." They are merely propositions and are either true or false. What we differ on when we discuss these claims is *whether* they are true or false. This may be difficult to determine; we would have to engage in a complex investigation and complex reasoning to determine their truth values, but it is the truth values of the propositions that we are trying to determine by these methods. They do not have any special kind of truth or falsity. Their truth or falsity no more depends on who asserts or denies, believes or disbelieves them than do the truth values of propositions about mathematics or the natural sciences.

There is another possible misunderstanding here, albeit a rare one, which would involve a confusion between the proposition and the state of affairs that the proposition seeks to describe. Someone might commit the subjectivist fallacy because they have confused the truth values of propositions with the states of affairs that propositions are about. It may be that Yuval is confused and merely means that the proposition "People who eat too much fast food tend to be unhealthy" may be true *about* Zara but that it is not true about him that eating too much fast food tends to be unhealthy. A proposition is true about a person if the proposition correctly describes that person. So, for example, the proposition "Yuval has blue eyes" is about Yuval, and if it is true, then it is true about him. If Yuval means that Zara's proposition is not true about him, then all he is saying is that he is an example of someone who is an exception to the general proposition that people who eat too much fast food tend to be unhealthy.

But if that is what Yuval means, he has stated the point in an extremely misleading and confusing way. He means to be talking about whether the proposition correctly describes a state of affairs in which he is an exception to the general claim the proposition makes. Yet what he says sounds like he means that the same proposition can be both true and false. If that is what he means, then the claim he makes would violate the *law of truth values*, that no proposition can be both true and false. Since laws of logic must be true before any proposition can be meaningful, Yuval's claim that the proposition is not true for him is meaningless. This point applies to subjectivist and relativist fallacies generally, namely, that they are meaningless because they violate the law of truth values. To say that one and the same proposition is both true for some people and not true for others would mean that the same proposition is both true and false and so would be nonsense.

Study Questions and Problems

Respond to each of the following questions and problems clearly and precisely.

1) What, in general, is the problem with appealing to people's motives or emotions?

2) What is a prudential reason?

3) Why do we sometimes need to appeal to authority?

4) State and explain the six standards for a legitimate appeal to authority.

5) Why is the appeal to what most people believe, do, or approve of an illegitimate appeal to authority?

6) Why is it illegitimate to conclude that a person is making a false claim because it is to their advantage to make the claim they make?

7) How is the fifth standard for a legitimate appeal to authority related to *ad hominem* circumstantial fallacies?

8) Using an example, explain what is wrong with saying the following: "Proposition **P** is true for me." Make sure you explain why people are tempted to say such things.

Exercises: Informal Fallacies

For each of the following paragraphs,

A) If the paragraph contains an argument that commits an informal fallacy, state what specific type of informal fallacy is most prominently committed. If the paragraph does not contain a fallacy, then say so.

B) Write the argument out in premises and conclusion form (see Chapter I, Part II, Section A), paraphrasing where necessary. Make sure you paraphrase the premises and conclusion in complete grammatical sentences.

c) Explain what goes wrong in the reasoning; that is, explain why the premises do not support the conclusion. Make sure that this explanation considers the specific content of the paragraph and does not merely give the general problem with informal fallacies of the sort committed in the paragraph. This will require explaining:
   (i) Why the premises of this particular argument do not support the conclusion, in other words, how it is possible for the premises to be true and the conclusion false.
   (ii) In the case of the informal fallacies in this chapter, give an example of what would be a relevant consideration instead of the irrelevancy given in the premises. This does not require giving a good argument (there may not be one) but merely explaining some considerations that would be relevant to determining the truth value of the conclusion.

Here are two examples of how these exercises are to be done:

Example 1: Smith had better not condemn Tory Party energy policies. Mr. Jones, who manages the office in which Smith works, is a dyed-in-the-wool Tory and has seen to it that opponents of Tory policies on issues of national importance have been dismissed from the firm or, at the very least, relegated to menial jobs with little chance of promotion.

A) This paragraph contains an argument that commits the informal fallacy of appeal to fear or force.

B) (1) If Smith opposes Tory energy policies, then his office manager is likely to get him fired or put into a dead-end job.
   _____
   Therefore, (2) Smith had better not oppose Tory energy policies.

C) (i) It is certainly possible for it to be true that if Smith opposes Tory energy policies, then his office manager is likely to get him fired or put into a dead-end job, and yet still be false that Smith had better not oppose Tory energy policies. For example, Smith may have an obligation as a good citizen to oppose the policies.

(ii) While the premise might give Smith a prudential reason for avoiding opposition to Tory energy policies (since Smith would be harmed by losing his job), it is strictly irrelevant to the correctness of those policies. For the argument never actually states what those energy policies are, and relevant support for those policies would have to consider their content. Nor does it consider any reasons that are concerned with energy or policy. The latter would, instead, provide reasons that actually would be relevant to the correctness of those energy policies.

Example 2: In his *New Introductory Lectures on Psychoanalysis*, Sigmund Freud said that "religion is an illusion and it derives its strength from the fact that it falls in with our instinctual desires." This shows that religion is an illusion.

A) This paragraph contains an argument that commits the informal fallacy of appeal to authority.

B) (1) In his lectures, Sigmund Freud said that "religion is an illusion...."

Therefore, (2) religion is an illusion.

C) (i) The appeal may violate the second standard of a legitimate appeal to authority, since it is not clear that psychoanalysts are the appropriate authorities qualified to judge the legitimacy of religious belief; that is, it is not clear that the legitimacy of religious belief is part of the subject matter in the field of psychoanalysis. While psychoanalysis does consider the appropriateness of such beliefs, for the most part it is concerned with their causes, not with their truth. In the quotation, Freud includes instinctual desires among these causes. Hence, it might be true that in his *New Introductory Lectures on Psychoanalysis*, Sigmund Freud said that "religion is an illusion and it derives its strength from the fact that it falls in with our instinctual desires" and still be false that religion is an illusion. (ii) Moreover, this appeal to Freud's authority is irrelevant to the conclusion because it violates the third standard for a legitimate appeal to authority: there is no adequate agreement among experts on whether religion is illusory. If there are such experts, it is also not clear who they are. This raises questions regarding the fourth standard for a legitimate appeal to authority: are these experts theologians, or religious leaders, philosophers, religions people, atheists, scientists, or some other experts? To determine whether Freud's arguments are good ones, we would have to examine those arguments explicitly and in detail.

Now apply this approach to the paragraphs that follow.

1) Mr. Allen is the administrator of the county street-repair program. When it is found that the program is permeated with corruption and bribery, Smith tells reporters, "The street-repair program has its difficulties, but what goes on in this program also goes on in most other county programs."

2) There has been some talk that the government is overstepping its legal powers by allowing police to arrest and detain people without the warrants traditionally required by the constitution. However, we now have to fear terrorism and proceed with the war on terror. I have in my office many letters from people who make it clear that they earnestly support the war against terror. Because of this compelling approval, it is clear that the police are acting correctly.

3) I am a single parent. I am wholly responsible for the financial support of my children. If you give me this traffic ticket, I will lose my license and be unable to drive to work. If I cannot work, my children and I will become homeless and may starve to death. So, you see, you should not give me this traffic ticket.

4) Claudette, I don't know why you still believe in divine providence. There cannot be any such thing as divine providence. After all, many terrorists are motivated by their belief in divine providence, and you don't want to be even remotely connected with terrorists.

5) We know that you are a person who understands the management of investments in financial derivative instruments, so I will not bother you with how our hedge fund operates with respect to such instruments. You are obviously an intelligent and knowledgeable investor.

6) It's not true that the government is innocent of wrongdoing regarding water pollution. I read the other day that government

agencies are responsible for more than 50% of the country's water pollution.

7) The governor says people should not get special tax credits for sending their kids to college. But look at how he's spending his salary—paid for by our tax dollars—sending his own children to some expensive college. Where does he get off saying we should not get the same break?

8) I know that many pundits think that President Obama's escalation of the war in Libya was a terrible mistake. Those pundits have a right to say what they want, but things are different for me. Whatever may be true for them, it's true for me that Obama acted in the best interest of the country.

9) You always say that people should not use their cellphones while driving, but you are always texting your sister while you are driving.

10) You say that the federal government need not try to balance its budget, but Senator Jones has vehemently argued on the floor of the Senate that failure to balance the budget will mortgage our children and grandchildren's future, since they will have to pay for the debt.

Chapter III

COMPOUND PROPOSITIONS AND TRUTH FUNCTIONAL CONNECTIVES

We now turn from a primary focus on critical thinking, which is concerned mainly with the truth and falsity of propositions, to a primary focus on logic, which is concerned with the relations between the possible truth values of propositions. In doing logic, all that matters about the values true and false is that they obey the laws of logic. **Logic is not concerned with the relationship between propositions and states of affairs; that is, logic is not concerned with the actual truth or falsity of propositions, but only with the possible and necessary relationships between the truth values of propositions** (whatever truth values they may have). This difference in modality—that is, logic's concern about the *possible* and *necessary* relations between the truth values of propositions as opposed to critical thinking's concern with the *actual* truth and falsity of propositions—is fundamental to understanding logic and logical relations.

We have distinguished propositions from states of affairs, on the one hand, and from people and their attitudes, on the other hand. Since arguments consist of propositions, we now turn to discussing how certain types of propositions differ from one another in their logical characteristics. We saw how the proposition "Lara believes that the door is open" was a complex proposition because it contained another proposition, "The door is open," as a part. However, we also saw that the truth values of these two propositions are independent of each other: the truth value of one does not depend on the truth value of the other. There are, however, other types of complex propositions that are a compound of simpler propositions, where the truth value of the compound (whole) proposition *does* depend on the truth values of its component parts.

We may define **simple and compound propositions** as follows.

DEFINITION OF SIMPLE PROPOSITION:
A proposition is simple if and only if it contains no parts that are also propositions.

DEFINITION OF COMPOUND PROPOSITION:
A proposition is compound if and only if it is composed of or contains parts that are also propositions.

So, for example, the proposition "Karen went to work today" is a simple proposition, since it has no parts that also are propositions, but the proposition "Karen went to work today and Karen was promoted" is a compound proposition, since it contains two parts that are themselves propositions: "Karen went to work today" and "Karen was promoted." A compound proposition may itself have compound propositions as its parts. So propositions may be of greater or lesser complexity depending on the complexity of the connections between their parts. For example, the proposition "If Karen went to work today and Karen was promoted, then Karen is happy" contains three simple propositions and includes the compound proposition "Karen went to work today and Karen was promoted" as a part.

For certain important compound propositions, their truth value depends *solely* on the truth values of their component parts. Compound propositions of this sort are composed by connecting simple propositions using the operator "not ..." or connective expressions such as "both ... and ...," "either ... or...," and "if ..., then...." Such expressions function to make compound propositions from simpler ones. When these expressions serve to construct compound propositions whose truth values are *solely* a function of the truth values of their parts, we call these expressions **truth functional operators** or **truth functional connectives**.

Here it should be noted that propositions constructed with the truth functional operator "it is not the case that ..." or "not ..." are compound propositions. The *only* difference between the truth functional operator "not ..." and the truth functional connectives "both ... and...," "either ... or...," and "if ..., then..." is that the "not ..." *operates* on a single proposition to produce a compound proposition, while the truth functional connectives *connect* two propositions together to produce a compound proposition.

DEFINITION OF TRUTH FUNCTIONAL OPERATOR AND CONNECTIVE:
An expression is a truth functional operator or a truth functional connective if and only if it functions to construct compound propositions such that the truth values of those compound propositions depend solely on the truth values of their component propositions.

The truth functional operator "not ..." and the truth functional connectives "both ... and ...," "either ... or ...," and "if ..., then ..." are especially important in logic. English is a complex language that often uses the same words for many different functions. Not every use of these words in ordinary English is a truth functional use. We will examine four main types of compound propositions with the aim of clarifying their logical features. To do this, we will have to distinguish the truth functional uses of the ordinary English terms "not ...," "... and ...," "... or ...," and "if ..." from other uses of these same terms. We will examine the operator "not ..." and the connective expressions "both ... and ...," "either ... or ...," and "if ..., then ..." in turn and identify their truth functional uses, which will be called **logical negation, logical conjunction, logical disjunction**, and **truth functional conditionals**, respectively.

Part I: Logical Negation

For clarity we will use the expression "It is not the case that **P**" to express the logical negation of a proposition **P** (no matter what or how complex the proposition **P** may be). By the expression "It is not the case that **P**," the whole of the proposition **P** is being negated. So we will treat both the proposition "It is not the case that Karen was promoted" as equivalent to the usual expression "Karen was not promoted." Both are logical negations of the proposition "Karen was promoted."

In order to understand the truth functional use of words like "not ...," we will now turn to the third and fourth laws of logic. Recall that a law of logic states a condition that is necessary before it is possible for any proposition to have a truth value (see Chapter II, Part I). The third and fourth laws of logic fix the way in which the truth value of the logical negation of any proposition depends on the truth value of the proposition it negates. The third and fourth laws of logic are the law of non-contradiction and the law of excluded middle.

3) **Law of non-contradiction: A proposition "P" and its negation "It is not the case that P" cannot both be true.**

4) **Law of (excluded middle: For every proposition "P" and its
   negation "It is not the case that P," either "P" is true or its
   negation "It is not the case that P" is true.**

We will wait until Chapter IV, Part I to discuss the meaning of the term "contra-diction" in detail, and we will wait until Chapter V, Part II to see why the law of non-contradiction is a law of logic; that is, why this law must be true as a condition for any proposition to have a truth value. For now, we will use these two laws to show how logical negation works.

The proposition "The stars do not appear to move" (or "It is not the case that the stars appear to move") logically negates the proposition "The stars appear to move." If the latter is true, then the former is false, and if the latter is false, the former is true.

The third and fourth laws of logic combine with the first two laws of logic to provide a definition of logical negation. We saw in Chapter II that the law of bivalence and the law of truth values gave us the simple truth table for any proposition "**P.**"

$$\frac{P}{\begin{array}{c} T \\ F \end{array}}$$

The law of non-contradiction, *together with* the law of bivalence, implies that when "**P**" is true, its negation "It is not the case that **P**" cannot have the value true. It follows, given the law of bivalence, that when the proposition "**P**" is true, its negation "It is not the case that **P**" must be false. (Note that neither the third nor the fourth law of logic mentions the value false; each considers only the value true, hence the need for appeal to the law of bivalence.) The law of excluded middle says that of the two propositions "**P**" and "It is not the case that **P**," one of the two must be true. This implies that when the proposition "**P**" is false, its logical negation "It is not the case that **P**" must be true. Putting these together, then, gives the following rule for logical negation.

RULE FOR LOGICAL NEGATION:
The logical negation of a proposition is true if and only if the proposition is false, and the logical negation of a proposition is false if and only if the proposition is true.

We can see more rigorously how this rule is derived if we spell out the arguments given for it in premises and conclusion form and use those arguments to construct the truth table for the logical negation of a proposition P. The first argument for constructing the truth table for the logical negation of a proposition P can be presented in premises and conclusion form as follows:

1) A proposition "P" and its negation "It is not the case that P" cannot both be true. (This is the law of non-contradiction)

2) A proposition must be either true or false. (This is the law of bivalence)

3) The proposition "P" is true. (This is the first line of the truth table for "P").

Therefore, (4) the proposition "It is not the case that P" is false. (This will be the first line of the truth table for "It is not the case that P")

This argument demonstrates that, given that a proposition **P** is true, it follows that its logical negation must be false. Notice that we needed the law of bivalence as a premise in this argument in addition to the law of non-contradiction. This is because, if the proposition **P** is true then its logical negation cannot also be true, as the law of non-contradiction tells us, but this does not tell us what truth value to assign to "It is not the case that P." We need the law of bivalence to tell us that there is only one other choice, namely the value false.

The second argument for constructing the truth table for the logical negation of a proposition P can be presented in premises and conclusion form as follows:

1) For every proposition "P" and its negation "It is not the case that P," either "P" is true or its negation "It is not the case that P" is true. (This is the law of excluded middle)

2) The proposition "P" is false. (This is the second line of the truth table for "P")

Therefore, (3) the proposition "It is not the case that P" is true. (This will be the second line of the truth table for "It is not the case that P")

These arguments define the logical use of negation by assigning truth values to the proposition "It is not the case that P" as follows:

P	It is not the case that P
T	F
F	T

This truth table defines logical negation; it displays the assignments of truth values for "It is not the case that P" given the truth values for "P" as determined by the rule for logical negation; that is, it maps the possible truth values for **P** onto the corresponding possible truth values for **It is not the case that P**.

Operators like "not ..." and connective terms like "... and ...," "... or ...," and "if ..." do not refer to anything in the world in the way that words like "chair" or "tree" do. The operator "not ..." and the connective terms get their meaning from what they do—that is, the functions they perform—in connecting component propositions to determine the corresponding possible truth values of compound propositions. When the operator and connectives are truth functional, their meaning is given by how they function to operate on the truth values of component propositions to determine the truth value of the compound propositions that result from their operation. Such definitions in terms of the functioning of a connective or operator were already contained in the definition of truth functional connective or operator given above. In the case of logical negation, the operator functions to assign the contrary truth value to the logical negation of a single proposition on which it operates. (Notice again that we can confirm that "It is not the case that P" is a compound proposition, since it has the proposition **P** as a part.) If the proposition **P** is true, then its logical negation is false, and if the proposition **P** is false, then its logical negation is true. This is exactly what is displayed in the truth table.

Notice that negation is not the same as falsehood. Propositions of the form "It is not the case that P" can be true. For example, the proposition "One hundred is not a larger number than one thousand" is true. Logical negation is an operator term that constructs compound propositions and is expressed by words or phrases in a language. It operates on propositions to assign truth values to the logical negation of a proposition (the compound proposition), given the truth value of the proposition being negated. Logical negation is a truth function belonging solely to language, whereas falsehood is a truth value, and as such it concerns the relation between a proposition and the state of affairs it attempts to describe. Falsehood is a relationship between language and the world.

Logical negation always operates on the truth value of a proposition and functions to assign a truth value to the compound proposition that it produces. We can make this point clearer by constructing the logical negation for the proposition "It is not the case that P." We express the logical negation of "It is not the case that P" in the proposition "It is not the case that it is not the case that P." We then construct the truth table for that proposition by applying the rule for logical negation to the proposition "It is not the case that P" as follows:

P	It is not the case that P	It is not the case that it is not the case that P
T	F	T
F	T	F

This truth table shows that the logical negation of the logical negation of a proposition **P** always has the same truth value as the original proposition **P** (this is sometimes called the rule of double negation, such that "**P**" is logically equivalent to "It is not the case that it is not the case that **P**"). The truth tables we have given for the propositions "**P**," "It is not the case that **P**," and "It is not the case that it is not the case that **P**" are perfectly general. It does not matter what proposition the variable "**P**" stands for (or how complex that proposition is). These truth tables show how the truth values of the compound propositions depend on the truth values of their parts.

However, it is important to notice that ordinary English does not always use negative indicators like the word "not ..." to express logical negation. Frequently, negative prefixes such as "dis-," "il-," and "un-" only deny that some feature belongs to some thing. For example, consider the propositions "Dissatisfaction unsettles people" and "Noncompliance will be subject to prosecution." In the former, the negative prefixes "dis-" and "un-" do not indicate logical negations since they negate only the terms "satisfaction" and "settles," respectively, and not the whole proposition. In particular, notice that the latter does not say the same thing as "It is not the case that compliance will be subject to prosecution." The former says that one will be prosecuted when one does not comply, while the latter says that one will not be prosecuted when one does comply but leaves it open as to what will happen if one does not comply. Ruling out such features is not equivalent to asserting logical negation, because what is negated in these cases is not a whole proposition. Moreover, in ordinary English we sometimes use more than one negative expression to emphasize and to intensify the rhetorical importance of the negation. So when the old song lyric says "I ain't got nobody," this does not mean I have got somebody. But if the two negative expressions (the "not ..." in "ain't" and the "no-" in "nobody") were logical negations, the lyric would have to mean that I have got somebody.

Since the English word "not ..." does not always express logical negation, and because writing out the phrase "It is not the case that ..." is cumbersome, we will use the sign "~" (called a tilde) placed immediately to the left of a proposition to indicate the logical negation of that proposition. So the truth table given immediately above will be written as follows:

P	~P	~(~P)
T	F	T
F	T	F

Study Questions and Problems

Respond to each of the following questions and problems clearly and precisely.

1) Define each of the following:
   (a) simple proposition
   (b) compound proposition

2) Define truth functional connective and truth functional operator.

3) Why is the logical negation of a proposition a compound proposition?

4) State the rule for logical negation. Give an example of the logical negation of a proposition.

5) Why do we need to define truth functional operators and connectives by using truth tables?

6) Name and state all four laws of logic. What is a law of logic?

7) Give arguments that demonstrate that the truth table for logical negation can be derived from the laws of logic.

8) Distinguish logical negation from falsehood.

9) Using an example, show that not all uses of negative indicators in English are logical negations.

Part II: Logical Conjunction

The first connective expression we will consider is the connective best expressed by the English word "... and ..." or the words "both ... and ...." Our interest in the connective "... and ..." is in its use to connect two whole propositions, but without any implications other than that the two propositions are both true. This is the truth functional use of "... and...." In the compound proposition "I bought a new coat and I bought a new hat," the word "... and ..." simply connects the proposition "I bought a new coat" with the proposition "I bought a new hat" in such a way that the resulting compound proposition is true only if both component propositions are true; otherwise the compound proposition is false. This use of the word "... and ..." is truth functional because the truth value of the compound proposition is solely a function of the truth values of its component propositions. We call a compound proposition connected by the truth functional use of "... and ..." a **logical conjunction**. (For the sake of brevity, logical conjunctions are often referred to merely as conjunctions.) The example proposition "I bought a new coat and I bought a new hat" is a logical conjunction. We call each of the component propositions connected by logical conjunction a **conjunct**. In the example, the two propositions "I bought a new coat" and "I bought a new hat" are the conjuncts belonging to the whole logical conjunction.

To represent the truth functional use of connectives like "... and ..." that combine two propositions to make a more complex compound proposition, we use a truth table that displays all the possible ways in which the two propositions can be true or false together. To do this, we begin by constructing a truth table for two propositions whose truth values are independent of one another. We have already seen an example of this in the previous chapter when we considered the two propositions "The door is open" and "Lara believes that the door is open." However, let us consider the matter more closely. Take, for example, the two propositions "The sun is shining" and "I am at the beach." It is possible for either one of these propositions to be true while either the other proposition is true or the other proposition is false. It is possible for either one of these propositions to be false while the other proposition is true or the other proposition is false. That all these combinations are possibilities is what we mean when we say that their truth values are independent of one another; that is, the truth value of one proposition does not determine the truth value of the other proposition. We can represent this situation in the following manner.

It is sunny	I am at the beach	s	b
☼	🏖	T	T
☼	⛱	T	F
🌧	🏖	F	T
🌧	⛱	F	F

In the first two columns on the left, the picture of the sun depicts the state of affairs when it is sunny and thus indicates the state of affairs when the proposition "It is sunny" is true. The picture of the cloud depicts the state of affairs when it is not sunny and thus indicates the state of affairs when the proposition "It is sunny" is false. The picture of the stick figure and the beach umbrella depict the state of affairs when I am at the beach and thus indicates the state of affairs when the proposition "I am at the beach" is true. The picture of the beach umbrella without the stick figure depicts the state of affairs when I am not at the beach and thus indicates the state of affairs when the proposition "I am at the beach" is false. The four rows of the table list all of the possible ways in which the states of affairs might occur. First, it could be that it is both sunny and I am at the beach. Second, it could be that it is sunny and I am not at the beach. Third, it could be that it is not sunny and I am at the beach. Lastly, it could be that it is not sunny and I am not at the beach. There are no other possible ways the world could be regarding the two states of affairs: it being sunny and my being at the beach.

In the two right-hand columns (which compose the truth table for the two propositions "It is sunny" and "I am at the beach"), the letter "s" stands for the proposition "It is sunny" and the letter "b" stands for the proposition "I am at the beach." The letters "T" and "F" stand for true and false, respectively, as usual. So the truth table gives all the possible combinations of truth values for two independent propositions. First, both propositions could be true. Second, the first proposition could be true and the second proposition false. Third, the first proposition could be false and the second proposition true. Lastly, both propositions could be false. There are no other possible assignments of truth values to two independent propositions.

Notice that for one simple proposition there are two possibilities (the proposition is either true or false), while for two propositions the number of possible assignments of truth values doubles. The reason for this is that for each of the two possible truth values assignable to the first proposition, the second proposition may be true, and for each of the two possible truth values assignable to the first proposition, the second proposition may be false. This means that each additional proposition doubles the number of possible assignments of truth values to the set of propositions, and so doubles the number of rows in the truth table—for two propositions four rows, for three propositions eight rows, for four propositions sixteen rows, and so on, and in general for n propositions 2^n rows. Thus the rows of a truth table represent all the *possible* ways states of affairs may be, that is, all the possibilities with respect to the propositions represented by the truth table.

We can now give the rule for the combination of independent propositions using logical conjunction.

RULE FOR LOGICAL CONJUNCTION:
A conjunction is true if and only if both conjuncts are true; otherwise the conjunction is false (i.e., if and only if either one of its conjuncts is true and the other false, or both of its conjuncts are false).

Since the English word "... and ..." does not always express logical conjunction, we will use the ampersand sign "&" placed between the two conjuncts to indicate their logical conjunction. According to this rule, if a proposition is a conjunction it will have the following truth table, in which "P" and "Q" stand for any two propositions and "P & Q" stands for their conjunction.

P	Q	P & Q
T	T	T
T	F	F
F	T	F
F	F	F

English contains several words that may express logical conjunction. The meanings of the words "but," "however," "while," and "even though" include logical conjunction and also indicate that the conjunction may run contrary to our expectations. So "It is not sunny, but I am at the beach" expresses the conjunction "It is not sunny, and I am at the beach" along with the suggestion that this conjunction runs contrary to expectation. The same can be said of the proposition "Even though it is not sunny, I am at the beach." In all these cases, and for the purposes of logical analysis, we will treat each of these words as expressing logical conjunction and ignore the additional meanings layered on top of the truth functional meaning.

Like "not ...," the English word "... and ..." is not always used to express logical conjunction in ordinary English. For example, in the proposition "Sigmund Freud and Emile Durkheim were contemporaries," the word "... and ..." indicates a relationship between the two names "Sigmund Freud" and "Emile Durkheim." Here the word "... and ..." does not connect whole propositions. (It makes no sense to say "Sigmund Freud was a contemporary" without saying who Freud was related to in that way.) This use of the word "... and ..." is not truth functional as it stands. We could, however, reconstruct a truth functional use of "... and ..." by making the relationship explicit as follows: "Sigmund Freud was a contemporary of Emile Durkheim *and* Emile Durkheim was a contemporary of Sigmund Freud." We also sometimes use the word "... and ..." to indicate temporal order. In such cases the word "then" (here indicating temporal sequence) is often left out; we say "... and ..." and mean "and then afterward." In many contexts, the proposition "Mila got married and had a baby" means that Mila got married first and then had a baby afterward. In this sense, "Mila got married and had a baby" does not mean the same as "Mila had a baby and got married." In these propositions, the word "... and ..." means the same as "and then" or "and afterward." This use of the word "... and ..." does contain a truth functional use of "and," but it also contains more than that use since it also includes an indication of temporal order. Again we will ignore this additional meaning layered on top of the truth functional meaning.

INFORMAL FALLACY: COMPLEX QUESTION

So far we have considered only the logic of conjunctions, that is, how the truth value of a conjunction is a function of the truth values of its conjuncts. However, since conjunctions can connect any two propositions whatsoever, they can be misused to produce misleading, but too often rhetorically effective, arguments. This produces an informal fallacy called **complex question**. This fallacy and the other two fallacies in this chapter are valid arguments, unlike the fallacies in Chapter II, and the rhetorical tricks that seduce people into accepting these fallacious arguments concern their soundness, and in particular the truth of their premises. It is a legitimate argument to conclude that when a conjunction is true, since each of the conjuncts in a true conjunction is true, one of the conjuncts will be true. Such arguments have the form

(1) **P & Q**

∴ (2) **P**

While these are valid argument forms (so any argument in this form is valid), it is a sound argument only if the conjunction that forms its premise is actually true. (We will look at argument forms of this sort in more detail in Chapter V. The symbol ∴ is conventionally used to mean therefore.) When, because they are conjoined, two unrelated propositions get treated as a single proposition, the speaker may seduce the audience into treating the whole conjunction as true, when it is not, and then persuade the audience to accept one of the conjuncts as true. Often this occurs when the speaker seduces the audience into treating the whole conjunction as true by demanding an answer to a complex question, that is, a question that really contains two different questions in one, as in the following example.

Example 43:   Lawyer: "Have you stopped using illegal sales practices?"
Demi: "Yes."
Lawyer: "Then you did once use illegal sales practices."

We can see the fallacy clearly when we paraphrase this example as an argument in premises and conclusion form. To do so we must turn the question into a proposition (since an argument can only contain propositions) as follows:

(1) Demi once used illegal sales practices and now she has stopped using illegal sales practices.

Therefore, (2) Demi once used illegal sales practices.

The question "Have you stopped using illegal sales practices?" really contains two questions: "Have you used illegal practices?" and "If so, have you stopped using illegal sales practices?" If Demi is tricked or forced into answering either "Yes" or "No" to the whole complex question, she has in effect answered "Yes" to the question "Have you used illegal practices?" as well. In the example, if Demi had answered "No," the lawyer would have concluded, "Then you still do use illegal sales practices." Complex questions are not fallacies by themselves; they become fallacies only when the conclusion is drawn that the respondent has answered the embedded question. So in Example 43, the lawyer has committed the fallacy of complex question by drawing the conclusion that Demi used illegal sales practices.

When confronted with a complex question, we should divide the question into its component questions and answer them separately. If Demi were innocent, then she should have refused to give a simple "Yes" or "No" answer to the complex question and replied that she has never used illegal sales practices, so the question of whether she has stopped does not arise.[1]

---

1 That the second question does not arise here shows that the situation is really more complicated than a simple conjunction. The relation between the two claims is not simply a relation of conjunction. A specific answer to the hidden question (in the example the answer "Yes") must be given before it makes sense to even ask the second question. The relation between the two questions, then, is that the second question presupposes an (affirmative) answer to the first question. This is the point of the phrase "If so, ..." used in expressing the second question in the complex question. We will not discuss the difficult logic of presupposition in this text and will treat complex questions as if they merely contained logical conjunctions.

Parliamentary procedure recognizes the importance of avoiding complex questions. In most parliamentary bodies, a motion to divide the question is a privileged motion. This means that when voting on any proposal, before the original proposal can be brought to a vote, the parliamentary body must first vote on whether to separate the proposal into its component proposals and vote on each component separately. This precaution protects the group from being forced to accept unsatisfactory proposals conjoined with measures the group may want to accept.

We saw in Chapter II, Part II (D) that the question "Is that a fact or an opinion?" is really a complex question, since it presupposes (in the figurative sense of the question that we discussed in the previous chapter) that the only way to settle the truth value of a proposition is to appeal to some person as an authority. The two questions are "Is this issue to be settled by appealing to authority?" and "If so, is the authority reliable?" The complex question gives us a choice between dogmatism and extreme skepticism. If we answer the complex question either way, we are tacitly forced to accept that we cannot reason matters out for ourselves and must either dogmatically obey some authority (this is what was misleadingly expressed by the question "Is that a fact?") or be reduced to hopelessly arbitrary skepticism (this is what was misleadingly expressed by the question "Is that an opinion?"). We should therefore reject the question "Is that a fact or an opinion?" as containing a misleading complex question. Instead, we should divide the question and consider the appropriate arguments for answers to each question separately and consider whether appealing to authority is appropriate in the case before us according to the six criteria for a legitimate appeal to authority.

Study Questions and Problems

Respond to each of the following questions and problems clearly and precisely.

1) Explain how to construct a truth table for two independent propositions.

2) Give an example (in English) of a logical conjunction.

3) Using examples, show that not all uses of the word "... and ..." are logical conjunctions.

4) State the rule for logical conjunction. Using the rule, construct the truth table for the conjunction of two propositions. Explain what you have done, and why.

5) Explain what has gone wrong when someone commits the fallacy of complex question.

6) Why does the question "Is that a fact or an opinion?" commit a complex question fallacy?

Part III: Logical Disjunction

Like the English word "... and ...," the English word "... or ..." (or the words "either ... or ...") functions to connect pairs of propositions together to make compound propositions. We call a compound proposition connected by a truth functional use of "... or ..." a **logical disjunction**, and we call each of the propositions connected by logical disjunction a **disjunct**. (For the sake of brevity, logical disjunctions are often referred to merely as disjunctions.)

We use the word "... or ..." (or the words "either ... or ...") to indicate that the states of affairs represented by the disjuncts are alternatives. However, the connective "... or ..." is ambiguous in English. There are two primary uses of the word, both of which are truth functional; that is, the word "... or ..." can be used to express either one of two different truth functional connectives, which are outlined below.

For example, in the disjunction "Employees may have paid days off either for illness or for family emergencies," the two disjuncts are "Employees may have paid days off for illness" and "Employees may have paid days off for family emergencies." If an employee takes a paid day off for illness, the disjunction correctly describes the state of affairs, and so the disjunction is true. If an employee takes a paid day off for a family emergency, the disjunction again correctly describes the state of affairs, and so the disjunction is again true. Also, if an employee takes a paid day off for both illness and a family emergency, the disjunction correctly describes the state of affairs, and so the disjunction is true; given this disjunction as a policy, it would be counterintuitive to deny that one should get a paid day off when one had both an illness and a family emergency. The disjunction is false only in the case where an employee does not get a paid day off and is either ill or has a family emergency. A disjunction that functions to connect its two disjuncts so that the whole disjunction is true if one of its disjuncts is true, or the other disjunct is true, or both of its disjuncts are true is called an **inclusive disjunction**. A disjunction of this sort is called inclusive because it includes the case where both of its disjuncts are true; that is, it includes the case where the whole disjunction is true when both of its disjuncts are true. The connective "... or ..." in an inclusive disjunction is a truth functional connective because it is governed by the following rule.

RULE FOR INCLUSIVE DISJUNCTION:

An inclusive disjunction is false if and only if both its disjuncts are false; an inclusive disjunction is true otherwise (i.e., if and only if either one of its disjuncts is true, or its other disjunct is true, or both of its disjuncts are true).

If a proposition is an inclusive disjunction, it will have the following truth table, in which "P" and "Q" stand for any two propositions and "P v Q" stands for their inclusive disjunction (we will use the lower case "v" as the sign for inclusive disjunction).

P	Q	P v Q
T	T	T
T	F	T
F	T	T
F	F	F

The inclusive sense of disjunction must be sharply distinguished from the other truth functional form of disjunction, **exclusive disjunction**. In the disjunction "Either Anna will go to the concert at 8:00 tonight, or she will go across town to the movie at 8:00 tonight," the two disjuncts are "Anna will go to the concert at 8:00 tonight" and "Anna will go across town to the movie at 8:00 tonight." Since Anna can do one or the other, these disjuncts represent states of affairs that are genuine alternatives. But these states of affairs also exclude one another, because Anna cannot both go to the concert and also go to the movie across town at the same time, since she cannot be in two places at once. The disjunction that expresses these exclusive alternatives is called an exclusive disjunction. While exclusive disjunctions often do represent states of affairs that exclude one another by nature (as in the example), they need not. Exclusive disjunctions are forms of propositions and may be used whenever we wish to present two states of affairs as alternatives that exclude one another. *To use a disjunction in the exclusive sense, one always needs to be able to give an argument to exclude the case where both disjuncts are true.* In the example, the following argument eliminates the possibility of both disjuncts being true:

(1) If Anna were to go to the concert at 8:00 tonight, and Anna were also to go across town to the movie at 8:00 tonight, then Anna would be in two places at the same time.

(2) Anna cannot be in two places at the same time.

Therefore, (3) Anna cannot both go to the concert at 8:00 tonight and go across town to the movie at 8:00 tonight.

The connective "... or ..." in an exclusive disjunction is a truth functional connective because it is governed by the following rule.

RULE FOR EXCLUSIVE DISJUNCTION:
An exclusive disjunction is true if and only if exactly one of its disjuncts is true, while an exclusive disjunction is false if both its disjuncts are true and the exclusive disjunction is false if both its disjuncts are false.

Since the English word "... or ..." may be used to express either an inclusive or an exclusive disjunction, we have to mark the difference between these uses. While in English we only have the single word "... or ..." to express both inclusive and exclusive disjunction, Latin has two different words: "vel" for inclusive disjunction and "aut" for exclusive disjunction.[2] We use the sign "v" (for the Latin "vel") placed between the two disjuncts to indicate their inclusive disjunction. We do not need a special sign for exclusive disjunction because an exclusive disjunction may be expressed (for any two propositions "P" and "Q") as "Either P is true (inclusive) or Q is true, but it is not the case that both P and Q are true." We can, therefore, symbolize P exclusive-or Q as $[(P \text{ v } Q) \text{ \& } (\sim (P \text{ \& } Q))]$. This formula uses only the signs we have developed for negation, conjunction, and inclusive disjunction. It says, "Either P or Q, and it is not the case that both P and Q," where the "... or ..." is an inclusive disjunction.

We already know from the rule governing exclusive disjunction that it *should* have the following truth table:

P	Q	P exclusive-or Q
T	T	F
T	F	T
F	T	T
F	F	F

---

2 This is actually an idealization of the Latin terms. The meaning of the Latin words is more complicated than stated in this exposition, as we should expect from words in a natural language.

However, by applying the truth table definitions and rules for negation, conjunction, and inclusive disjunction to this formula one at a time, we can build up the truth table for exclusive disjunction. In the first two columns (starting on the left of the table below), we see the truth tables for the independent propositions "**P**" and "**Q**." In the third column, we see the truth table for the inclusive disjunction of the propositions "**P**" and "**Q**," and in the fourth column we see the conjunction of the propositions "**P**" and "**Q**." In the fifth column, we see the truth table for the negation of the conjunction "**P & Q**" by following the rule for logical negation: in every row of the truth table for column four, "**P & Q**," where "**P & Q**" has the value "**T**," we write "**F**" for its negation "**~ (P & Q)**," and also in every row of the truth table for "**P & Q**" where "**P & Q**" has the value "**F**," we write "**T**" for its negation "**~ (P & Q)**." Finally, we follow the rule for logical conjunction to conjoin the disjunction "**P v Q**" from the third column with the negation of the conjunction "**~ (P & Q)**" from the fifth column. In every row where "**P v Q**" and "**~ (P & Q)**" both have the value "**T**," we write "**T**" for the conjunction [(**P v Q**) & (~ (**P & Q**))]. In every row where either "(**P v Q**)" has the value "**F**" or "**~ (P & Q)**" has the value "**F**," or both have the value "**F**," we write "**F**" for the conjunction [(**P v Q**) & (~ (**P & Q**))]. The result gives us the following truth table.

P	Q	P v Q	P & Q	~ (P & Q)	[(P v Q) & (~ (P & Q))]
T	T	T	T	F	F
T	F	T	F	T	T
F	T	T	F	T	T
F	F	F	F	T	F

When the method for constructing truth tables for complex formulae is spelled out in English as we have done above, it may seem more complicated than it is. Notice that the truth table we have arrived at for the formula for the exclusive disjunction [(**P v Q**) & (~ (**P & Q**))] is the same as the truth table we got from the rule for exclusive disjunction. This illustrates that the method for constructing truth tables using the truth functional connectives corresponds with our understanding of the operators and connectives stated in the rules for their use.

It is a common mistake in critical thinking to assume that disjunctions are exclusive when really they are inclusive. When an inclusive disjunction is misread as an exclusive disjunction, this conceals the possibility that both disjuncts may be true. This misreading leads to unnecessarily cramped and rigid thinking in that it systematically conceals available possibilities and so closes off alternative possibilities for thought and action. To avoid this sort of difficulty when *translating* disjunctions from English into our notation, <u>we shall always assume that a disjunction is inclusive unless it is explicitly stated as an exclusive disjunction.</u> This means that unless the text clearly and explicitly excludes the case where both the disjuncts are true, we will translate the disjunction as an inclusive disjunction. No harm will arise if a disjunction is intended as exclusive and we translate it as inclusive.

However, when someone illegitimately assumes that a disjunction is exclusive when it is really inclusive, they fall prey to a fallacy called **affirming the disjunct** (because the second premise asserts one of the disjuncts). This type of argument is a formal fallacy: it is fallacious because of its formal structure. The fallacy can be displayed formally as follows:

(1) **P v Q**
(2) **P**
∴ (3) **~ Q**

This argument form is invalid; it would be valid only if the disjunction were an exclusive disjunction that ruled out the possibility that both disjuncts could be true. However, since disjunctions should be read as inclusive unless they are explicitly stated to be exclusive, this argument has an invalid form. (Hence, this is a formal fallacy; it does not depend on a rhetorical trick, but is invalid because of its form. This invalidity will be demonstrated in Chapter V.) The symbol "v" always symbolizes an inclusive disjunction, so in the above argument form, the premise includes the possibility that both **P** and **Q** are true. But the conclusion denies exactly that possibility and so cannot follow from the premise. Here is an example of the affirming the disjunct fallacy in English.

Example 44a: (1) Bill is treasurer or he is vice president.

(2) Bill is treasurer.

∴ (3) Bill is not vice president.

There is no reason given in the premises that Bill could not hold both offices. If there is such a reason, say that the club rules forbid anyone holding more than one office at a time, then that amounts to a separate and additional premise that explicitly rules out the case where Bill could be both treasurer and vice president. In that case, we would have a different argument, the first premise of which would say "Bill is treasurer or he is vice president, but he cannot hold both offices." In this case, we make explicit that both alternatives are not true together. But that would be a different argument than the one given in Example 44a, which is actually invalid. A common example of this fallacy often arises in discussions of human traits such as intelligence or sexual orientation, when the question is asked whether such traits are due to our natural or genetic endowment, or whether they are due to influences in our education, training, or habits. This is usually put in terms of an alternative between nature or nurture and can fall prey to fallacies of affirming the disjunct, as in the following example:

Example 45: (1) Either this human characteristic is due to nature or this human characteristic is due to nurture.

(2) This human characteristic is due to nature.

Therefore, (3) this human characteristic is not due to nurture.

The flaw in this argument is that many (perhaps most) human characteristics arise out of *both* our natural endowment and our conditioning. So the fact that a human characteristic arises partly because of our nature does not exclude the possibility that it also arises partly out of our education, training, or habits.

INFORMAL FALLACY: FALSE DILEMMA

So far we have considered only the logic of disjunctions, that is, how the truth value of a disjunction is a function of the truth values of its disjuncts. However, since disjunctions need not give all the possible alternatives, they can be misused to produce misleading, but too often rhetorically effective, fallacious arguments, specifically an informal fallacy called a false dilemma. It is a legitimate—that is, valid—argument to conclude from a disjunction and the negation of one of the disjuncts that the other disjunct must be true. Such an argument has the form:

(1) $P \vee Q$
(2) $\sim P$
∴ (3) Q

This argument form is valid (and so any argument in this form is valid) because it is impossible for it to have true premises and a false conclusion. (We shall demonstrate that arguments of this form are valid in Chapter V.) Here is an example:

Example 44b: (1) Bill is president or he is vice president.

(2) Bill is not president.

∴ (3) Bill is vice president.

However, arguments in this form are sound arguments only if the disjunction "**P v Q**" exhausts all of the legitimate alternatives and the disjunction "**P v Q**" is true. When there are other legitimate alternatives, both the disjuncts offered in the argument could be false (and so the whole disjunction would be false). So, in Example 44b, if we are considering officers of our club, Bill might also be the treasurer. For an additional example, consider the following argument:

> **Example 46:**   Either you can afford this stereo, or you are going to have to do without music for a while. Since you don't have enough money for this stereo, you are just going to have to do without music for a while.

We can paraphrase this example as an argument in premises and conclusion form as follows:

(1) Either you can afford this stereo, or you are going to do without music for a while.
(2) You cannot afford this stereo.

Therefore, (3) you are going to do without music for a while.

In this argument, the speaker has failed to take account of other reasonable alternatives. One could, for instance, buy another more affordable stereo, rent a stereo, listen to the radio, or play an instrument oneself instead of either buying this stereo or doing without music. When confronted with false dilemmas, we should respond by *explicitly specifying* other alternatives and showing that they are reasonable options.

When there is a third alternative, the argument should really be written in the form:

(1) **P v (Q v R)**
(2) **~ P**

∴ (3) **Q v R**

where from the first premise combined with the negation of "**P**" in the second premise we are justified in concluding only that either one or the other of the remaining alternatives "**Q**" or "**R**" is true. Similarly, if there are more alternatives, we should make them explicit in the argument. When a speaker conceals or neglects other reasonable alternatives, that speaker may trick or seduce the audience into accepting a proposition as true, when the argument only genuinely supports a disjunction between that proposition and propositions expressing the other alternatives.

Study Questions and Problems

Respond to each of the following questions and problems clearly and precisely.

1) Using examples, explain the difference between inclusive and exclusive uses of the word "... or ...."

2) State the rule for inclusive disjunction.

3) State the rule for exclusive disjunction.

4) Under what conditions do we translate the English word "... or ..." as an exclusive disjunction?

5) What fallacy may arise if we confuse an inclusive disjunction with an exclusive disjunction? What goes wrong in this fallacy?

6) Explain why **not** every argument of the form

   (1) P v Q
   (2) ~ P
   _____
   ∴ (3) Q

   is an example of a false dilemma.

7) Explain what has gone wrong when someone commits the fallacy of false dilemma.

Part IV: Truth Functional Conditionals

The most important, and most difficult, of the connectives we will study are **truth functional conditionals**, which are forms of conditional propositions. Conditional propositions (we will call them "conditionals" for the sake of brevity) are compound propositions most clearly expressed when component propositions are connected by the English words "if ..., then...." For example, the proposition "If Fiona goes to the store, then she will buy bread" is a conditional proposition. Its two component propositions are "Fiona goes to the store" and "Fiona will buy bread." Such propositions are called conditionals because the second component proposition (following the "then ...," which is called the consequent) is claimed to be true only on the condition that the first component proposition (following the "if ...," which is called the antecedent) is true. When a conditional proposition is asserted, neither of the component propositions is asserted; in other words, our example "If Fiona goes to the store, then she will buy bread" asserts *neither* that Fiona will go to the store *nor* that she will buy bread. It only claims that *on the condition* that Fiona goes to the store, she will buy bread, but the condition may not hold. While the truth values of truth functional conditionals are determined by the truth values of their parts, as in all truth functions, here there is no way to get from the actual truth of the whole compound proposition alone to the truth values of the component propositions.

There is an important formal difference between conditionals, on the one hand, and conjunctions and disjunctions, on the other. In both conjunctions and disjunctions the connective is symmetrical. This means that propositions of the form "**P & Q**" say exactly the same thing (express exactly the same truth function) as "**Q & P**," and propositions of the form "**P v Q**" say exactly the same thing (express exactly the same truth function) as "**Q v P**." This is not the case for conditionals: *conditionals are not symmetric.*

Propositions of the form "if P, then Q" do not say the same thing as propositions of the form "if Q, then P." Conditional propositions in which the component propositions are interchanged are called *converses* of one another. In general, any two conditionals of the forms

If P, then Q.
If Q, then P.

are converses of one another, and have different meanings and different implications. So, for example, the proposition "If Helen is a citizen of Colorado, then she is a citizen of the United States" does not mean the same thing as its converse, "If Helen is a citizen of the United States, then she is a citizen of Colorado." After all, even when the first of these propositions is true, the second may be false. If Helen is a citizen of Colorado she is, indeed, a citizen of the United States. But if Helen is a citizen of the United States, she may not be a citizen of Colorado; she could be a citizen of some other state. So Helen being a citizen of the United States is not a condition sufficient for her being a citizen of Colorado. Here we can enunciate a general principle about propositions as the meanings of sentences: **if it is possible for one sentence to be true while another sentence false, the two sentences must express different propositions**—that is, the two sentences must have different meanings; the two propositions cannot be interchanged.

So while compound propositions that connect pairs of component propositions with the connective of the standard form "if ..., then ..." are called conditionals, we need to have two different terms to designate the component propositions connected in a conditional. If the conditional is in standard form we call the proposition governed by the "if..." the **antecedent** of the conditional, and we call the proposition governed by the "then" the **consequent** of the conditional. So, in the example "If Helen goes to the store, then she will buy bread," the component "Helen goes to the store" is the antecedent, and the component "Helen will buy bread" is the consequent. We can sketch the standard form of the conditional, then, as follows:

If (antecedent), then (consequent).

In general, in any conditional proposition of the form

If P, then Q,

"**P**" is the antecedent and "**Q**" is the consequent.

(A) VARIOUS USES OF CONDITIONALS

Conditional propositions are particularly complicated because there are several different uses for conditionals and several different types of conditionals, all with their own logical features. It is important when analyzing a text to identify how the conditional propositions are used, because different types of conditionals will have different implications. We may use conditional propositions to express various sorts of conditional relations, for instance, conditional predictions, conditional bets, conditional promises, and causal relations. These are only a sampling of the uses we make of conditionals; we will later also consider the use of conditionals in definitions and logical implications. In each of the following four cases, however, the differences are due to extra meanings layered on top of the core truth functional meaning. We will now consider these uses in order to extract a **truth functional core** common to all the various uses of conditionals and underlying any meanings layered on top of their core truth functional meaning, and also to make clear why the truth functional conditional has the truth table it does.

Conditional Predictions

Example 47:   An economist predicts, "If Britain's unemployment subsides, the British pound will rise in value."

A conditional prediction concerns what will happen in the future under some specified condition. In the example, the economist predicts that the British pound will rise in value, but only on the condition that Britain's unemployment subsides. The prediction clearly would turn out to be true if Britain's unemployment rate were to fall and the British pound were to rise in value. The prediction clearly would turn out to be false if Britain's unemployment rate were to fall, but the British pound failed to rise in value: *the conditional would be false if the antecedent were true and the consequent false.* However, suppose that the pound rises but British employment does too, or that neither the value of the pound rises nor the British rate of unemployment subsides. In either of these cases, we can say only that the prediction has not turned out to be false, for it was predicted only that the British pound would rise on the condition that Britain's unemployment subsides. In effect, when the antecedent is false, no prediction has been made, and the prediction has not been falsified. Here the conditional prediction expresses the claim that the state of affairs described in the consequent will occur on the condition that the state of affairs described by the antecedent occurs. The conditional prediction adds an additional meaning to the truth functional meaning of the conditional, namely the claim that the future event predicted will occur if the condition holds (in our example, that the future value of the British pound will go up if the condition holds that Britain's unemployment falls).

Conditional Bets

Example 48:   Jess bets Tom money by saying, "If the Rockies beat the Dodgers next week, then they will win the pennant."

Notice that Jess makes the bet that the Rockies will win the pennant only under the condition that they beat the Dodgers next week. She may collect on the bet only where the state of affairs is that the Rockies beat the Dodgers next week and the Rockies do win the pennant, that is, when both the antecedent and consequent turn out to be true. Jess commits to paying off the bet only should the state of affairs turn out to be that the Rockies beat the Dodgers next week but do not win the pennant; in other words, *the conditional is false just in the case where the antecedent of the conditional is true and the consequent is*

false. If the Rockies do not beat the Dodgers next week, then neither Jess nor Tom may win the bet, no matter who wins the pennant. If the condition that the Rockies beat the Dodgers fails to come about, then the bet is off. Again, a meaning has been added to the truth functional meaning of the conditional. Here the additional meaning is that in making the bet, Jess and Tom take on the obligation to pay the other the amount bet, depending on the truth value of the conditional given the truth of the antecedent.

As in the above example, conditional bets are typically a type of conditional prediction. Their logic is very similar. However, a bet need not be about something in the future. For example, someone may make the bet, "If the word 'furze' is in this dictionary, then the only definition is that a furze is a gorse." The truth of this claim depends on what is already in the dictionary, not on something in the future.

Conditional Promises

> **Example 49:**   Greta promises Hans, "If it is sunny, then I'll be at the beach."

Conditional promises are similar to conditional bets in that the only case where we would count Greta as breaking her promise is where the state of affairs occurs that it is sunny and she is not at the beach. *The conditional is false just in the case where the antecedent of the conditional is true and the consequent is false.* Greta has promised to be at the beach on the condition that it is sunny. She will have kept her promise by being at the beach when it is sunny, that is, when both the antecedent and the consequent of the conditional are true. However, she has not committed herself to anything if that condition fails. If it is not sunny, she will not have broken her promise regardless of whether she goes to the beach or not. Here, the fact that Greta is obligated to make the conditional true on the condition that the antecedent is true is a meaning added to the truth functional meaning of the conditional.

Causal Conditionals and Causal Explanations

Causal relations connect states of affairs or events in the world so that one event, the cause, brings about the occurrence of the other event, the effect. That causal relations hold between states of affairs or events of certain types is completely independent of any propositions we assert about them. However, we often use conditional propositions to present causal explanations and describe causal relations.

Example 50:   If the drought continues, then the wheat harvest will be poor.

This conditional claims that there is a causal connection between a cause—the state of affairs of the drought continuing—and an effect—the state of affairs of a poor wheat harvest. The continuation of the drought is a causal condition of the poor wheat harvest. The conditional proposition would be true should the continuation of the drought bring about a poor wheat harvest. The conditional proposition would be false were the drought to continue and the wheat harvest be a good one; that is, once again, *the conditional proposition is clearly false in the case where the antecedent is true and the consequent is false.*

Causal propositions are complicated, because when the causal condition fails to occur—that is, when the antecedent of the conditional is false—it is difficult to assess the truth value of the conditional. We often state causal and other explanatory conditionals in the subjunctive mood. In English grammar, conditionals using the subjunctive mood of the verb are formed differently from propositions in the indicative mood. In the subjunctive mood, we would say, for example, "If I *were* able, then I would vote," whereas in the indicative mood we might say, "I *am* able to vote." So even when the drought breaks and does not continue, we may still hold that continued drought would have caused a poor wheat harvest. We would express this by saying "If the drought had continued, then the wheat harvest would have been poor." The subjunctive mood of the conditional indicates that its antecedent may be false, that the conditional sentence expresses a proposition that may run counter to fact. We call conditionals that run counter to fact **counterfactual conditionals** and often express them in the subjunctive mood. There is no simple adequate account of how to assign truth values to subjunctive and counterfactual conditionals. They are sometimes true and sometimes false (usually the counterfactual conditional will be true, even if the antecedent is false when there is a causal law governing the relationship between events of the appropriate types). The causal laws of the universe partly determine whether these counterfactual and subjunctive conditionals are true or false and constitute an additional meaning added to the truth functional meaning of the conditional, which is solely a matter of the truth values of the antecedent and consequent. The causal laws of the universe are aspects of states of affairs, not aspects of the logic of propositions. However, as noted above, when not stated in the subjunctive mood *causal conditionals are clearly false whenever their antecedent is true and their consequent is false.*

(B) TRUTH FUNCTIONAL CONDITIONALS

While there are other uses for conditional propositions (for example, we will examine definitions below and implicational conditionals in Chapter IV), the types of conditionals given above will suffice for our present purposes. None of the uses we have examined are quite truth functional, for in each case there are difficulties assigning truth values to the conditionals when the antecedent is false. When the antecedent of the conditional is false, the truth value of causal conditionals can be settled only by appealing to the causal laws of the universe, conditional promises are not binding, conditional bets are off, and all we can say regarding conditional predictions is that they have not been falsified.

However, one feature that all these types of conditionals share is that **when the antecedent is true and the consequent is false, the conditional proposition is false.** This is the one clear case where all conditional propositions are false. We can use this feature to extract a truth functional core from these various types of conditional propositions. Moreover, in the case where the antecedent and consequent are both true, all conditional propositions are true.

The difficulties arise only when the antecedent is false. However, for the most part, when the antecedent is false, we can say that the conditional has not been falsified. In each of our exemplary types of conditionals, when the antecedent is false, for the conditional to be falsified we would have to consider something besides the truth values of the component propositions. For causal conditionals, for example, we must consider causal laws. For conditional promises and conditional bets, we must consider the obligation incurred in undertaking the promise or bet. For conditional predictions, we must consider what will happen in the future. This means that when the antecedent of a conditional proposition is false, we should not hold that the conditional has been falsified purely as a matter of the truth values of its component propositions, its antecedent and its consequent. The law of bivalence tells us that we must assign one of the two truth values to every proposition. Moreover, the truth values of truth functional conditionals depend solely on the truth values of their component parts. Therefore, since, as we have seen, when their antecedents are false, conditionals are not falsified purely as a matter of the truth values of their component propositions, we hold that purely truth functional conditionals are true when their antecedents are false.

This, then, lays out the strategy we will take in assigning truth values to truth functional conditionals.[3] Just as we extracted a truth functional core

---

3   Truth functional conditionals are sometimes also called material conditionals. We will discuss this nomenclature in Chapter IV.

from the different senses of negation and conjunction in English, we may extract a truth functional core from the various uses of conditional propositions. So we may assume that every conditional proposition has a truth functional core to which other meanings and uses accrue. Since the truth functional conditional is not strictly equivalent to the English words "if ..., then...," we use an arrow "→" placed after the antecedent, on the left, and pointing toward the consequent, on the right, to indicate the truth functional conditional. The truth functional conditional will have the following truth table, where "**P**" and "**Q**" stand for any two propositions and "**P → Q**" stands for the truth functional conditional in which "**P**" is the antecedent and "**Q**" is the consequent, that is, for the conditional "If P, then Q."

P	Q	P → Q
T	T	T
T	F	F
F	T	T
F	F	T

In this truth table, the conditional proposition "**P → Q**" is false only in the case where the antecedent "**P**" is true and the consequent "**Q**" is false. Notice that this table reflects the lack of symmetry of the conditional. When we switch the antecedent and the consequent of the conditional and construct the truth table for the converse "**Q → P**," we get the following truth table:

P	Q	P → Q	Q → P
T	T	T	T
T	F	F	T
F	T	T	F
F	F	T	T

Since the conditional "**P → Q**" and its converse "**Q → P**" do not have the same truth table, they are not equivalent: it is possible for a conditional to be true and its converse to be false, as is clear in the second and third rows of the truth table, and therefore the two have different meanings and different implications. This is just what we would expect from our earlier discussion of the relation between a conditional and its converse. This rests on the previously enunciated principle: if it is possible for one sentence to be true and another sentence false, the two sentences must express different propositions—that is, the two sentences must have different meanings.

> **RULE FOR TRUTH FUNCTIONAL CONDITIONALS:**
> A truth functional conditional is false if and only if its antecedent is true and its consequent is false; otherwise the truth functional conditional is true.

(C) NECESSARY AND SUFFICIENT CONDITIONS

We have seen that propositions of the form "If P, then Q" are conditional propositions. But it is not yet completely clear what conditional propositions state is a condition of what, since they assert that the consequent is true only on the condition that the antecedent is true. This is because every conditional proposition expresses not just this one conditional relationship but two different sorts of conditions: **necessary conditions** and **sufficient conditions**.

A condition is sufficient for the truth of a proposition if it is enough that the condition occur for the state of affairs for which it is a condition also to occur. This is the sense in which we have already seen that conditional propositions assert that the consequent is true on the condition that the antecedent is true. So, for example, that Helen is a citizen of Colorado is a sufficient condition for her to be a citizen of the United States.

> **DEFINITION OF SUFFICIENT CONDITION:**
> A state of affairs or event S is a sufficient condition for a state of affairs or event N if and only if the occurrence of S is enough for N to occur.

In addition to expressing a sufficient condition, a conditional proposition expresses a necessary condition relationship. A condition is a necessary condition for the truth of a proposition if that condition must occur for the state of affairs for which it is a condition to occur. So, for example, that Helen is a citizen of the United States is a necessary condition for her to be a citizen of Colorado.

> **DEFINITION OF NECESSARY CONDITION:**
> A state of affairs or event N is a necessary condition for a state of affairs or event S if and only if N must occur for S to occur.

While it is enough for a sufficient condition, **S**, to occur for the state of affairs for which it is a condition, **N**, to also occur, it is *not* necessary that **S** occur for **N** to occur. So, for example, while it is true that Helen's being a citizen of Colorado is a sufficient condition for her being a citizen of the United States (i.e., it is enough for her to be a citizen of Colorado for her to be a citizen of the United States), it is not necessary for her to be a citizen of Colorado to be a citizen of the United States. She could instead be a citizen of Utah or Iowa, for example, and still be a citizen of the United States. Being a citizen of Utah and being a citizen of Iowa are also sufficient, but not necessary, conditions for being a citizen of the United States.

Moreover, while a necessary condition, **N**, must occur for the state of affairs for which it is a condition, **S**, to occur, it is not sufficient that **N** occur for **S** to occur. So, for example, while it is true that Helen's being a citizen of the United States is a necessary condition for her being a citizen of Colorado, it is not sufficient for her to be a citizen of the United States to be a citizen of Colorado. Helen would have to fulfill other requirements besides being a citizen of the United States to qualify as a citizen of Colorado. In addition to being a citizen of the United States, she would, for example, also have to have established residency in Colorado. There may also be other conditions that Helen must fulfill to be a citizen of Colorado.

Notice that if **S** is a sufficient condition for **N**, then **N** is a necessary condition for **S**, and if **N** is a necessary condition for **S**, then **S** is a sufficient condition for **N**. Conditional propositions give ways of expressing, in language, conditional relations between states of affairs, and this makes clear why conditionals express *both* necessary and sufficient conditions. The antecedent of a conditional claims to be a sufficient condition for the state of affairs described by its consequent to occur—that is, for the truth of the consequent—and the consequent of a conditional claims to be a necessary condition for the state of affairs described by its antecedent to occur—that is, for the truth of the antecedent.

We can sketch conditional propositions as stating necessary and sufficient conditions as follows:

If (sufficient condition), then (necessary condition).

Or, where **S** is a proposition that stands for a sufficient condition for the truth of the consequent of the conditional and **N** is a proposition that stands for a necessary condition for the truth of the antecedent of the conditional:

If S, then N.

The following rule states the relation between conditional propositions and necessary and sufficient conditions:

S is a sufficient condition for N and N is a necessary condition for S only if the conditional proposition "If S, then N" is true.

This says that the truth of the conditional proposition is a *necessary* condition for the truth of its antecedent to be a sufficient condition for the truth of its consequent and for the truth of its consequent to be a necessary condition for the truth of its antecedent. It does *not* say that the truth of the conditional proposition is a *sufficient* condition for the truth of its antecedent to be a sufficient condition for the truth of its consequent and for the truth of its consequent to be a necessary condition for the truth of its antecedent. The reason for this is that what makes any condition a sufficient condition or a necessary condition for the truth of another proposition requires more than the truth functional aspects of a conditional proposition. For example, that the presence of oxygen is a necessary condition for there to be a fire may be expressed in the conditional proposition "If there is a fire, then there is oxygen present." But, what *makes* the presence of oxygen a necessary condition for there to be a fire are the causal laws of nature that govern combustion. These causal laws are features of states of affairs and not truth functional features of conditional propositions.

(D) IDENTIFYING CONDITIONALS

We must again emphasize that conditional propositions are asymmetric. The conditional "If S, then N" does not say the same thing as its converse "If N, then S." If **S** is a sufficient condition for **N** and **N** is a necessary condition for **S**, the first of these conditionals may be true while its converse may be false. This shows that in using conditionals, we must be careful not to confuse the antecedent with the consequent. Such confusions mistake necessary for sufficient conditions, and vice versa, and can confuse true with false propositions, and vice versa. Confusing necessary and sufficient conditions often arises as a mistake about the form of conditional propositions, and leads to the most common formal mistake in reasoning: *The most common mistake in reasoning occurs when we confuse necessary with sufficient conditions.* This is the same as saying that the mistake is *confusing which proposition is the antecedent and which the consequent* of a conditional, or in other words, *mistaking a conditional for its converse.*

This is a formal mistake because it arises when we fail to correctly identify the antecedent and the consequent of conditionals. These are formal aspects of conditionals, and as such they are independent of the conditionals' content. It is easy to become confused about which component of a conditional proposition is the antecedent and which component is the consequent because in ordinary English there are a great many different ways of expressing conditionals. So far, for the sake of clarity, we have confined ourselves to expressing all conditionals in the standard form "If P, then Q," but this is not always the case in everyday English. Consider the following list of instructions for responding to traffic signs and indicators.

(1) If you approach a red octagonal sign, slow down and come to a stop before you get to the sign.
(2) Proceed only if a traffic light is green.
(3) When you come to a traffic light that is red or yellow, come to a stop.
(4) Yield to approaching traffic whenever you come to a triangular sign that is pointing down.
(5) In the event there is a double continuous line in the center of the road, do not pass other vehicles in your lane.
(6) You have got to signal first in order to make a legal lane change.

Each of these instructions expresses a conditional proposition, but none of them is in the standard form "If P, then Q." However, any conditional can be translated into the standard form "If P, then Q," although sometimes this translation requires some grammatical adjustments.

Here is a list of different sentence forms in ordinary English that say exactly the same as the conditional proposition "If S, then N." In other words, each of these forms of English sentences expresses the same conditional proposition as "If S, then N," where **S** claims to be a sufficient condition for **N** and **N** claims to be a necessary condition for **S**.

List of English Equivalents of "If S, then N"

1) If S, then N.
2) N, if S.
3) S only if N.
4) Only if N, S.
5) S is a sufficient condition for N.
6) N is a necessary condition for S.
7) N, provided that S.
8) Whenever S, then N.
9) When S, N.
10) N, when S.
11) In the event that S, N.
12) S only when N.
13) A requirement for S is N.

14) S requires N.
15) S depends on N.
16) A prerequisite for S is N.
17) You have got to have an N in order to have an S.
18) One must have N in order to have S.
19) You cannot have S without N.
20) If not N, then not S.
21) Either not S or N.
22) S is not the case unless N.
23) Not S unless N.
24) You cannot have both S and not N.
25) All Ss are Ns.
26) If something is an S, then that same thing is an N.
27) Being S requires being N.
28) Only Ns are Ss.

Some of these ways of expressing conditional propositions call for special comment.

Expressions 3 and 4 contain the phrase "… only if …." While this phrase contains the word "if …" in English, **the phrase "… only if …" should never be confused with the word "if …."** When the word "if …" comes before a component proposition in a conditional, that component proposition is the *antecedent* of the conditional and indicates a sufficient condition for the truth of the consequent. On the other hand, when the phrase "… only if …" comes before a component proposition in a conditional, that component proposition is the *consequent* of the conditional and indicates a necessary condition for the truth of the antecedent. It is best to think of "… only if …" as a single expression in order to avoid this confusion. (It is sometimes useful to think of "… only if …" as replacing the word "… then …" in the standard form of the conditional "if …, then….")

Expressions 5 and 6 both explicitly state conditionals in terms of necessary and sufficient conditions. We could add slight grammatical variations to these sentences also, such as "A sufficient condition for N is S" and "A necessary condition for S is N." In any case, we should always read the antecedent of a conditional as claiming to be a sufficient condition for the truth of the consequent and the consequent of a conditional as claiming to be a necessary condition for the truth of the antecedent.

In expressions 7 to 11, the words "provided that" (often used in legal contexts), "in the event that," "when," and "whenever" function like "if…."

The phrase "... only when ..." functions like "... only if ...." Expressions 12 to 19 all use phrases that indicate necessity. So such phrases indicate that the components they govern indicate necessary conditions for the truth of the consequent of the conditionals.

Expressions 20 to 24 are all truth functional equivalents of the truth functional conditional. In other words, if we treat these expressions truth functionally, they have the same truth tables as the conditional "If S, then N." We can illustrate this with expression 21, "Either not S or N." We can construct the truth table for this expression using the rules for logical negation and inclusive disjunction as follows:

S	N	~S	(~S) v N	S →N
T	T	F	T	T
T	F	F	F	F
F	T	T	T	T
F	F	T	T	T

In the third column, we construct the truth table for "It is not the case that S" or "~ S" by writing the truth value "T" wherever "S" is false and writing the truth value "F" wherever "S" is true, using the rule for logical negation. This means that we write "F" in the first two rows and "T" in the third and fourth rows of the column for "~ S." We then combine the third and second columns using the rule for inclusive disjunction. This rule instructs us to write "F" in the fourth column for "(~ S) v N" wherever both "~ S" and "N" are false and to write "T" in the column for "(~ S) v N" otherwise. This means that we write "F" in the second row of the column for "(~ S) v N" and write "T" in all other rows. But this produces exactly the same truth table as that of the conditional proposition "S → N." So the disjunction "(~ S) v N" and the conditional "S → N" are (logically) equivalent truth functions; that is, they can *never* have different truth values. (We will say more about truth functional equivalence when we discuss truth functional biconditionals below, and in more detail in Chapter IV.)

It should also be noted in connection with expression 23 that the word "unless" means the same as "if not." This means that a proposition such as "Ella will return, unless the repairman arrives" means the same thing as "Ella will return, if it is not the case that the repairman arrives." To put this in standard "if ..., then ..." form, we may rearrange this sentence so that the antecedent comes first, and write "If it is not the case that the repairman arrives, then Ella will return."

Finally, expressions 25 to 28 are special cases of conditional propositions. In particular, in expressions 25 and 26 the letters "S" and "N" do not stand in for component *propositions*. Instead, they stand for general terms that pick out classes of objects. A **class** is any group of objects. The objects in a class are usually grouped together because they exhibit some feature or property in common. So, for example, the class of dogs consists of all (possible) dogs and the class of mammals includes all (possible) mammals. When propositions using the words "all," "some," and "no" are concerned with the relations between classes of objects, they are called **categorical propositions**. So, for instance, an example of 25 would be "All dogs are mammals." This says that all (possible) things that belong to the class of dogs also belong to the class of mammals. This is equivalent to the corresponding example for expression 26, "If something is a dog, then that same thing is a mammal." This may be shortened to "If something is a dog, then it is a mammal," where the pronoun "it" indicates that the consequent refers to exactly the same thing as the antecedent. These sorts of conditionals refer in a general way to all members of some class. They say that for each member of a particular class of objects, should that object belong to the class indicated in the antecedent, it will also belong to the class indicated in the consequent. So all members of the class of dogs belong to the class of mammals. Other examples include the following:

(a) All malingerers will be shot.
(b) If anyone is malingering, then that person will be shot.
(c) No numbers that lie between 31 and 37 are prime numbers.
(d) If a number lies between 31 and 37, then that number is not a prime number.

Here examples (a) and (c) are not in standard form but are stated as categorical propositions. Examples (a) and (b) say the same thing as each other, as do examples (c) and (d). Examples (c) and (d) contain negations. In (c), the negative term "No" means that no members of the class of numbers that lie between 31 and 37, indicated in the antecedent, belongs to the class prime numbers, indicated in the consequent of the conditional proposition. So, when translated into the standard form "If S, then N," the logical negation attaches to the consequent of the conditional.

The logic of categorical propositions can become quite complicated because they involve relations between general classes of objects. Difficulties arise from the generalized character of these relations between classes; they refer generally to the members of an entire class, each member of which stands in a specified relation to members of another class. However, by translating categorical propositions into conditionals, we can display their conditional form. Conditionals of this sort are called **generalized conditionals**. Generalized conditionals are very important, as, for example, in their use in scientific and mathematical reasoning. A thoroughgoing analysis of their logic takes more sophisticated tools than will be developed in this book (for a list of the simplest valid categorical arguments, see the Appendix to this chapter).

One exception is worth pointing out. There are rare and atypical cases where we use conditionals to express the proposition that the antecedent and consequent are both necessary and sufficient for each other. For example, when the commercial says "When you're out o' Schlitz you're out o' beer," the advertisers intend to convey that having no Schlitz is exactly the same as having no beer, that being out of Schlitz is both necessary and sufficient for being out of beer. While cases of this sort do occur, we should avoid speaking and writing in this manner and be wary of propositions that do this, because these forms of expression encourage the confusion of necessary and sufficient conditions. These uses of language blur this important logical difference, and the difference between conditional propositions and biconditional propositions (for which see the next section).

Exercises

Put each of the following sentences into standard conditional form, "If P, then Q," and then state each as a necessary condition claim in the form "Q is a necessary condition for P" and state each as a sufficient condition claim in the form "P is a sufficient condition for Q." (Hint: sometimes stating claims in necessary or sufficient condition form can seem awkward in English, but this awkwardness can be removed by stating that "Q is a necessary condition for P to be true" and that "P is a sufficient condition for Q to be true.")

1. If the big cities voted Democratic, then the Democratic candidate won.

2. Bill's success depended upon Frank helping him.

3. You've got to be a member of the band to get a backstage pass.

4. There will be no dance unless we get a band.

5. Being a single parent is a requirement for taking the earned income credit.

6. To get to New York from Detroit all you have to do is to go through Canada.

7. A good library is a **sine qua non** for greatness in a university.

8. All who use words have abstract general ideas.

9. Only doctors and hospital administrators are eligible.

10. You can't graduate unless you have enough credits.

(E) TRUTH FUNCTIONAL BICONDITIONALS AND DEFINITIONS

We have emphasized the lack of symmetry of the conditional, noting that the conditional "**P → Q**" does not say the same thing as its converse "**Q → P**." However, there are times when we want to indicate both that "**P → Q**" and "**Q → P**" are true. For example, consider the definition of a valid deductive argument:

A deductive argument is a valid argument if and only if it is impossible for the premises to be true and the conclusion false.

This definition expresses the conjunction between two conditionals.

(1) A deductive argument is a valid argument, if it is impossible for the premises to be true and the conclusion false.

and

(2) A deductive argument is a valid argument only if it is impossible for the premises to be true and the conclusion false.

We can make the logical structure of this definition clearer by substituting variables for the propositions as follows:

P = A deductive argument is a valid argument.
Q = It is impossible for the premises to be true and the conclusion false.

Substituting into the whole definition, the definition has the form of the conjunction

P if and only if Q.

Substituting into (1) and (2) we get the following sentence forms:

(1) **P, if Q.**
and
(2) **P only if Q.**

If we read the conditionals as truth functional conditionals, (1) and (2) will be symbolized as

(1) **Q → P**
and
(2) **P → Q**

The definition as a whole (P if and only if Q) will then be symbolized by the conjunction

(P → Q) & (Q → P)

This expression is called a **biconditional**, since it is the conjunction of two converse conditionals (the prefix "bi-" means two). Since the two conditionals conjoined in the biconditional are truth functional, we can now construct the truth table for the **truth functional biconditional** as follows:

P	Q	P →Q	Q →P	(P →Q) & (Q →P)
T	T	T	T	T
T	F	F	T	F
F	T	T	F	F
F	F	T	T	T

NOTE ON SYMBOLISM:
Since the truth functional biconditional has important and common uses, the symbolized form (P → Q) & (Q → P) is sometimes given a special symbol (a double-headed arrow "↔") to indicate that the conditional goes both ways; thus the biconditional is written as P ↔ Q. We will sometimes find it convenient to use this alternative symbolism.

Notice that the truth table for the truth functional biconditional—called a "biconditional" for the sake of brevity—counts the whole proposition as true only in the cases where the two simple component propositions "**P**" and "**Q**" have the same truth value, that is, where both "**P**" and "**Q**" are true or where both "**P**" and "**Q**" are false. The truth functional biconditional is false when the two component propositions have different truth values, that is, where "**P**" is true and "**Q**" is false or where "**P**" is false and "**Q**" is true. (It is worth noting that this truth table reverses the truth values in the truth table for exclusive disjunction, and it is a worthwhile exercise to confirm this by constructing the truth table for the negation of an exclusive disjunction.)

RULE FOR TRUTH FUNCTIONAL BICONDITIONALS:
A truth functional biconditional is true if and only if the component propositions it connects have the same truth value; otherwise it is false.

This means that the truth functional biconditional **P** ⟷ **Q** is true if and only if **P** and **Q** have the same truth value.

That truth functional biconditionals are true when the two component propositions have the same truth value makes them suitable for stating definitions of terms. There are several different types of definitions. For our purposes, we will only distinguish between three types of definitions as follows:

1) **Real definitions** tell us what the sort of thing (in the world), designated by the general term being defined, really is.

2) **Nominal definitions** tell us how the term being defined has actually been used (in the language) in the past.

3) **Stipulative definitions** arbitrarily assign a term to designate some thing (in the world) for which we already have criteria of identification.

Stipulative definitions are arbitrary assignments of a general term to some sort of thing that we already know how to pick out. This means that the definition tells us nothing about what sort of thing the term designates, nor about the history of language use, but only provides a new term for something already understood. The new term may be arbitrarily chosen and may only be used temporarily for some specific purpose, as when a mathematician says "Let X stand for a number between 10 and 20" for the purpose of a particular demonstration. An example comes from the late 1960s, when physicists discovered a previously unknown sub-atomic particle, which they came to be able to identify empirically and theoretically but for which they lacked a name. So, they took a word from James Joyce's *Finnegans Wake* and stipulated that this particle be called a quark. *It is a common misconception to think that all definitions are stipulative*, but this cannot be true. Most meanings in language do not arise from stipulation, nor could they, since one needs to already have a working language in order to do the stipulating. In fact, very few words get their meanings by stipulation.

The definitions given in dictionaries are nominal definitions. Dictionaries are empirical works that report on the history of past word usage. Lexicographers, people who, among other things, make up dictionaries, study how words have actually been used. It is worthwhile to read the introductory material in a good dictionary, which explains how the uses of words were selected, often by seeing when words were first used in print with a particular meaning. Hence, contrary to some common misconceptions, *dictionaries are not authorities on the correct use of words; they do not prescribe word use but rather only describe past uses.* Instead, when one comes across a word whose meaning one does not know, the dictionary definition gives hints about what the word may mean in the context. However, these hints seldom meet the standards of a real definition, since they do not give both necessary and sufficient conditions for applying a general term to its examples. It is a worthwhile exercise to test some actual dictionary definitions to determine if they give both necessary and sufficient conditions for applying the general term. Most actual dictionary definitions fail to do so.

While there are other sorts of definitions, what we will be concerned with here are only real definitions, since real definitions are true or false and can be tested for their truth or falsity. A real definition gives conditions that are both necessary and sufficient for applying a term to all its possible examples, and thus they can be stated as biconditionals. We can read the biconditional "$P \leftrightarrow Q$" as stating that P is both a necessary condition and a sufficient condition for Q, and that Q is both a necessary condition and a sufficient condition for P. In stating a definitional claim, a real definition of a general term is supposed to give both necessary and sufficient conditions for applying that general term to its examples:

> **An adequate definition must pick out ALL and ONLY those examples that fit the general term it claims to define.**

Since an adequate real definition must pick out *all* examples that fit the general term it claims to define, an adequate real definition must give conditions that are *necessary conditions* for counting as examples of that sort of thing.

Since an adequate real definition must pick out *only* examples that fit the general term it claims to define, an adequate real definition must give conditions that are together *sufficient conditions* for counting as examples of that sort of thing.

So the real definition of a general term may be expressed in the form of a biconditional connecting the proposition stating the definition with a proposition stating that the general term applies to its examples. The following **definitional proposition** states a definition for the mathematical term "prime number":

> **Example 51:**   Something is a prime number if and only if it is an integer that has only itself and 1 as divisors without remainder.

We can extract the general form of such definitions by substituting the phrase "example of the sort of thing to which the term to be defined applies" for the general term "prime number" and substituting a set of variables $\{x_1, x_2, x_3...\}$ for the defining conditions. The general form of a definition, then, will be the following:

> **Something is an example of the sort of thing to which the term to be defined applies if and only if that thing meets the defining conditions $\{x_1, x_2, x_3...\}$.**

If T is the term to be defined, then this says that the conditions $\{x_1, x_2, x_3...\}$ are both necessary and sufficient conditions for something to be an example of a T. If we use the letter "W" as a variable that stands for the proposition "Something is a T" and use the letter "D" as a variable that stands for the proposition "That thing meets the defining conditions $\{x_1, x_2, x_3...\}$," then we can symbolize the definition in the form of a biconditional as follows:

$$\mathbf{W \longleftrightarrow D}$$

This biconditional will be true only when **W** and the conjunction of the conditions $\{x_1, x_2, x_3...\}$ **D** have the same truth value. This means that the definition will be true only when the definition picks out exactly the same objects as are picked out by the term to be defined, and that is exactly what we want from a definition.[4]

Perhaps this will be clearer if we return to our example, the definition of a prime number. The biconditional will be true when some example is a prime number (for example, the number 7) and it meets the conditions that it is an integer (7 is an integer) and that it has only itself and 1 as divisors without remainder (7 may be divided by only 7 and 1 without remainder). The

---

4 There is an important assumption in stating definitions this way, namely that we are confining definitions only to those general terms that are extensional, that is, terms whose meanings are understood only in relation to the things that fall under—are picked out by—the term.

biconditional will also be true when some example is a not prime number (for example, the number 8) and it fails to meet at least one of the defining conditions. Because 8 may be divided by 2 and 4 as well as by 8 and 1, the number 8 fails to meet the condition that it be divisible by only itself and 1 without remainder. This means that the definition truly sorts out which numbers are prime and which are not prime, since it is true of every number. The only cases where the definition is false are where something is supposed to be a prime number but it is either not an integer or has divisors other than itself and 1, or where something is not supposed to be a prime number and yet is an integer and has only itself and 1 as divisors. The biconditional is false in these cases, and these would be just the cases—were it possible for them to occur—where a proposed definition would fail to adequately give the meaning of prime number.

This last point might be clearer if we consider a definition that is false and hence inadequate as a definition. Consider the following proposal for a definition of a triangle:

Example 52:   Something is a triangle if and only if it is a plane figure with three equal sides.

This definition is false because it fails to state necessary and sufficient conditions for something to be a triangle. It fails to give a necessary condition for something to be a triangle, because there are triangles that do not have equal sides, for example, scalene triangles. So it is true that a scalene triangle is a triangle, yet it is false that a scalene triangle is a plane figure with three equal sides. This means the definition is inadequate because the conditional proposition "If something is a triangle, then it is a plane figure with three equal sides" is false. For the example of a scalene triangle, the antecedent of this conditional is true and the consequent is false, and we know that whenever a conditional has a true antecedent and a false consequent, the conditional is false. The definition also fails to give a sufficient condition for something to be a triangle, because there are plane figures with three equal sides that are not triangles. Consider, for example, a plane figure composed of three lines of equal length connected by two right angles and open at the top like so: ⊔. This figure shows that the proposition "If something is a plane figure with three equal sides, it is a triangle" is false. For the example of the open box figure, the antecedent of this conditional is true and the consequent is false, and again we know that whenever a conditional has a true antecedent and a false consequent, the conditional is false. These are cases where the two component propositions have different truth values, and it is just when there are cases of this sort that the definition is false. (The appendix to Chapter V examines arguments for testing definitional claims in more formal detail.)

(F) INFORMAL FALLACY: SLIPPERY SLOPE

As with logical conjunctions and disjunctions, conditionals can also be misused for their rhetorical effects. The following argument form is a legitimate argument, and all arguments with this form are valid. (We will look at arguments of this sort in more detail in Chapter V.)

(1) $P \rightarrow Q$
(2) $Q \rightarrow R$
———————
∴ (3) $P \rightarrow R$

In arguments of this form, conditional propositions are chained together in the premises because the consequent of the conditional in the first premise is identical with the antecedent in the conditional in the second premise. Furthermore, conditionals may continue to be chained together in this manner, yielding arguments of similar valid forms with more premises. For example, the following is an argument form with four such premises.

(1) $P \rightarrow Q$
(2) $Q \rightarrow R$
(3) $R \rightarrow U$
(4) $U \rightarrow W$
———————
∴ (5) $P \rightarrow W$

Arguments of this form are valid. However, as we know from Chapter I, an argument may well be valid and not be sound because one or more of the premises may be false. For arguments of this sort to be sound, each of the conditional premises in the argument must be true.

Unfortunately, it is too often a rhetorically effective argument to present a sequence of conditionals that state a series of steps or gradations between events and make it seem that the intervening steps or gradations will inevitably occur, that is, that all the conditionals are true. This sort of argument is an informal fallacy called a **slippery slope fallacy**. Slippery slope arguments are fallacious because they presume that the intermediate conditional propositions are true when they may not be; they presume that just because one conditional in the series is true, the other conditionals are inevitably true; that is, it is assumed that one event in a series will inevitably lead to the others.

Example 53:   You should never gamble. Once you start gambling, you will find it hard to stop. Soon you are spending all your money on gambling, and eventually you will turn to crime to support your earnings.

We can translate this argument into a series of conditionals as follows:

(1) If you start gambling, then you will find it hard to stop.

(2) If you find it hard to stop, then you will spend all your money on gambling.

(3) If you spend all your money on gambling, then you will eventually turn to crime to support your gambling habit.

Therefore, (4) if you start gambling, then you will eventually turn to crime to support your gambling habit.

In this argument, the speaker assumes that each of the steps, stated in premises (1)–(3), will inevitably occur once you start gambling. But each of these conditional propositions would have to be true for the argument to be sound. The rhetorician is counting on the audience failing to understand that the truth values of the premises of a deductive argument do not determine the truth values of one another; it is only the truth of the premises *taken together* that is supposed to necessitate the truth of the conclusion of the argument. Yet, since each of these steps may or may not occur, there is nothing inevitable about the sequence of events proposed by premises (1)–(3). It is dubious that premises (2) and (3) are true of many people, and concerning quite a few people it is doubtful that even premise (1) is true. In any case, there is nothing inevitable about this sequence of steps: even if (1) is true, that does not tell us anything about the truth values of the other premises.

Since these steps are not inevitable, the speaker needs to show that each will occur—that all of the premises are true—for the argument to be sound. So, without a great deal of further argument to support these premises, it remains dubious whether the argument is sound. Arguments in this form are sound arguments only if each of the conditional premises is true and the events described in the antecedents will actually lead to the events described in the consequents. However, by portraying these steps as inevitable, the speaker may trick the audience into accepting the conclusion by getting the audience to accept the first premise (or sometimes even just the antecedent of the first premise) as true, and then tricking the audience into thinking that once they have accepted this, all the premises must inevitably be true. But, of course, the truth or falsity of one premise does not depend on the truth or falsity of the other premises. Instead, the truth or falsity of the conclusion depends on all of the premises being true together (and of course on the validity of the argument). When the speaker fails to give good reasons for thinking that each of the steps will actually occur, we should not assume that the steps are inevitable.

Study Questions and Problems

Respond to each of the following questions and problems clearly and precisely.

1) Give an example of a conditional proposition, and identify its antecedent and consequent.

2) What is the formal difference between conditionals, on the one hand, and disjunctions and conjunctions, on the other hand?

3) In determining the truth value of any sort of conditional proposition (whether it is predictive, a conditional bet, a conditional promise, a causal conditional, or a truth functional conditional), when can we clearly assert that the conditional proposition is false?

4) Explain the relationship between causal relations and causal conditionals.

5) State the rule for truth functional conditionals. Give the truth table for a truth functional conditional and explain how the truth table displays the rule.

6) Using an example, explain how the converse of a conditional is formed. Give an example of two propositions that are converses of each other.

7) Using an example, explain why a conditional proposition and its converse do not always have the same truth value.

8) How, in general, is the truth value of a conditional related to the truth value of its converse? (Hint: compare the truth table of a conditional with that of its converse.)

9) What is the most common formal mistake in reasoning?

10) Define and give an example of each of the following:
    (a) a sufficient condition
    (b) a necessary condition

11) What kinds of propositions express necessary and sufficient conditions?

12) Explain the relationship between necessary and sufficient conditions and conditional propositions (this can be done by stating the rule for the relation between conditional propositions and necessary and sufficient conditions).

13) Using an example, explain why a sufficient condition need not also be a necessary condition.

14) Using an example, explain why a necessary condition need not also be a sufficient condition.

15) State the rule for truth functional biconditionals.

16) Explain why biconditionals are appropriate for stating definitions. Describe and explain the general form of such definitions.

17) Explain what has gone wrong when someone commits the fallacy of slippery slope.

Summary of the Logical Operator and Logical Connectives: Their Symbols, Rules, and Truth Tables

We have identified five logical connectives and assigned separate symbols to their truth functional uses. The following list summarizes these symbols and their translations into English.

For any propositions **P** and **Q**:

~ P	It is not the case that P.
P & Q	P and Q.
P v Q	Either P (inclusive) or Q.
P → Q	If P, then Q.
P ↔ Q	P if and only if Q.

Suppose

P = Beth arrives.   and   **Q = The meeting will begin.**

then the symbols would translate the following English sentences:

~ P	**It is not the case that Beth arrives.**
P & Q	**Beth arrives and the meeting will begin.**
P v Q	**Either Beth arrives or the meeting will begin.**
P → Q	**If Beth arrives, then the meeting will begin.**
P ↔ Q	**Beth arrives if and only if the meeting will begin.**

The rules and truth tables for the truth functional operator "not ..." and for each of the truth functional connectives are as follows:

RULE FOR LOGICAL NEGATION:
The logical negation of a proposition is true if and only if the proposition is false, and the logical negation of a proposition is false if and only if the proposition is true.

P	~ P
T	F
F	T

RULE FOR LOGICAL CONJUNCTION:
A conjunction is true if and only if both conjuncts are true; otherwise the conjunction is false.

P	Q	P & Q
T	T	T
T	F	F
F	T	F
F	F	F

RULE FOR (INCLUSIVE) DISJUNCTION:
An inclusive disjunction is false if and only if both its disjuncts are false; otherwise the disjunction is true.

P	Q	P v Q
T	T	T
T	F	T
F	T	T
F	F	F

RULE FOR TRUTH FUNCTIONAL CONDITIONALS:

A truth functional conditional is false if and only if its antecedent is true and its consequent is false; otherwise the truth functional conditional is true.

P	Q	$P \rightarrow Q$
T	T	T
T	F	F
F	T	T
F	F	T

RULE FOR TRUTH FUNCTIONAL BICONDITIONALS:

A truth functional biconditional is true if and only if the component propositions it connects have the same truth value; otherwise it is false.

P	Q	$P \leftrightarrow Q$
T	T	T
T	F	F
F	T	F
F	F	T

PUNCTUATION: PARENTHESES

When we symbolize complex propositions, we often have to indicate which propositions are connected with which connectives to which other propositions. This may not always be clear. To avoid confusions, we use parentheses to group propositions together and indicate which propositions are connected together by which connectives. (We will discuss fallacies that arise from confusions of these sorts in Chapter IV, Part III, when we discuss fallacies of amphiboly.)

We need not place parentheses around symbols for propositions containing only one logical connective. So the following symbols do not require parentheses:

~ P

P & Q

P v Q

P → Q

P ↔ Q

However, we need to use a pair of parentheses for symbols with two or more logical operators or connectives. For example, without parentheses the sequence of symbols

P & Q v R

does not indicate whether & is the main connective connecting P with Q v R, or whether v is the main connective connecting P & Q with R. A pair of parentheses will determine which of these two readings is intended. We may distinguish between the following two sequences of symbols:

P & (Q v R)
(P & Q) v R

These two sequences of symbols will have different truth tables and so have different meanings, as may be demonstrated by constructing the two truth tables.

The primary rule for using parentheses is

RULE FOR USING PARENTHESES:
For n logical operators and connectives in the symbol for a compound proposition, the symbol should contain n–1 pairs of parentheses.

This rule means that for two logical operators or connectives, there should be one pair of parentheses, and for each additional logical operator or connective there should be an additional pair of parentheses. For example, in the following sequence of symbols there are five logical operators or connectives and so there should be four pairs of parentheses:

P & Q v R & ~ P → R

Where the parentheses should be located depends entirely on the meaning of the natural language sentence the symbol translates into our notation. The placement of commas and other punctuation marks and the other grammatical features of the sentence provide clues to where the parentheses should be placed.

One exception to the above rule for using parentheses should be mentioned. When a symbol for a single proposition (a single letter like **P** or **Q**) is preceded by the symbol for negation (~) in the farthest position to the right of a complex symbol, there is no need to enclose the negated proposition in parentheses. So in the formula

P → ~ Q

it is not strictly necessary to enclose ~ **Q** in parentheses, since there is only one way to read the negation. While parentheses are not necessary in this case, as a matter of practice the parentheses will be included. Such consistency with the rule will do no harm and may help us avoid unnecessary confusions. For instance, when the negation does not precede the symbol for a single proposition in the farthest position to the right of a complex symbol, parentheses are necessary. So in the formula

$$\sim P \rightarrow Q$$

it is necessary to add a pair of parentheses to distinguish between the formulae

$$\sim (P \rightarrow Q)$$

and

$$(\sim P) \rightarrow Q$$

These two formulae have different truth tables and so have different meanings that must be distinguished. In the first formula the logical negation negates the whole conditional, while in the second the logical negation negates only the antecedent of the conditional.

Exercises

A. For each of the following English sentences, if the operators or connectives are truth functional (or if the operators and connectives can be treated truth functionally despite extra meanings), translate the sentences into our notation (including parentheses for punctuation in the appropriate places). Make sure you explicitly identify which variables stand for which simple propositions, and convert appropriate clauses into complete grammatical sentences.

1) I'll play, if you play.

2) Marjorie was not prepared for the audition.

3) Either she loves me or she doesn't.

4) I want toast and I want eggs, but I do not want steak.

5) A prerequisite for getting into PHIL-410 is that a student pass PHIL-110.

6) Jane passed the GRE and was admitted to graduate school, and either the school is lucky or Jane is.

7) Our only alternative to binding arbitration is to withhold our labor.

8) Neither the state house nor the state senate will pass health-care legislation this year.

9) Dino got on the horse and was thrown, yet got back on even though Kim begged him not to do it.

10) Mary left for Kansas although she should have gone to Iowa.

11) Either the dictator will be deposed and suffer ignominy, or he will force the people to accept him and continue his iron rule.

12) Hugh and Cathy carried the couch up the stairs together.

13) Filing a formal intent to open a business is a necessary condition for getting a business license.

14) If people are guided by their sense of duty or by their desire for pleasure, then they act only in their own interest.

15) Unless I get more hours, I won't work here anymore.

16) It can't be that you voted and didn't get registered in time.

17) You will be convicted only if you continue to try to bribe the jury.

18) Players' eligibility will expire only when they either have not played for three consecutive matches or have violated club rules.

19) If an item is a business expense, it can be deducted only if it has not been reimbursed by the taxpayer's employer and it is an expense required for the taxpayer's continued employment.

20) If there are more books published every year and the small local bookstores cannot afford to stock them, the Internet bookstores will flourish only if they offer more personal service.

B. Do the same with this set of sentences.

1) Either Iran or Libya raised the price of oil.

2) Joe, Jane, Sam, and Sue missed class on Thursday.

3) Humans are not immortal.

4) Rome is neither the capital of Spain nor of France.

5) Either London is the capital of England and is rainy, or London is the capital of Morocco and is sunny.

6) Whenever Venus is conjunct with Jupiter, the two planets are on the same side of the sun.

7) Either no one is responsible, or Mildred is responsible and should be punished.

8) Stealing is both illegal and immoral.

9) The contract is not signed, but either it will be signed tomorrow or the company won't make a profit.

10) It's not true that either the negotiations will fail and there will be a strike, or that the union will give up and return to work.

11) The union will organize only if the workers are not suspicious of it.

12) Unless there is a change in the weather, the crops will fail.

13) If there are no new elections, the country will remain a dictatorship.

14) When the sun shines and the air is warm, the flowers bloom and they begin to pollinate.

15) If the prime minister dies, she will be replaced by the minister of state unless there are new elections.

16) If Nigeria's turmoil continues only if the present government stays in power, then if the opposition comes to power, there will be reform.

17) If neither chemical compound is stable, then the experiment will fail or another program won't be feasible.

18) Only if we continue to squabble will the organization dissolve, but if we can reach a consensus then it will not.

19) If the rainforests are not preserved, there will be more diseases released into the human population unless the lower oxygen levels destroy us first.

20) If you earn over $10,000 in taxable income, then you may file the short form only if you do not also claim the earned income tax credit.

C. For each of the following English sentences:

(a) Translate the sentences into our notation. Make sure you identify which letters stand for which simple propositions.
(b) Construct the truth table for each sentence.

1) It is not the case that the bill will pass the committee, and it is not the case that the bill will come to a vote.

2) The court will not release the prisoner, or they will not release the prisoner right away.

3) It is not the case both that troops will remain and that the war will wind down.

4) It is not the case either that the banks fail or that unemployment will decrease.

5) If it is true both that the climate is changing and that if the climate is changing, then food supplies will decline, then it is true that food supplies will decline.

6) If the legends are true, then the moon is made of green cheese, and if the moon is made of green cheese, then the moon is edible, but the legends are true and the moon is not edible.

D. For each of the following paragraphs:

(a) If the paragraph contains an argument that commits a fallacy, name the type of fallacy most prominently committed. If the paragraph does not contain a fallacy, then say so. (Fallacies may include any of those presented in either Chapter II or Chapter III.)
(b) Write the argument out in premises and conclusion form (see Chapter I, Part II, Section A). Make sure you paraphrase the premises and conclusion in complete grammatical sentences.
(c) Explain what goes wrong in the reasoning; that is, explain why the premises do not support the conclusion. Make sure that this explanation considers the specific content of the paragraph and does not merely give the general problem with fallacies of the sort committed in the paragraph. This will require explaining, in the case of the fallacies in this chapter, what rhetorical trick is being used to make the argument forms, while valid, to also seem to be sound.

1) Studying philosophy is a dangerous thing to do. It makes you critical, which in turn makes you skeptical of your religious beliefs. And once you've begun to lose faith in your religion, then you become an atheist. From there it's a small step to immorality and a life of the damned.

2) I know that John Smith is a candidate for president of the United States. He must be the Democratic Party candidate, since he isn't the Republican Party candidate.

3) If students are allowed to serve on faculty committees, they will next want to be members of departments, and then members of the governing board. Before you know it, they will be hiring and firing the faculty.

4) Have you tried to stop watching too much television? If so, then you admit that you do watch too much television. If not, then you must still be watching too much television. Therefore, you watch too much television.

5) Our newsletter certainly deserves the support of every good American. We will forward copies of it to you and hope that you will not want to expose yourself to unfortunate consequences in the case of cancellation.

6) Have you taken office equipment home with you more than once? You know that that is still theft.

7) If we let the politicians take away our automatic weapons, then soon they will come after our rifles, and then our hand guns, and we will inevitably be left defenseless.

8) The way health insurance costs are going, either we adopt a national health insurance system like Canada's, or else pretty soon only millionaires will be able to pay their insurance premiums. But if most people didn't have health insurance, then America would be no better than some third-world country. So we need to adopt a Canadian-style system.

9) The crime lab could not find blood on your clothes or figure out how it was removed. What did you use to get the blood out of your clothes?

10) If Congress lets people have automatic weapons, they will soon let people have cannons, and then tanks, and eventually everyone will have their own nuclear bombs.

Appendix: Valid Forms of Categorical Syllogisms

In each of the following valid categorical argument forms (syllogisms), the letters S, M, and P stand respectively for the subject term of the conclusion, the predicate term of the conclusion, and the middle term, which appears in both premises but not in the conclusion.

1) All M is P.
2) All S is M.

Therefore, all S is P.

1) No M is P.
2) All S is M.

Therefore, no S is P.

1) All M is P.
2) Some S is M.

Therefore, some S is P.

1) No M is P.
2) Some S is M.

Therefore, some S is not P.

1) All P is M.
2) No S is M.

Therefore, no S is P.

1) No P is M.
2) All S is M.

Therefore, no S is P.

1) All P is M.
2) Some S is not M.

Therefore, some S is not P.

1) No P is M.
2) Some S is M.

Therefore, some S is not P.

1) All M is P.
2) Some M is S.

Therefore, some S is P.

1) Some M is P.
2) All M is S.

Therefore, some S is P.

1) No M is P.
2) Some M is S.

Therefore, some S is not P.

1) Some M is not P.
2) All M is S.

Therefore, some S is not P

1) All P is M.
2) No M is S.

Therefore, no S is P.

1) Some P is M.
2) All M is S.

Therefore, some S is P.

1) No P is M.
2) Some M is S.

Therefore, some S is not P.

Chapter IV

LOGICAL RELATIONS

_____

Up to this point we have identified propositions and demonstrated how to determine the truth values of compound propositions as a function of the truth values of their component propositions. Moreover, as we have seen, an argument is a *set* of propositions such that the truth of one proposition, the conclusion, is supposed to be supported by the truth of the other propositions, the premises. So an argument not only is composed of propositions but also consists of a set of propositions in which the truth of the conclusion is supposed to depend upon the truth of the premises; that is, the truth of the conclusion is supposed to depend on the relations between the truth values of more than one proposition. So we must now investigate sets of propositions (rather than single propositions) and how their truth values are related to one another. In particular, we will investigate in what ways the truth values of propositions may depend on one another. When the truth value of one proposition depends upon the truth value of another, we say the propositions are **logically related**. Logical relations are what make reasoning so powerful as a tool for discovering and justifying truths.

DEFINITION OF A LOGICAL RELATION BETWEEN TWO PROPOSITIONS: Two propositions are logically related if and only if the truth value of one proposition depends on the truth value of the other.

For example, contradictory pairs of propositions are two propositions that are logically related. A specific example of two such contradictory propositions is the following:

(1) The earth revolves around the sun.
(2) The earth does not revolve around the sun.

These two propositions cannot both be true, nor can they both be false, hence the truth value of one depends upon the truth value of the other. The definition of logical relation can be generalized to any number of propositions in a set of propositions as follows:

DEFINITION OF A LOGICAL RELATION BETWEEN PROPOSITIONS:
Given a set of propositions, the propositions are logically related if and only if the truth value of any one proposition in the set depends on the truth values of the other propositions in the set.

For example, any set of propositions that can be true together are logically consistent. Since logical relations link the truth values of propositions so that these determine the truth values of other propositions, propositions do not have truth values in isolation from the truth values of other propositions. This is important in logic because these **logical links often allow us to establish the truth values of propositions without having to directly investigate the states of affairs those propositions are about.** (This point will become clearer once we recognize that logical relations hold independent of any actual states of affairs.) Most of the propositions in whose truth values we are interested cannot be determined to be true or false merely by observing the states of affairs they purport to describe. Most states of affairs cannot be directly observed, so we must discover the truth values of propositions purporting to describe them by reasoning, that is, by following the logical relations between propositions. For example, the truth values of propositions about the distant past, the future, events at great distances, mathematical states of affairs, and evaluative propositions cannot be determined to be true or false by direct observation. Consequently, the truth values of such propositions must be discovered and justified by reasoning. Even when the actual truth value of a proposition cannot be determined by the truth values of other propositions, the logical relations a proposition enters into can restrict the possibilities and show us what needs to be investigated further. We will see examples of such restrictions in Part II (A) below.

That propositions cannot be true or false in isolation from the truth values of other propositions distinguishes propositions even more completely from people and their attitudes. A person may believe that a proposition is true completely independently from whether they believe other propositions to be true. Moreover, the all too common assumption that such isolated opinions can be true regardless of what other propositions are true cannot be justified. While a person could believe or disbelieve any particular list of propositions, the truth values of propositions themselves necessarily determine the truth values of certain other propositions. So it may not be justified to believe such a list, since it may be that not all of the propositions on the list can be true together (see Part I (A) below). Here we must recall the distinction between someone's propositional attitude and the proposition that attitude is directed toward (see Chapter II). It is a psychological possibility that someone may believe any arbitrary set of propositions, but that is a point about human psychology and has no bearing on the truth values of the propositions that person believes.

While it may be the case that the beliefs (doubts, wishes, etc.) someone has may be isolated from one another and so may be acquired or dismissed regardless of any other beliefs (doubts, wishes, etc.) someone may or may not have, it is false to assume that a proposition's truth value can be isolated from the truth value of every other proposition. Instead, the truth values of propositions stand in logical relations to other propositions and so their truth values depend on one another. Confusion between propositional attitudes and propositions and their truth values explains why people tend to repeat the false cliché that there are two sides to every issue. This false cliché may arise from confusing propositions with attitudes directed toward those propositions. Such attitudes may be isolated from one another. For any proposition, a person may believe it to be true or not regardless of whether they believe any other proposition is true. But the truth values of propositions cannot be isolated from one another, since there will always be other propositions to which any given proposition is logically related such that the truth value of the given proposition is dependent on the truth value of other propositions.

While it may be possible for someone to believe an arbitrary set of propositions, it is not necessarily possible for all these propositions to be true together, since they may be logically inconsistent (see Part I below), so it could not even be possible to be justified in believing that set of propositions to be true together. In this way, **the logical relations between propositions put a constraint on what anyone could be justified in believing to be true.** That this is so further demonstrates the importance of logic, since it shows us that if we want our beliefs to be true, the logical relations between propositions have priority over our beliefs and opinions.

For example, consider the issues around the practice of abortion, which are often portrayed as if there were just two sides (which is why we pick the issue as an illustration). Here, we are not concerned with settling the issue or with finding the answer to these problems, but rather we are concerned with the structure of the issues as such, as problems, prior to any attempt to resolve them. Hence, we are going to grossly oversimplify the issues at stake so that we can see, even in such oversimplified versions, that there are many more than two sides to the issue. Our first oversimplification is to suppose that there are only three questions that bear on the issue (of course there are many more important questions involved in the issue than just these three):

(1) Is the fetus a person?

(2) Is it morally allowable to abort a fetus?

(3) Should the practice of abortion be a matter of law?

While it is clear that the answers to such questions will be long and complex, we are going to even more blatantly oversimplify these issues by supposing that the only answers that can be given to each of these questions are "Yes" or "No." We are also going to assume—again grossly oversimplifying—that the answers to each of these questions are independent of the answers to the other questions. This gives us eight possible positions or sides to the issue as follows:

(1)	(2)	(3)
Yes	Yes	Yes
Yes	Yes	No
Yes	No	Yes
Yes	No	No
No	Yes	Yes
No	Yes	No
No	No	Yes
No	No	No

Notice, first of all, that there are eight, not six, possibilities, which shows that even though the answers to the questions are (as assumed above) independent of one another, the number of possibilities is not simply additive; we do not simply add the "Yes" or "No" of each question to the "Yes" or "No" of the others. What we get here amounts to a truth table for the propositions embedded in the questions, and that gives us eight sides to the issue. This means, even in this grossly oversimplified example, that there are at least eight possible positions or sides to the issue. Now, if we relax our assumptions, we find that for every question in addition to those listed above, the number of sides to the issue doubles. The same holds if we relax the restriction of the answers to merely "Yes" or "No," since for every prior possibility the additional proposition contained in an additional question or the additional propositions given in fleshing out more adequate answers may be true or false (or be answered "Yes" or "No," if what is added is a question). Since any serious issue involves more than a single proposition, there will be more, usually many more sides to an issue than merely the two presupposed in the cliché that there are (only) two sides to every issue. The cliché likely arises because propositional attitudes are confused with propositions. While in the case of propositional attitudes such as belief that a proposition is true, the belief may be held in isolation, as a matter of psychology, so that it appears as if the truth value of the proposition believed were also isolated from all other propositions. Since propositions are always logically related to other propositions, the truth values of any proposition will depend on the truth values of others. This is so simply because more than one proposition is always in question in any serious issue. Therefore, even in the case of independent propositions, the number of sides to the issue doubles with every additional proposition, and these sides only get more complicated the more logical relations between propositions are taken into account, where the truth values of some propositions depend on the truth values of other propositions. Perhaps it would be best to stop talking about sides at all.

It is crucial, then, to understand that logical relations are relations between the truth values of propositions. Furthermore, such logical connections should be strictly distinguished from both causal relations between events and merely psychological associations and habits of thought. In Chapter II, we distinguished between causal laws and laws of logic, and the distinction between causal relations and logical relations runs along similar lines. Causal relations are relations between events or states of affairs in the world. When one event or state of affairs brings about another event or state of affairs, the two events are causally related. The first event or state of affairs is the cause; the event or state of affairs that the cause brings about is the effect. Such relations occur among states of affairs regardless of whether we know about them, understand them, or speak about them at all. For example, the causal relations that hold between the moon's motion and the ocean tides existed even before there were people to notice them, and they would have existed even had there never been anyone to notice or say anything about them.

Logical relations are not relations between events or states of affairs, nor are they mere psychological associations (in which a person connects propositions out of habit, training, familiarity, or the contingencies and accidents of experience). Logical relations are relations between the truth values of propositions. Logical relations hold only between propositions (i.e., between things that can have a truth value and so are meaningful). Logical relations between propositions do not occur in space or time. Two propositions whose truth values are logically related are not primarily states of affairs nor events that occur in the world. Propositions are true or false descriptions of such states of affairs. Logical relations between propositions express the dependency of the truth values of propositions (not only on the states of affairs they describe, but also) on the truth values of other propositions. This means there are two constraints on the truth values of propositions: their truth values depend both on states of affairs and on the truth values of certain other logically related propositions. Logical relations order and constrain the latter.

Part I: Definitions of Some Logical Relations

We will now list, discuss, and give examples of several important logical relations. We will consider four general groups of logical relations: (A) logically inconsistent propositions of four kinds; (B) logically consistent propositions, tautologies, and contingent propositions; (C) logical implications; and (D) logical equivalences.

A) LOGICALLY INCONSISTENT PROPOSITIONS

We will begin by discussing a group of logical relations in which it is impossible that a whole set of propositions can be true together.

> DEFINITION OF LOGICALLY INCONSISTENT PROPOSITIONS:
> A set of propositions is logically inconsistent if and only if it is not possible for all its members to be true.

Any number of propositions may be included in a set of logically inconsistent propositions, so long as the whole set of propositions cannot be true together. However, logical inconsistency will become clearer if we first consider cases limited to one or two propositions before we consider sets of propositions with more than two members. We begin by considering sets of two propositions that are logically inconsistent. There are two important, but fundamentally different, ways in which two propositions may be logically inconsistent with each other. Logically inconsistent pairs of these two kinds of inconsistent pairs of propositions differ significantly, so it is important that we keep them distinct, and as usual, in order to respect the distinction we give them different names. Two propositions that cannot have the same truth value, we call **contradictory** pairs of propositions; two propositions that cannot both be true, although they may both be false, we call **contrary** pairs of propositions. We start with the former.

DEFINITION OF CONTRADICTORY PROPOSITIONS:

Two propositions are contradictories if and only if it is not possible for both propositions to be true and it is not possible for both propositions to be false.

This definition entails that it is impossible for contradictory propositions to ever have the same truth value. Given a pair of contradictory propositions, one must be true and the other false. The following pair of propositions are contradictories.

Example 54:   (i) We are holding class.

(ii) It is not the case that we are holding class.

As in Example 54, the simplest contradictory pairs of propositions are two propositions where one is the logical negation of the other. Every pair of propositions of the form

(i) **P**
(ii) ~ **P**

are contradictories, as can be seen from the truth table.

P	~ P
T	F
F	T

Since the rows of the truth table exhaust all the possibilities, and in no row do the propositions have the same truth value, these propositions can never have the same truth value. This is the simplest case, but there are indefinitely many contradictory pairs of propositions with different (more complex) forms. Some of these are truth functional forms of propositions that we can easily model using only simple propositions and truth functional operators and connectives (others are not so simple). So, for example, the following pairs of propositions are contradictory pairs:

Example 55a: (i) Either Helga will pay her taxes, or she will go to jail.

(ii) Helga will not pay her taxes, and she will not go to jail.

Example 55b: (i) All birds have feathers.

(ii) Some birds do not have feathers.

Example 55c: (i) No grains are poisonous.

(ii) Some grains are poisonous.

In Example 55a we can translate these propositions into truth functional forms as follows:

P = Helga will pay her taxes.
Q = Helga will go to jail.

(i) **P v Q**
(ii) **(~ P) & (~Q)**

Constructing the truth tables for (i) and (ii) we get the following:

P	Q	~ P	~ Q	P v Q	(~ P) & (~ Q)
T	T	F	F	T	F
T	F	F	T	T	F
F	T	T	F	T	F
F	F	T	T	F	T

Notice that in no row of the truth table do **P v Q** and (~ P) & (~ Q) have the same truth value. Since the rows of the truth table exhaust all the possibilities, these propositions can never have the same truth value; if one is true the other is false, so they are contradictory propositions.

We cannot so easily model Examples 55b and 55c in truth functional form because these are categorical propositions and their truth values depend on the complex logic of the terms "all" and "some." Propositions of this sort depend on the grammatical structure internal to simple propositions and are the subject matter of categorical logic, since the general terms A and B, etc. (which stand for general terms, not whole propositions) are connected by "All ... are ..." and "Some ... are ...," as in "All A are B" or "Some A are B."

However, we can see intuitively that both pairs of propositions constitute contradictories. Moreover, if we translate the propositions into conditionals, we can give an approximate model in truth functional form as follows.

Example 55b: (i) If something is a bird, then that thing has feathers.

(ii) There is a bird and that bird does not have feathers.

Example 55c: (i) If something is a grain, then that grain is not poisonous.

(ii) There is a grain, and that grain is poisonous.

With some difficulties,[1] these propositions can be symbolized in our notation, and their truth tables would show that they are contradictory pairs of propositions.

The second way in which pairs of propositions can be logically inconsistent with one another is that they form a pair of contraries, which are defined as follows:

DEFINITION OF CONTRARY PROPOSITIONS:
Two propositions are contraries if and only if it is not possible for both propositions to be true while it is possible for both propositions to be false.

Contrary propositions are similar to contradictory propositions in that both propositions cannot be true. At least one of a pair of contrary propositions must be false. This is why contraries count as logically inconsistent propositions. However, contraries differ from contradictories in that contraries can both be false. The most simple and common examples of contrary pairs of propositions attribute incompatible properties to the same thing, as in the following example.

Example 56: (i) The book is red.

(ii) The book is blue.

In this example, we assume that we are talking about the same book and the color of the book's whole cover at a particular time. (These are differences in meaning and so differ in which propositions are expressed in different sentences. We will examine these restrictions in Part III below, when we deal with fallacies of equivocation.) If that is so, then both (i) and (ii) cannot be true. However, it is possible for the book to be some other color, green for example, in which case both (i) and (ii) would be false. So while it is not possible for (i) and (ii) to both be true, it is possible that they both be false. Hence, (i) and

---

1 The difficulties here are that in each case the statement in the consequent must refer to the same thing as the statement in the antecedent, and the clause "something is a ..." may assert the existence of something, when truth functional conditionals do not.

(ii) are contraries. However, these examples are not truth functional and so we cannot display their relations using truth tables.

The following example *is* truth functional, since the truth values of the compound propositions turn on the logical operator and connectives:

Example 57:   (i) Farah is twenty years old and Abdul is twenty-one.

(ii) It is not the case that either Farah is twenty years old or Abdul is twenty-one.

P = Farah is twenty years old.

Q = Abdul is twenty-one years old.

(i) **P & Q**

(ii) ~ **(P v Q)**

P	Q	P v Q	~ (P v Q)	P & Q
T	T	T	F	T
T	F	T	F	F
F	T	T	F	F
F	F	F	T	F

So, while (i) and (ii) can never both be true (there is no row in the truth table in which both are true, and the truth table exhausts the possibilities), they can both be false, as we can see from the second and third rows of the truth table.

Here is a different sort of example, in this case of categorical propositions that turn on the internal structure of the propositions.

Example 58:   (i) All even numbers are prime numbers.

(ii) No even numbers are prime numbers.

In this example, it is not possible that all even numbers are prime numbers and also that no even numbers are prime numbers. So both (i) and (ii) cannot be true. However, it is possible that some even numbers are prime numbers and some even numbers are not prime numbers. In fact, this is actually true, since the number two is prime, even though no other even number is prime. Hence, propositions (i) and (ii) are contraries.

Although we are concerned here with the logical relations between several propositions, we should note that certain types of propositions have a special logical status. So far we have examined the ways in which pairs of propositions may be logically inconsistent. However, it is also possible for a single proposition to be logically inconsistent in itself. Such propositions are called **contradictions** and are necessarily false.

DEFINITION OF CONTRADICTION:
A proposition is a contradiction if and only if it is not possible for that proposition to be true.

Contradictions cannot possibly be true; they must be false (they are necessarily false). The truth value of contradictions then does not depend on any states of affairs. Contradictions are false regardless of what states of affairs occur in the world. No matter what the world is like or how it may change, contradictions remain false. The clearest truth functional examples of contradictions are compound propositions consisting of the conjunction of a pair of contradictory propositions. (The conjunction of a pair of contrary propositions will also be a contradiction, and contradictions may have other forms besides.) For example, the pair of contradictories in Example 54 above may be conjoined to form the contradiction "We are holding class, and we are not holding class." We can see that this proposition cannot possibly be true by constructing its truth table.

P = We are holding class.

P	~P	P & (~ P)
T	F	F
F	T	F

The rows of the truth table exhaust all possibilities, and in each row the compound proposition **P & (~ P)** is false. There are no possible ways in which states of affairs could be arranged such that the contradiction would turn out to be true. So the proposition **P & (~ P)** must be false: it is necessarily false, and it cannot possibly be true.

Not all contradictions are so simple or so obvious. Consider a proposition of the form

$$(P \,\&\, (\sim Q)) \,\&\, (P \rightarrow Q)$$

The truth table for this proposition is:

P	Q	~Q	(P & (~Q))	P → Q	(P & (~Q)) & (P → Q)
T	T	F	F	T	F
T	F	T	T	F	F
F	T	F	F	T	F
F	F	T	F	T	F

Since the truth table shows that (**P** & (~ **Q**)) & (**P** → **Q**) is false no matter which of the possibilities exhaustively represented by the rows of the truth table is actual, the proposition is a contradiction.

Up till this point, we have examined limited sets of propositions that are logically inconsistent. Contradictions are single propositions that cannot possibly be true. Contradictory propositions and contrary propositions are pairs of propositions in which members of the pair cannot both be true. Now we are ready to consider sets of propositions containing more than two propositions. Here we are interested primarily in cases where the whole set of propositions are logically inconsistent and so cannot all be true, while at the same time any proper subset of the set of propositions can all be true. So, for instance, there could be a set of ten propositions that cannot all be true, even though if we select any nine propositions from those ten, all nine could be true. To illustrate the point that a set of proposition can be logically inconsistent even though none of its proper subsets are logically inconsistent, we will examine an example of the simplest case: a set of three propositions that are logically inconsistent, even though no pair of propositions in the set is logically inconsistent.

Example 59:   (i) Either the room is big enough or we will use another room.

(ii) The room is not big enough.

(iii) We will not use another room.

In this example, we can demonstrate that these propositions cannot all be true, even though any two of them may be true. Suppose that (i) and (ii) are true, then it is true that the only alternatives are that the room is big enough and that we will use another room, and it is also true that the room is not big enough. If these are both true it follows that the proposition "We will use another room" must be true. But that proposition is the contradictory of (iii). Consequently, since contradictory propositions cannot have the same truth value, if (i) and (ii) are true, then (iii) must be false. Now suppose that (i) and (iii) are true, then it is true that the only alternatives are that the room is big enough or that we will use another room, and we will not use another room. If these propositions are true it follows that the proposition "The room is big enough" must be true. But that proposition is the contradictory of (ii). Consequently, since contradictory propositions cannot have the same truth value, if (i) and (iii) are true, then (ii) must be false. Finally, suppose that (ii) and (iii) are true, then it is true that the room is not big enough, and that we will not use another room. But if these are both true it follows that the proposition "Either the room is big enough or we will use another room" must be false. Consequently, if (ii) and (iii) are true, then (i) must be false. The result of all this is that while any two of these propositions may be true, it is impossible that all three be true.

We can represent this situation more clearly by constructing a truth table. If we assign variables to the simple propositions as

P = The room is big enough.
Q = We will use another room.

then we can symbolize the three propositions as follows:

(i) **P v Q**
(ii) **~ P**
(iii) **~ Q**

This gives the following truth table for these propositions:

P	Q	~ P	~ Q	P v Q
T	T	F	F	T
T	F	F	T	T
F	T	T	F	T
F	F	T	T	F

Examining this truth table, we find that in the last row ~ **P** and ~ **Q** are both true but **P v Q** is false, in the third row ~ **P** and **P v Q** are both true but ~ **Q** is false, and in the second row ~ **Q** and **P v Q** are both true but ~ **P** is false. This shows that it is possible for any two of the three propositions to be true. However, there is no row of the truth table where all three propositions are true (in the first row both ~ **P** and ~ **Q** are false). Since the rows of the truth table exhaust all of the possibilities, it is not possible for all three of these propositions to be true; at least one of them *must* be false. Hence the set of three propositions is logically inconsistent, even though no pair of propositions in the set is logically inconsistent.

Logically inconsistent propositions are important, since as we have already seen, they put a constraint on what can justifiably be believed or be part of a coherent and justifiable description or theory. Let us make this clearer by considering an example. It is psychologically plausible that someone may believe the following three propositions:

(1) **We cannot choose our desires.**
(2) **Thou shalt not covet.**
(3) **Ought implies can.**

It is plausible, psychologically (see Chapter II on the differences between psychology and logic), that someone may believe these three since they are associated with different areas of our lives. The first is a claim about our psychology, saying that while one may desire many different things—food, sex, a career, for example—and choose what to eat, whether to have sex, which career to pursue, we cannot choose whether to have the desire for those things. The second claim is a claim usually associated with religion and is put in traditionally religious terms; it says that we ought not to want things that do not belong to us. The third is a philosophical slogan from the study of morality, saying that if one ought to do some act (call the act A), then that act must be in one's power to do. So (3) claims that we can be morally responsible and so culpable only for doing things that are in our power to do. For example, if one is at present in North America and someone is at present drowning in Lake Baikal, which is in Russia, one is not morally culpable for not saving them, since no one would be able to save them in such circumstances, unlike the situation where, if someone was drowning in a pool right before one where one could easily reach down and pull them out.

Therefore, as a first approximation we could translate and clarify the three propositions as follows:

(1) **We cannot choose our desires.**
(2) **Thou shalt not covet.**
(3) **Ought implies can.**

(1′) **It is not the case that it is in our power to choose which desires to have (or not to have).**
(2′) **It is a moral obligation that we choose not to have desires for things that do not belong to us.**
(3′) **If some action A is a moral obligation, then it must be in our power to do A.**

We may now consider the case where instead of the specific act of choosing our desires, we consider more generally doing some action A, of which choosing our desires is only one instance of A. Then we can further clarify what is at stake by reformulating the three propositions as follows:

(1″) **It is not the case that it is in our power to do A.**
(2″) **It is a moral obligation to do A.**
(3″) **If it is a moral obligation to do A, then it is in our power to do A.**

These last formulations can be translated into truth functional form as follows:

P = It is in our power to do A.
Q = It is a moral obligation to do A.

(1‴) ~ P
(2‴) Q
(3‴) Q → P

But these three can be demonstrated to be logically inconsistent by examining the truth table for (1‴), (2‴), and (3‴):

		2‴	1‴	3‴
P	Q	~ P	Q → P
T	T	F	T
T	F	F	T
F	T	T	F
F	F	T	T

This table shows that since (1‴) is false in the first and second rows, (3‴) is false in the third row and (2‴) is false in the fourth row (as well as the second row), there is no row in the truth table in which all three propositions have the value true. And since the rows of the truth table exhaust all of the possibilities, it is not possible for all three of these propositions to be true; at least one of them *must* be false. Hence, although it is psychologically plausible that someone might believe all three of these propositions, it is not possible for them all to be true together, and so no one could ever be *justified* in believing them to be true or including them in a single coherent description or theory. Thus logical inconsistency puts a constraint on what could justifiably be believed or could justifiably be part of a coherent description or theory. It is worth noting here (see Chapter II) that not only are the truth values of propositions independent of any attitudes anyone might have toward these propositions, but also the logical relations are prior to and must be considered before one could justifiably come to have such an attitude.

(B) TAUTOLOGIES, LOGICALLY CONSISTENT PROPOSITIONS, AND CONTINGENT PROPOSITIONS

We have seen that contradictions are single propositions that cannot possibly be true; they are, therefore, necessarily false; it is a logical necessity that they be false no matter what the circumstances, that is, no matter what states of affairs there are. There are also propositions that are necessarily true: propositions that cannot possibly be false. We call such propositions **tautologies**.

> DEFINITION OF TAUTOLOGY:
> A proposition is a tautology if and only if it is not possible for that proposition to be false.

A tautology is a proposition that cannot possibly be false, and this remains so no matter how states of affairs in the world stand or how they may change. The simplest truth functional case of a tautology is the disjunction of a proposition and its negation.

Example 60: "Either we are holding class or we are not holding class."

In this example, we can show that the proposition cannot possibly be false by constructing the truth table.

P = We are holding class.

P	~ P	P v (~ P)
T	F	T
F	T	T

The rows of the truth table exhaust all the possibilities, and in each row the compound proposition **P v (~ P)** is true. There are no possible ways states of affairs could be arranged in which the tautology would turn out to be false. So the proposition **P v (~ P)** must be true—it is necessarily true—in every possible state of affairs.

Not all tautologies are so simple or obvious. Consider a proposition of the form **(P & Q) → Q**. The truth table for this proposition is as follows:

P	Q	P & Q	(P & Q) → Q
T	T	T	T
T	F	F	T
F	T	F	T
F	F	F	T

Since the truth table shows that **(P & Q) → Q** is always true, the proposition is a tautology.

Tautologies and contradictions have special logical status, because they have their truth values as a matter of necessity. We have noted that this means that tautologies are true and contradictions are false no matter what states of affairs occur in the world. More importantly, tautologies are true and contradictions are false no matter what states of affairs could *possibly* occur, that is, no matter how states of affairs could possibly be arranged, change, or be different. Since this is the case, tautologies and contradictions can tell us nothing about how the world is; they are empty of informational content (or rather tautologies are empty and contradictions are too full; see Chapter V, Part II (D)(2)). However, despite this peculiarity, tautologies and contradictions are of special logical importance. In the case of contradictions, and indeed in the case of all forms of logical inconsistency, these logical relations are important because they help us eliminate certain sets of propositions from our descriptions and theories about the world as logically impossible. No matter what the world is like, it cannot possibly be as a set of logically inconsistent propositions purports to describe it.

It is more difficult to see why tautologies are important even though they tell us nothing about states of affairs in the world. Tautologies express the necessity of logical relations, so they require us to accept certain propositions as true and others as false, depending on the truth values of other propositions. These relations of necessity are important because following the lines of necessary connections in the logical relations between propositions is a fundamental skill in thinking for ourselves and not having to rely on authority. Following these necessary connections is to a large extent what it means to think for ourselves. The necessary connections between the truth values of propositions constrain which propositions can be true together, and so they constrain what can justifiably be thought to be true. This will become clearer when we discuss logical implication below, when we discuss modal concepts below, and when we discuss validity in the next chapter.

If a set of propositions is logically inconsistent, it is not possible for all the propositions in that set to be true together. If, instead, it is possible for all the propositions in a set of propositions to be true together, we call the set logically consistent.

DEFINITION OF LOGICALLY CONSISTENT PROPOSITIONS:
A set of propositions is logically consistent if and only if it is possible for all the members of that set to be true.

If all the members of a set of propositions can be true together, then the set of propositions is logically consistent. For example, the following set of propositions is logically consistent.

Example 61: (i) The executive committee is in session.
(ii) The executive committee will select the nominees.
(iii) The executive committee session will last several hours.

It is clearly possible that all of these propositions could be true together. A single proposition may also be called logically consistent. A single proposition is logically consistent if and only if it is *possible* for it to be true, that is, that the proposition is not a contradiction.

In the above example, the propositions are **contingently related** to one another. This means that no matter what the truth value of any one of these propositions is, each of the other propositions may be either true or false.

We can see that logically consistent propositions can all be true together more clearly in a truth functional example such as the following:

Example 62: (i) The door is open and the lights are on.
(ii) The door is open or the lights are on.
(iii) If the door is open, then the lights are on.

Given that **P = The door is open** and that **Q = The lights are on**, we get the following truth table.

P	Q	P & Q	P v Q	P → Q
T	T	T	T	T
T	F	F	T	F
F	T	F	T	T
F	F	F	F	T

In the first row of the truth table, each of the three propositions is true. Since each row of a truth table represents one possible way state of affairs may be, it is possible for all of the propositions in Example 62 to be true together. They are, therefore, logically consistent.

DEFINITION OF CONTINGENTLY RELATED PROPOSITIONS:
Two propositions are contingently related if and only if the truth value of one does not depend on the truth value of the other.

A single proposition that can be either true or false, that is, a single proposition that is neither necessarily true nor necessarily false, is called a **contingent proposition**. Consequently, neither contradictions nor tautologies are contingent propositions.

DEFINITION OF CONTINGENT PROPOSITION:
A proposition P is contingent if and only if it is neither necessarily true nor necessarily false.

If a proposition is contingent, then its truth or falsity depends on how things are in the world. For example, the proposition "We are holding class" is a contingent proposition, since the truth or falsity of the proposition depends on the state of affairs it purports to describe. Contingent propositions are neither necessarily true nor necessarily false, so the truth table for a contingent proposition will have some rows that have the value true and also some rows that have the value false. Therefore, contingent propositions are both possible truths and possible falsehoods.

When we discussed the nature of truth and falsity in Chapter II and defined truth and falsity as relationships between a proposition and the state of affairs that proposition purports to describe, we were saying what it is for contingent propositions to be true or false. If a contingent proposition is true, it describes the state of affairs it is about just as that state of affairs is, and we call that proposition a **contingent truth**. If a contingent proposition is false, it fails to describe the state of affairs it is about just as that state of affairs is, and we call that proposition a **contingent falsehood**. As we will see in Part II, this means we have to broaden our definitions of truth and falsehood so as to include both contingent truths and falsehoods and necessary truths (tautologies) and falsehoods (contradictions).

(c) LOGICAL IMPLICATION

Two propositions may be related so that if one of the propositions is true, the other proposition cannot possibly be false. In cases of this sort, we say that the first proposition **logically implies** the second proposition.

> **DEFINITION OF LOGICAL IMPLICATION:**
> One proposition logically implies another proposition if and only if it is impossible for the implying proposition to be true and the implied proposition to be false.

So if one proposition logically implies another proposition, then if the proposition doing the implying is true, the proposition being implied *must* be true. Notice that this does not say that the proposition doing the implying is true; it only says that *if* that proposition is true, then the implied proposition *must* be true. Furthermore, when one proposition logically implies another, it is *not* merely that when the first *is* true the second *is* true. The relationship between the truth of the implying proposition and the truth of the implied proposition is one of *necessity*; if the implying proposition is true, then it is *impossible* that the implied proposition be false. This means, as we will see, that not every conditional proposition is a logical implication. Moreover, it is possible for it to be true that the implying proposition logically implies the implied proposition and false that the implied proposition logically implies the implying proposition. Logical implication is not a symmetric relation.

In Example 63, proposition (i) logically implies proposition (ii):

> **Example 63:**   (i) Socrates was an Athenian philosopher.
> (ii) Socrates was a philosopher.

It would be impossible for it to be true that Socrates was an Athenian philosopher and false that Socrates was a philosopher. Moreover, proposition (ii) does not logically imply proposition (i). It is possible for it to be true that Socrates was a philosopher and false that Socrates was an Athenian philosopher; it could have been that Socrates was a philosopher, but that he was from some other place besides Athens. This example is not truth functional, but we can also give a simple truth functional example as follows:

> **Example 64:**   (i) It is Tuesday and class is in session.
> (ii) It is Tuesday.

In this example, proposition (i) logically implies proposition (ii). It would be impossible for it to be true that it is Tuesday and class is in session and false that it is Tuesday. But proposition (ii) does not logically imply proposition (i). It is possible for it to be true that it is Tuesday and false that it is Tuesday and class is in session (just in the case where it is Tuesday and class is not in session).

NOTE:
For the sake of brevity, logical implications are often referred to merely as implications, and "implies" is often used rather than "logically implies."

Because implication is not a symmetrical relation (one proposition may imply another, without the second implying the first), we sometimes need to emphasize which proposition is doing the implying while at other times we need to emphasize which proposition is being implied. We say "**A** implies **B**" when we wish to emphasize that **A** is the proposition doing the implying. But when we wish to emphasize that **B** is the proposition being implied, we say that **B** is a **logical consequence** of **A**.

DEFINITION OF LOGICAL CONSEQUENCE:
A proposition is a logical consequence of a second proposition if and only if that second proposition logically implies the first proposition.

Logical implication and logical consequence are two names for the same logical relation. The only difference between them is that the former emphasizes the proposition doing the implying, while the latter emphasizes the proposition being implied.

Insofar as they are relations between propositions, logical implications exhibit three important features:

1) Logical implications are *not symmetric*. This means that although **A** implies **B**, it need not be true that **B** implies **A**.

2) Logical implications are *reflexive*. This means that every proposition implies itself; that is, for every proposition **A**, **A** implies **A**.

3) Logical implications are *transitive*. This means that for any three propositions **A**, **B**, and **C**, if **A** implies **B** and **B** implies **C**, then **A** implies **C**.

These three features describe logical implication as a relation in general, while the definition of logical implication gives the specific nature of that relation by saying how the truth values of propositions stand in a relation of *necessity*.

When we discussed conditionals in Chapter III, we saw that there were other types of conditional besides the ones we discussed there. Logical implications may be expressed by conditional propositions. However, logical implications are not simple truth functional conditionals, because the implied proposition is implied with *necessity*. If the logical relationship between two propositions is genuinely a logical implication, then that relationship is not merely one in which if the one proposition is true, then the other proposition merely is true, but one in which if the implying proposition is true, then the implied proposition *must* be true. So the necessity involved in logical implications requires that logical implication be not merely an ordinary truth functional conditional but a conditional that is also a tautology or necessary truth. While logical implications may be truth functional, they differ from truth functional conditionals that are not necessary truths. In order to mark this distinction, truth functional conditionals that are not necessary truths are often called **material** (or contingent) **conditionals**, which means only that their truth values are determined by the states of affairs that they purport to describe: their subject matter (so this name has nothing specifically to do with physical matter).

When we wish to explicitly express a logical implication, we express it in the form of a conditional proposition, with the proposition doing the implying as the antecedent and the proposition being implied as the consequent. To do this we need to add some indicator that the relation between the antecedent and the consequent is one of necessity so as to distinguish the logical implication from merely material conditionals. We could, then, express the logical implication in the example we gave above as follows:

Example 65:   If Socrates was an Athenian philosopher, then it must be the case that Socrates was a philosopher.

The conditional form of the proposition makes it clear that the relation is not symmetrical, since conditionals are not symmetric ("If **P**, then **Q**" does not mean the same as "If **Q**, then **P**"). The phrase "it must be the case that" indicates that the conditional is an implicational conditional, a necessary truth, and not a simple material (contingent) conditional.

However it is not enough merely to state a conditional in the form of a logical implication for that conditional to actually be a logical implication, that is it is not enough to add the word "must" or some other words indicating necessity (the issue here is not merely a matter of words). For a conditional to be a logical implication and not merely a material (contingent) conditional, it must be true that the conditional is a necessary truth—that the conditional is a tautology. Consider example **64** again. We can translate the example as follows:

(i) It is Tuesday and class is in session.
(ii) It is Tuesday.

P = It is Tuesday.
Q = Class is in session.

(i′) **P & Q**
(ii′) **P**

If we express the logical implication (i′) logically implies (ii′) in the form of a conditional proposition, we get

(**P & Q**) → **P**

This conditional expresses a logical implication because it is a tautology or necessary truth, as shown by the fourth column of the following truth table:

P	Q	P & Q	(P & Q) → P	P → Q
T	T	T	T	T
T	F	F	T	F
F	T	F	T	T
F	F	F	T	T

When we compare this truth table with the truth table for a simple material (contingent) conditional such as **P → Q** in the last column of the truth table, we see that **P → Q** is not a tautology, since it is possible for the conditional to be false, so it does not express a logical implication. This is so because the truth table for **P → Q** contains the truth value false in at least one row. So no matter how the conditionals are expressed in a sentence, (**P & Q**) → **P** is a logical implication and **P → Q** is not.

We will see in more detail in Chapter V that implicational conditionals are particularly important, when we compare the definition of logical implication with the definition of a valid argument. If we substitute "the premises" in for **P** in the definition for logical implication and we substitute "the conclusion" in for **Q**, we transform the definition of logical implication into the definition for valid argument. So when we claim that a deductive argument is valid, we are claiming that the premises taken together logically imply the conclusion.

(D) LOGICAL EQUIVALENCE

The last logical relation we will discuss is logical equivalence. In Chapter III, we saw that two propositions are equivalent when they have the same truth value. However, two propositions are **logically equivalent** when that equivalence is a necessary truth or tautology, that is, when it is impossible for two propositions to have different truth values.

> **DEFINITION OF LOGICALLY EQUIVALENT PROPOSITIONS:**
> Two propositions are logically equivalent if and only if it is not possible for one proposition to be true while the other is false.

Hence, when two propositions are logically equivalent, they *must* have the same truth value. No matter what states of affairs occur or how they may change, two logically equivalent propositions will have the same truth value. So for any two logically equivalent propositions, it is necessary that either both are true or both are false.

Example 66:   (i) If Elaine is a golfer, then she uses golf clubs.
(ii) If Elaine does not use golf clubs, then she is not a golfer.

In this example, proposition (i) is logically equivalent to proposition (ii). It is impossible for proposition (i) to be true while proposition (ii) is false, and it is impossible for proposition (i) to be false while proposition (ii) is true. The two propositions *must* have the same truth value no matter what the actual state of affairs is regarding Elaine's golfing and her use of golf clubs. We can show that this is so by constructing the truth tables for these propositions.

P = Elaine is a golfer.
Q = Elaine uses golf clubs.

P	Q	~P	~Q	P → Q	(~Q) → (~P)	(P → Q) ↔ ((~Q) → (~P))
T	T	F	F	T	T	T
T	F	F	T	F	F	T
F	T	T	F	T	T	T
F	F	T	T	T	T	T

The truth tables for **P** → **Q** and for (~ **Q**) → (~ **P**) are identical. Since the rows of the truth table exhaust all the possibilities, it is impossible for the two propositions **P** → **Q** and (~ **Q**) → (~ **P**) to have different truth values, so they are logically equivalent. Because of this, the biconditional connecting them will be a tautology, as shown in the last column.

The two logically equivalent propositions **P** → **Q** and (~ **Q**) → (~ **P**) exhibit an important logical relation between conditional propositions called contraposition, and the propositions related by contraposition are called **contrapositives** of one another. The contrapositive of a conditional proposition is formed by negating both the antecedent and the consequent of the conditional and reversing them so that the negation of the consequent of the conditional becomes the antecedent of the contrapositive and the negation of the antecedent of the conditional becomes the consequent of the contrapositive. In Chapter III, we discussed conditionals that were converses of one another; recall that propositions of the form **P** → **Q** and **Q** → **P** are converses of one another. In general converses are not equivalent; they do not necessarily have the same truth values (hence they cannot be logically equivalent, they do not mean the same thing, and one cannot legitimately be substituted for the other). However, propositions that are contrapositives of one another (propositions of the form **P** → **Q** and (~ **Q**) → (~ **P**)) are logically equivalent and necessarily have the same truth values.

We should also distinguish between logically equivalent propositions and merely contingently equivalent propositions. When it is contingent that two propositions have the same truth value, but it is possible for the two propositions to differ in truth value, the two propositions are said to be **materially** (or contingently) **equivalent**, on analogy with what was said about material (contingent) conditionals above. This distinction is exactly parallel to the distinction between logical implications and material conditionals. Two propositions are materially equivalent if and only if they contingently happen to have the same truth values, while logically equivalent propositions *must* have the same truth values.

Again, like the difference between logical implications and material conditionals, it is not enough merely to state an equivalence relation in the form of a logical equivalence for it to actually be a logical equivalence; that is, it is not enough to add the word "must" or some other words indicating necessity. For an equivalence to be a logical equivalence and not merely a material (contingent) equivalence, it must be true that the equivalence is a *necessary* truth—that the equivalence is a tautology.

Study Questions and Problems

Respond to each of the following questions and problems clearly and precisely.

1) Define and give an example of each of the following: (a) logical relation between two propositions, and (b) logical relation between propositions.

2) Explain why we may not be justified in believing just any list of propositions.

3) Explain the difference between logical relations and causal relations.

4) What two constraints determine the truth values of propositions?

5) Define and give an example, not already given above, of each of the following:
   (a) logically inconsistent propositions
   (b) contradictory propositions
   (c) contrary propositions
   (d) contradiction
   (e) logically consistent propositions
   (f) tautology.

6) Explain the difference between contradictory pairs of propositions and contrary pairs of propositions.

7) What do contradictions and tautologies tell us about the world? Why are contradictions and tautologies important?

8) Define and give an example, not already given above, of each of the following:
   (a) contingent propositions
   (b) contingently related propositions
   (c) logical implication
   (d) logical consequence
   (e) logically equivalent propositions
   (f) contrapositives.

9) What are the three important general formal features of relations of logical implication?

10) What is the difference between a conditional proposition that expresses a logical implication and a conditional proposition that expresses a material conditional?

11) What is the difference between two propositions that are logically equivalent and two propositions that are materially equivalent?

Part II: Modal Concepts

Throughout our discussion of logical relations (as well as in discussions in previous chapters), we have used the concepts of possibility and impossibility, necessity and contingency, and actuality. We have been concerned whether certain propositions or sets of propositions are actually true or actually false, possibly true or impossible, necessarily true, necessarily false, contingently true, or contingently false. Concepts of this sort are called **modal concepts**, because they indicate the manner (mode) in which a proposition has its truth value. For instance, when we distinguished valid arguments from sound arguments, we had to distinguish the *possibility* that the premises were true and the conclusion false from the *actual* truth or falsity of the premises of those arguments. In another instance, in cases of both logically inconsistent and logically consistent propositions, what is at issue are the *possible* truth values of the propositions, not their actual truth values.

Truth tables give us schemata that help make modal concepts clear. Since the rows of a truth table exhaustively list all the possible truth values for each proposition, truth tables display all the available *possibilities*. If the truth table for a proposition has some rows with the value true and some rows with the value false, then the proposition is contingent and its truth value depends on which states of affairs are *actual*. If the truth table for a proposition has the value true in every row, then it is *impossible* for the proposition to be false, and the proposition is a tautology or *necessary* truth. If the truth table for a proposition has the value false in every row, then it is *impossible* for the proposition to be true, and the proposition is a contradiction or *necessary* falsehood. As we shall see in (C) below, this is only a basic schema for understanding modal concepts, but it is a schema that constrains other senses of these modal concepts.

(A) MODAL CONCEPTS AND LOGICAL RELATIONS

Modal concepts are important because logical relations, and with them the validity and invalidity of deductive arguments, depend on modal differences.

The definitions of each of the logical relations contain one or more modal concepts. Each definition of a logical relation crucially depends on these modalities. For example, logical consistency and logical inconsistency depend on whether it is *possible* for a set of propositions to all be true. It is *impossible* for tautologies to be false. When one proposition logically implies another proposition, it is *impossible* for the implying proposition to be true and the implied proposition to be false, or alternatively, when one proposition logically implies another proposition, if the implying proposition is true then it is *necessary* that the implied proposition be true. Even contingent propositions are propositions that are *possibly* true or *possibly* false. *Logical relations*, then, *are inherently defined in terms of modal concepts.* In particular, logical relations are relations between truth values of propositions in the modes of possibility, impossibility, and necessity.

The assessment of deductive reasoning also depends fundamentally on different modalities, on what is *possibly* true and what is *necessarily* true or *necessarily* false. Determining the *actual* truth or falsity of the conclusion of an argument depends on the modalities of possibility and necessity. We assess deductive arguments by determining whether they are valid and whether they are sound. We say an argument is valid under the condition that if the premises are true, the conclusion *must* be true. Validity, then, requires that the relationship between the premises and conclusion be one of *necessity*; the truth of the premises necessitates the truth of the conclusion in a valid argument. Moreover, it does not matter for validity whether the premises are *actually* true. What matters is that, in a valid argument, if the premises were true, then the conclusion would have to be true. In a valid argument, it is *impossible* for the premises to be true and the conclusion false. In an invalid argument, is *possible* for the premises to be true and the conclusion false, and again, it does not matter for the invalidity of an argument whether the premises are *actually* true. None of these features of valid and invalid arguments could be explained without modal concepts. We say an argument is sound when it is both valid and all its premises are actually true. So in addition to the modalities involved in validity, determining soundness also requires considering the *actual* truth values of the premises.

Consider the following example of the use of logical possibilities in reasoning. In this example, we start with the logical possibilities and then use some given propositions to eliminate what is impossible so as to arrive at some actually true propositions.

Example 67:   Problem: In a certain bank, the positions of cashier, manager, and teller are held by Brown, Jones, and Smith but not necessarily in that order. We are given the following two propositions as true:

1) The teller, who was an only child, earns the least of the three.
2) Smith, who married Brown's sister, earns more than the manager.

The problem is to discover who is the cashier, who the manager, and who the teller.[2]

We reason as follows:

(a) There are nine *possibilities* (although not all nine are possible together): Brown could be the cashier, the manager, or the teller; Jones could be the cashier, the manager, or the teller; and Smith could be the cashier, the manager, or the teller.

(b) However, Smith cannot be the manager, because Smith earns more than the manager, and it would be a contradiction and so *impossible* for Smith to earn more than Smith.

(c) Brown cannot be the teller, because the teller was an only child and Brown has a sister. It is contradictory and so *impossible* for Brown to both have a sister and be an only child, and so have a sister and not have a sister.

(d) Finally, Smith cannot be the teller, because Smith earns more than the manager, and the teller earns the least of the three. These two propositions together logically imply that if Smith were the teller, then Smith would both earn the least of the three and earn more than the manager. This also contains a contradiction, namely that Smith earns more than the manager and Smith does not earn more than the manager. So, it is *impossible* for Smith to be the teller.

---

2 This problem is taken from C.R. Wylie Jr., *101 Puzzles in Thought & Logic*, Dover Publications, 1957, #1.

(e) At this point we have eliminated enough of the *possibilities* to solve the problem (note that we do not have to consider every possible case). Neither Brown nor Smith can be the teller (from (d) and(c)), which leaves only the possibility that Jones is the teller. So it must *actually* be true that Jones is the teller. Since Smith cannot be the teller and Smith cannot be the manager (from (b)), Smith *must* necessarily be the cashier. Finally, then, since Jones is the teller and Smith is the cashier, the only *possibility* left is that Brown is the manager.

We can display this reasoning by setting out the possibilities in the following table. The possibilities along the top row are that someone is the teller (T), or the cashier (C), or the manager (M), and down the far left column that the jobs are held by Brown (B), Smith (S), or Jones (J). The Xs show the possibilities we have eliminated with our reasoning, and the os show our conclusions as to who occupies which job.

	T	C	M
B	X		0
S	X	0	X
J	0		

We have been able to arrive at conclusions about what is actually true in the problem by relying on what is possibly true, what cannot possibly be true (given our information in (1) and (2)), and what is necessary as a matter of the logical implications of propositions (1) and (2). So our reasoning relied on using the modalities of possibility, impossibility, and necessity to sort out what was actually true (true in the mode of actuality). This is an important procedure for solving problems more generally. We begin by laying out all of the possibilities and then use the logical relations between the possible truth values of the various propositions so as to eliminate what is impossible. And as Sherlock Holmes famously said, when we have eliminated the impossible, whatever remains, no matter how improbable, must be the (actual) truth. It is important to note that in tracing out the logical relations, the only actual information we used was about who earns what and who has siblings. It was by considering what was possible, what was necessary, and what was impossible that got us to what was actually true. This explains how following out the logical relations between propositions can get us to actual truths without relying on authorities or guessing at what was actually true or false; in this sense, following out logical relations constitutes thinking for ourselves. Such thinking for ourselves is a matter neither of persons (i.e., it is not a matter of personality or psychology) nor of their propositional attitudes.

(B) IMPLICATIONS AMONG MODALITIES

Modal concepts stand in complex relations of implication. Consider the following propositions:

(a) Proposition **P** is necessarily true.
(b) Proposition **P** is necessarily false.
(c) Proposition **P** is contingently true.
(d) Proposition **P** is contingently false.
(e) Proposition **P** is actually true.
(f) Proposition **P** is actually false.
(g) Proposition **P** is possibly true.
(h) Proposition **P** is impossible (not possible).

These propositions stand in the following implication relations:

(a) implies (e)
(a) implies (g)
(b) implies (f)
(b) implies (h)
(c) implies (e)
(c) implies (g)
(d) implies (f)
(d) implies (g)
(e) implies either (a) or (c)
(f) implies either (b) or (d)
(g) implies either (a) or (c) or (d)
(h) implies (b)

These implication relations may be clearer if we represent them in the following table:

Possibly true			Impossible
Necessarily True	Contingently True	Contingently False	Necessarily False
Actually True		Actually False	

We read the table as follows:

(A) If a box is narrower than (and completely spanned by) a box immediately above or below it, then propositions governed by the modal notion in that box imply propositions with the same content and are also governed by the modal notion in the wider box. It is helpful to think of this as if we could slide the boxes up and down vertically, but not move them horizontally. For example, the proposition "It is necessarily true that four is divisible by two" implies "It is actually true that four is divisible by two."

(B) Likewise, if a box completely spans more than one box immediately above or below it, then propositions governed by the modal notion in that box imply the disjunction of the propositions with the same content except governed by the modal notions in the spanned boxes. So, for example, the proposition "It is actually true that whales are mammals" implies "It is either necessarily true that whales are mammals, or it is contingently true that whales are mammals."

(C) DIFFERENT TYPES OF POSSIBILITY AND IMPOSSIBILITY

In everyday speech, we tend to use modal notions in more than one sense. However, these different senses are systematically related to one another. For example, when the detective in a story says that it was not possible that the murderer entered the locked room, she is concerned with what it was technically possible for the murderer to do. She is concerned with whether there were any practical means for the murderer to get into the room. She is not considering, for example, that the murderer may have teleported into the room, since that is not something we have the practical means of doing. In fact, it may be impossible to do so within the constraints of the causal laws of nature. In that case, it would not only be technically impossible but it would also be causally or naturally impossible. However, even then, we understand what it would mean for the murderer to teleport into the room. The murderer would be somewhere else one instant, and then be in the room the next without taking time in traversing the intervening space. That is understandable, even if it is not causally or naturally possible. We can tell a coherent story in which the murderer teleports into the locked room. Much science fiction assumes that we can make sense of such propositions, regardless of the laws of nature. Since we can make sense of such propositions (that is, we know what states of affairs would be like if the propositions describing them were true), it is logically possible that such propositions are true.

This gives us several related senses of possibility. We can picture them as systematically related by a series of constraints.

The most fundamental sort of possibility is logical possibility, and this is the sort of possibility we are most concerned with in this book. Logical possibility is concerned with what can possibly be a true proposition—that is, with whether a proposition can be true. If a proposition can be true, then it is possibly true in the sense of logical possibility. *A proposition expresses a logical possibility if it obeys the laws of logic.*

However, not every proposition that is logically possible describes a state of affairs that obeys the laws of nature. For example, while it is logically possible to exceed the velocity of light, it is not possible to do so without violating the causal laws of nature (if the laws of nature are as contemporary physics proposes they are in the special theory of relativity). So we may say that exceeding the velocity of light is not naturally or causally possible, even though it is logically possible. *A proposition states a causal or natural possibility if what it describes is both logically possible and does not violate the laws of nature.* A proposition expresses a natural possibility if it obeys the laws of nature, and every natural possibility must also be a logical possibility.

Of course, not everything that obeys the laws of nature is something within our practical or technical capacity. For example, it is naturally possible to travel at half the velocity of light, but we have not been able to do so. We lack the technical means to travel that fast. So while it is logically and naturally possible to travel at half the velocity of light, it is not a practical or technical possibility for us. A proposition expresses a technical or practical possibility if what it describes is logically possible and naturally possible and does not exceed our productive capacities. *A proposition states a technical or practical possibility if what it describes does not violate the rules or limits of technical feasibility.*

Often, when people say that something is not possible, they mean that it is not practically or technically possible for us. This use is common, because in everyday affairs we focus on what we are concerned to do. However, this sort of possibility should not be confused with the other sorts. We need to be clear in any context what sort of possibility is relevant to our interests. Moreover, our technical capabilities change over time; what was not technically possible at one time may become technically possible later as our capabilities increase. For example, in the eighteenth century, people could not travel at even 100 miles per hour, but now any of us can do so driving a car (although it is not to be recommended). When evaluating deductive arguments, we need to be concerned only with what is logically possible, not with natural possibilities or with merely practical possibilities.

Finally, there is a sense in which much that is technically or practically possible is not morally possible. For example, it is technically possible for us to destroy all the people on Earth. However, this would not be morally permissible. Sometimes, we speak of this sort of circumstance in terms of what is possible. In these cases, we are concerned with what is morally possible. We may say, then, that destroying all the people on Earth is technically or practically possible, but that it is not morally possible.[3] *A proposition states a moral possibility if what it describes is logically possible, naturally possible, and technically possible, and does not violate the rules or laws of morality.*

In sum, the most basic sort of possibility is logical possibility. A proposition expresses a logical possibility if and only if it does not violate any of the laws of logic. Every other sort of possibility involves further restrictions due to the consideration of other types of laws or rules. These other types of laws or rules must be applied in an order of inclusion; more specific laws get constrained by more general laws. So laws of nature are constrained by the laws of logic; every natural possibility must also be a logical possibility. Rules of technical possibility are constrained by laws of nature; every technical possibility must also be a natural possibility (and so also a logical possibility). Finally, laws or rules of morality are constrained by rules of technical feasibility; every moral possibility must be a technical possibility (and so also a logical possibility and a natural possibility). We can picture these relationships as follows:

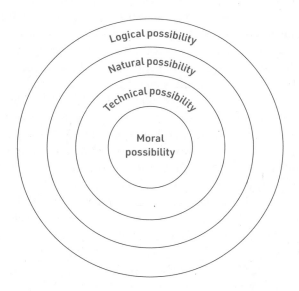

---

3 This assumes that what is morally possible must be within our power to do. Philosophers often express this assumption with the slogan "Ought implies can," which means that if some act is obligatory (we ought to do it), then it must be an act that we can do. See Part I (A) of this chapter.

Testing for deductive validity, strictly speaking, considers only logical possibility (and impossibility) when determining whether it is possible (or impossible) for the premises to be true and the conclusion false. However, it is often useful to test arguments that are not strictly deductive arguments by considering whether it is possible (or impossible) for the premises to be true and the conclusion false in the more restricted senses of possibility, natural possibility, technical possibility, or moral possibility and treating such arguments as deductive arguments with the laws of nature, the rules of our technical capabilities, or the laws of morality as additional unstated (that is, enthymemic; see Chapter VI) premises. Whether we do so will depend on the purpose of the argument and the context in which the argument arises. For example, in deciding on a course of action we may need to consider only technical or practical possibility. However, in trying to discover laws of nature, natural scientists have to consider logical possibilities that may be tested against empirical observations, while some sciences will have to consider what is naturally possible according to the laws of nature discovered by other sciences. For instance, in trying to discover laws of nature in biology, biologists accept the laws of physics and chemistry. In doing so, all we need to remember is that these other more restrictive laws are unstated premises in the argument, and in criticizing such arguments we need to keep in mind that these more restrictive laws may be false. For example, in arguing about whether we might travel to planets orbiting other stars, we would usually be assuming the laws of nature as unstated premises. However, under certain circumstances we may bring such laws into question.

Study Questions and Problems

Respond to each of the following questions and problems clearly and precisely.

1) What are modal concepts?

2) How are modal concepts connected with logical relations?

3) How are modal concepts connected with the assessment of deductive reasoning?

4) Explain whether each of the following is true or false by considering counterexamples (that is, are there examples where the antecedent is true and the consequent false?).

(a) If a proposition is contingently true, then it is actually true.

(b) If a proposition is contingently false, then it is possibly true.

(c) If a proposition is possibly true, then it is actually true.

(d) If a proposition is actually true, then it is necessarily true.

(e) If a proposition is actually false, then it is impossible.

(f) If a proposition is actually false, then it is possibly true.

5) Using examples, distinguish between logical possibility and natural or causal possibility.

6) Using examples, distinguish between natural or causal possibility and technical or practical possibility.

7) Using examples, distinguish between technical or practical possibility and moral possibility.

Part III: Informal Fallacies of Equivocation

We have seen that contradictions cannot possibly be true. We have also noted that the simplest example of a truth functional contradiction is a proposition of the form **P &** (**~ P**). However, we must be careful that when we use the form **P &** (**~ P**) the sentence represented by the letter "**P**" means the same thing, that is, expresses the same proposition, in the conjunct **P** as it does when it is negated in the conjunct (**~ P**). In ordinary speech, we sometimes say things like "Well, it is and it isn't" when we want to point out some neglected aspect of the situation. So, for instance, someone might say "My house is in Wyoming and my house is not in Wyoming" to point out that her house straddles the state line. These are not contradictions, and when someone says "My house is in Wyoming and my house is not in Wyoming," we can accept that she has said something true (or merely contingently false) even though the form of her sentence appears to be that of a contradiction (which would be a necessary falsehood). The reason the sentence can be true, even though no contradiction could possibly be true, is that the sentence does not really express a proposition which has the form **P &** (**~ P**). The proposition really says "*Part* of my house is in Wyoming and *another part* of my house is not in Wyoming." This proposition has the form **P &** (**~ Q**), which is not a contradiction. It is a contingent proposition and may well be true.

What this caution shows is that when we are concerned with sets of propositions, we must settle the meanings of the sentences (that is, settle which propositions they are expressing; see Chapter II) before we can sort out their logical relations or their truth values. In general, the meaning, logical relations, and truth values of propositions are interconnected such that we have to establish two of these factors in order to determine the third. It is easy to generate confusion in discussing an issue by putting more than one of these factors in question at the same time. So it is important to be clear, in any dispute, whether what is at issue is the truth value of a proposition, the meaning of a sentence, or the logical relations between propositions, and neither to confuse these different issues nor to try to settle more than one at a time. We must consider only one of these questions while provisionally holding the answers to the other two constant. In this section, we are concerned only with questions of meaning—that is, questions about which propositions are expressed in sentences.

We can be seduced into fallacious reasoning when propositions or some of the words expressing propositions have more than one meaning. Fallacies that arise out of multiple uses or meanings of sentences (that is, which propositions they are expressing) or words in sentences are called **fallacies of equivocation**. We will discuss four sorts of fallacies of equivocation: fallacies of ambiguity, fallacies of amphiboly, fallacies of composition, and fallacies of division.

(1) *Fallacy of Ambiguity*

A word, phrase, or sentence that has more than one meaning is called **ambiguous**. A sentence might be ambiguous because it contains a word or phrase that is ambiguous. For example, the word "check" can mean a bill, as in a restaurant, or a draft on a bank directing the bank to pay out money. In the sentence "Hilda wrote out a check," it is not clear whether the proposition expressed is that Hilda wrote out a bill or that she wrote out a draft on a bank. Usually, in cases of this sort, we can settle the meaning by considering the context in which the sentence appears. However, this is not always the case, and sometimes we fail to notice the ambiguity. This can lead to fallacious reasoning when a word or phrase is used with one meaning in one sentence in an argument and with another meaning in another sentence in that same argument. The two sentences may seem to be connected by the use of the same word or phrase, but they really are not connected since the word or phrase has different meanings in the two sentences. The following is not a valid argument for the claim that a salami sandwich is better than lasting happiness:

Example 68: (1) A salami sandwich is better than nothing.

(2) Nothing is better than lasting happiness.

Therefore, (3) a salami sandwich is better than lasting happiness.

This argument looks like it has the valid form

(1) A is better than B.

(2) B is better than C.

Therefore, (3) A is better than C.

But (1) means that having a salami sandwich is better than having nothing at all, while (2) means that for any thing in the universe none of those things is better than lasting happiness. This difference of meaning arises from the ambiguity in the word "nothing," which has different meanings in (1) and (2). So Example 68 really has the invalid form

(1) A is better than B.

(2) **D** is better than C.

Therefore, (3) A is better than C.

Hence the argument in Example 68 is fallacious; it is not a valid argument even though the ambiguity might at first make it seem valid. Here is another example:

Example 69a: (1) Being fired is the end of the job.

(2) The end of anything is its purpose.

Therefore, (3) being fired is the purpose of the job.

In this example, the word "end" is ambiguous; it is used with two different meanings. In (1), "end" means termination, while in (2) it means the goal something seeks to achieve. The argument is invalid, because while the two premises seem to be connected by the notion of an end, they really are not connected in this way because of the different meanings of "end" in (1) and (2). This can be seen more clearly if we substitute the different meanings of "end" in the argument as follows:

Example 69b: (1) Being fired is the termination of the job.

(2) The goal of anything is its purpose.

Therefore, (3) being fired is the purpose of the job.

This argument is clearly invalid.

(2) Fallacy of Amphiboly

A proposition may also have more than one meaning, not because the words in the sentence that expresses the proposition have more than one meaning, but rather because the words or phrases in the sentence can serve more than one grammatical function. So, for example, in linguist Noam Chomsky's famous example "Flying planes can be dangerous," the word "flying" can be either a verb or an adjective. If we read "flying" as a verb, then the sentence expresses the proposition that piloting planes can be dangerous, but if we read "flying" as an adjective, then the sentence expresses the proposition that planes that are in the act of flying can be dangerous. Here the sentence can express different propositions because it can be read as having different grammatical structures. Sentences that can express different propositions due to differences in grammatical structures are called **amphibolous**. Amphibolies can lead to fallacious reasoning when a sentence, used in an argument, has different meanings due to words or phrases that can serve different grammatical functions.

Example 70:   (1) It is important to save water and waste paper.

Therefore, (2) it is important to waste paper.

In this example, the word "waste" can function as either a verb or an adjective. In the premise, the word "waste" functions as an adjective, and we are admonished to save two sorts of things: water and a certain type of paper, waste paper. In the conclusion, the word "waste" functions as a verb, and we are admonished to do something with paper, namely, to waste it. Hence, the argument is invalid.

Many amphibolies arise because of misplaced modifiers in sentences. A notorious story tells us that a letter sent to the editor of a music magazine claimed,

"I've looked everywhere in this area for a book on how to play the crumhorn without success."

To which the editor's jocular reply was:

"You need no instruction, just plunge boldly ahead!"

The point of the joke is that in the letter the phrase "without success" modifies the phrase "how to play the crumhorn" because of its placement in the sentence. Of course one needs no instruction on how to fail to play the crumhorn. To correct this and to express the intended meaning, the phrase "without success" should be moved so that it modifies the verb "looked" rather than the verb "play." Then the sentence would read,

"I've looked without success everywhere in this area for a book on how to play the crumhorn."

These sorts of amphibolies are all too common in people's writing and speaking, often with equally humorous effects. However, amphibolies constitute fallacies only when the equivocation they produce affects the validity or strength of an argument.

(3) Fallacy of Composition

When something is a whole composed of parts, we cannot take it for granted that the features of the parts are also features of the whole composed of those parts. For example, while it may be true that I am able to lift each part of my car, it does not follow that I am able to lift my car. When we argue from the properties of the parts to the properties of the whole they compose, we commit the fallacy of composition. Examples of fallacious arguments of this sort include the following:

Example 71: (1) Every part of this machine weighs less than two ounces.

Therefore, (2) this machine weighs less than two ounces.

and

Example 72: (1) Human beings are composed of atoms.
(2) Atoms are not alive.

Therefore, (3) human beings are not alive.

Example 72 tries to conclude that human beings are not alive because their parts, atoms, are not alive. This is an invalid argument and a fallacy of composition, because it is not legitimate to assume that because the parts of human beings are non-living, human beings as wholes are non-living.

(4) Fallacy of Division

Similarly, when something is a whole composed of parts, it cannot be taken for granted that the features of the whole are also features of the parts out of which the whole is composed. For example, while it may be true that the United States is a rich country, it does not follow from this that every person in the country is rich. This does not follow even though the wealth of the country as a whole is composed of the wealth of its people. For the wealth of the country is not equally distributed among the people. When we argue from the properties of the whole to the properties of the parts that compose it, we commit the fallacy of division. Here is another example:

Example 73:   (1) The condor is vanishing.
(2) This animal is a condor.
_____
Therefore, (3) this animal is vanishing.

This argument tries to conclude that this particular condor is vanishing because the species of which it is a member is vanishing. This is an invalid argument and a fallacy of division because it is not legitimate to assume that because the whole species is vanishing, this particular member of the species is vanishing. This example makes clear how the fallacy contains an equivocation: the word "condor" in premise (1) refers to the species that is vanishing because individual members are dying off, while in premise (2) "condor" refers to an individual bird. For a single bird to vanish means for it to fade away or disappear.

Exercises: Informal Fallacies

For each of the following paragraphs:

(a) If the paragraph contains an argument that commits a fallacy, name the type of fallacy most prominently committed. If the paragraph does not contain a fallacy, then say so. (Fallacies may include any of those presented in Chapters II, III, or IV.)
(b) Write the argument out in premises and conclusion form (see Chapter I, Part II, Section A). Make sure you paraphrase the premises and conclusion in complete grammatical sentences.
(c) Explain what goes wrong in the reasoning—that is, explain why the premises do not support the conclusion. Make sure that this explanation considers the specific content of the paragraph and does not merely give the general problem with fallacies of the sort committed in the paragraph. This will require explaining:
(i) Why the premises do not support the conclusion, that is, how it is possible for the premises to be true and the conclusion false.
(ii) In the case of the fallacies in this chapter, what mechanism produces the equivocation in the argument (grammatical structure, difference in word meaning, confusing parts with wholes, etc.). Be specific about how the specific content of the argument uses one of these mechanisms; specify the reasons that this particular equivocation

occurs (for example, if the fallacy is a fallacy of ambiguity, then state the different meanings of the words or phrases in question; if the fallacy is a fallacy of amphiboly, then state the grammatical difference in question, etc.).

1) It is very likely that someone will win this week's lottery. So why not me?

2) I don't want to attend a college that puts students into large classes. Since the University of Colorado is such a large university with over 40,000 students, I don't think I should apply there.

3) The men's ice hockey team must be the best team in the conference. After all, it has the best goalie in the conference. It also has the best center, best wingmen, and best defensemen in the conference. How could any of the other teams compete with that?

4) This contract says that the builders expect the sum of $500 before and after the completion of the project. So we can get more interest on our money by paying them $50 before they start and $450 after the project is completed.

5) What could be more affordable than free software? But to make sure that it remains free, that users can do what they like with it, we must place a license on it to make sure that it will always be freely distributable.

6) "Seeing that eye and hand and foot and every one of our members has some obvious function, must we not believe that in a like manner a human being has a function over and above these particular functions?" (Aristotle).

7) People gamble every day: they take chances driving on the highways and even walking across the street. Gambling is an unavoidable part of human life. So gambling should be legalized.

8) Since the average American family has two children and the Jones family is an average American family, the Jones family must have two children.

9) The Empire State Building must be in Greenwich Village. The tour guide said that standing in Greenwich Village, the Empire State Building could be clearly seen.

10) "The only proof that something is visible is that people see it. The only proof that something is audible is that people hear it. So, similarly, the proof that something is desirable is that people desire it" (John Stuart Mill).

Chapter V

ARGUMENT FORMS AND THEIR EVALUATION

We have identified propositions by distinguishing them from propositional attitudes (from who says something) and from states of affairs (what propositions are about). We have seen how to determine the truth values of compound propositions from the truth values of their component propositions. We have also found that, in sets of propositions, the truth values of propositions stand in certain logical relations to one another, so that the truth values of some propositions depend upon the truth values of other propositions. We have defined an argument as a set of propositions such that the truth of one proposition, the conclusion, is supposed to be supported by the truth of the other propositions, the premises. It is now time to examine what it means for the truth of the premises of an argument to **support** the truth of its conclusion; that is, for deductive arguments we need to understand how to determine when deductive arguments are **valid** and when they are **invalid**. This means we need to develop means for testing whether it is impossible for the premises of a deductive argument to be true and its conclusion false. Since a deductive argument consists of a set of propositions in which the truth value of one proposition (the conclusion) depends upon the truth value of the others (the premises), the support relation is a logical relation between the premises and conclusion of an argument. To construct a schema of the validity of deductive arguments, we begin by abstracting the forms of arguments from their content.

Part I: Argument Forms

One of the crucial insights of logical theory is that the validity of a deductive argument does not depend on its content, but only on its form or structure. This may be surprising, since our practical interest in arguments is to determine the truth of their conclusions. Usually what we are interested in is their subject matter, and what is true about that subject matter. Indeed, the content of propositions is relevant to determining the soundness of arguments, since a sound argument must have all actually true premises. However, the relevance of the content of an argument only (and only partially) applies to determining the truth values of its premises. The support relationship between the premises and the conclusion does not depend on an argument's content. The claim that the premises of an argument support its conclusion amounts to the claim that a logical relation holds between the argument's premises and its conclusion. In a deductive argument, the supposition is that the premises, when taken together, logically imply the conclusion. If this supposition is true, then the argument is valid; if this supposition is false, then the argument is invalid. Since logical implications are necessarily true, their truth values cannot depend on how states of affairs happen to be arranged and so cannot depend on the content of the propositions of which the argument is composed. When we abstract from the content of an argument, we are left with a formal structure. It is that formal structure that determines whether the argument is valid or invalid.

Consider the following example from the history of astronomy. At the end of the sixteenth century, the Danish astronomer Tycho Brahe argued, using the following argument, that the Copernican theory—that the Earth revolves around the Sun—was flawed.

Example 74:   The Earth does not move around the sun. For if the Earth moves around the sun, then the stars would appear to move with respect to one another. But the stars do not appear to move with respect to one another.[1]

---

1   The astronomical issue here arises from the consideration that if the position of a star is measured while the Earth is on one side of the Sun (for example, during the summer solstice), and then the position of the same star is measured while the Earth is on the other side of the Sun (for example, during the winter solstice), then the star will appear to have moved. This phenomenon is called parallax, and it can be easily seen by closing one eye and holding one's finger so it lines up with some object on a wall, and then closing the open eye and opening the formerly unopened eye. If this is done, then the object on the wall will appear to have shifted even though that object has not moved.

We can rewrite this argument in premises and conclusion form as follows:

(1) If the Earth moves around the Sun, then the stars would appear to move with respect to one another.
(2) The stars do not appear to move with respect to one another.

Therefore, (3) the Earth does not move around the Sun.

Now we can replace the content of the argument by assigning variables to the simple propositions as follows:

P = The Earth moves around the Sun.
Q = The stars appear to move with respect to one another.

This gives us the following intermediary form for the argument:

(1) **If P, then Q.**
(2) **It is not the case that Q.**

Therefore, (3) it is not the case that P.

The logical operators and connectives in this argument are truth functional, so we can give the form of the argument, or more properly the **logical form**, of this argument as follows:

(1) $P \rightarrow Q$
(2) $\sim Q$

$\therefore$ (3) $\sim P$

This represents the logical form of Tycho's argument completely abstracted from its content regarding the movement of the Earth and the apparent movement of the stars. We will see that by testing this logical form we can conclusively determine the validity of this argument and show that Tycho's argument is a valid deductive argument. While Tycho's argument is valid, it turns out not to be sound because the second premise is not true. Tycho, while famous for the precision of his astronomical observations and his development of the most precise instruments of his time for measuring astronomical relationships, did not have the tools to make fine enough measurements of the apparent motion of the stars. But in spite of this flaw, Tycho reasoned well; his argument is valid. If the premises were true, it would be impossible for the conclusion to be false. Moreover, **by testing the logical form of this argument, we also**

determine the validity of all arguments with the same form. For example, if Tycho's argument is valid, then so is the following argument:

> **Example 75:**   (1) If plagiarism is ethical, then theft is ethical.
>
> (2) Theft is not ethical.
>
> ___
>
> Therefore, (3) plagiarism is not ethical.

This argument has the same form as Tycho's argument, even though it is about a completely different subject matter. It still has a conditional proposition for its first premise, the negation of the consequent of the conditional for its second premise, and the negation of the antecedent of the conditional for its conclusion. As we will see, any argument with this form is valid.

The logical form of Tycho's argument turns entirely on the structures of the truth functional propositions it contains. Not every deductive argument depends on these structures. We have neglected the internal grammatical and logical structure of the simple propositions that combine to compose the truth functional compound propositions. We have also neglected any forms that are not truth functional. Consider the following arguments:

> **Example 76a:**   (1) Every boy loves some girl.
>
> (2) Juan is a boy.
>
> ___
>
> Therefore, (3) there is some girl whom Juan loves.

> **Example 76b:**   (1) Maria is a good golfer.
>
> ___
>
> Therefore, (2) Maria is a golfer.

In Example 76a, the internal grammar of the sentences makes a difference to the validity of the argument. Whether this argument is valid depends on how the words "every," "there is," and "some" function and on their grammatical arrangement. In Example 76b, the validity of the argument depends on how the adjective "good" functions. While it is clear that the argument is valid, its validity is not due to the use of any truth functional operators or connectives.

These examples show that the logic of many arguments is more complicated than what we can formalize using only simple propositions and truth functional operators and connectives. Logicians have developed more complicated formal systems that test the validity of arguments like Example 76a. In the case of arguments like Example 76b, logicians are still working to develop formal systems that can adequately capture their logic. Logic is an ongoing enterprise in which people are still doing research, developing and adding to our understanding of how to separate valid from invalid arguments and how to represent those arguments purely in terms of their logical forms.

For our purposes, we will consider only deductive arguments that can be formalized by our simple formal tools, representing simple propositions with variables, truth functional operators and connectives with our symbols for negation, conjunction, disjunction, and conditionals, and punctuating the resultant propositions with parentheses. This system formalizes arguments that turn on the truth functional connections between whole propositions, and hence it is called **propositional logic**. It is surprising how many real arguments can be modeled with this system. Indeed, with careful paraphrasing (discussed in Chapter VI), we can use propositional logic to test the validity of an indefinitely large number of arguments commonly found in everyday contexts.

Study Questions and Problems

Respond to each of the following questions and problems clearly and precisely.

1)   How do we abstract the form of an argument?

2)   What is the importance of abstracting the form of an argument?

Part II: Testing for Validity

(A) USING TRUTH TABLES TO DETERMINE VALIDITY

The definition of a valid argument states that an argument is valid if and only if:

(V) If the premises are true, then the conclusion must be true.

Proposition (V) is itself a conditional proposition. But it is not in the form of a contingent truth functional conditional, since it contains the word "must," a modal term indicating that, if true, the conditional is an implicational conditional and so necessarily true. This means that the logical relation that holds between the premises and the conclusion of a valid argument is that the premises *together* logically imply the conclusion. If the premises together do not logically imply the conclusion, then proposition (V) is false and the argument is invalid. If the premises together do logically imply the conclusion, then proposition (V) is true and the argument is valid. Let us consider the following simple argument as an example:

(1) The bill will pass the committee and it will be brought to a vote on the floor of the Senate.

Therefore, (2) the bill will be brought to a vote on the floor of the Senate.

The simple propositions in this argument are

P = The bill will pass the committee.
Q = The bill will be brought to a vote on the floor of the Senate.

And the form of the argument is

(1) **P & Q**

∴ (2) **Q**

(This argument form is called **simplification**; see (C) below.) Now let us take proposition (V), which expresses the claim that the argument is valid,

(V) If the premises are true, then the conclusion must be true,

and substitute in the premise of our example where (V) says "the premises" and substitute in the conclusion of our example where (V) says "the conclusion." This gives us the following proposition:

(A) If P & Q are true, then Q must be true.

Proposition (A) says that our example is a valid argument; that is, if proposition (A) is true, then our example has a valid argument form and is a valid argument. But if proposition (A) is false, our example does not have a valid argument form and is invalid. Our problem is, then, to determine if proposition (A) is true. Since proposition (A) claims to be a logical implication, we need to be able to show when one proposition logically implies another. We can do this using truth tables.

Compare proposition (A) with proposition (B) as follows:

(A) If P & Q are true, then Q must be true.
(B) If P & Q are true, then Q is true.

Proposition **(B)** is an ordinary truth functional (contingent or material) conditional. It says that if **P & Q** are true, then **Q** *is* true. Hence we can rewrite proposition (B) in our notation as

(C) (P & Q) → Q

Proposition (A) is different from proposition (B) because proposition (A) asserts that if **P & Q** are true, then **Q** *must be* true. The difference between the two propositions, then, is a modal difference: while proposition (B) claims that there is only a contingent relation between its antecedent and its consequent, proposition (A) claims that there is a necessary connection between its antecedent and its consequent. Which of these is correct? Is there a necessary connection between the antecedent and the consequent (such that the truth of **P & Q** necessitates the truth of **Q**) or only a contingent connection? If there is a necessary connection between the antecedent and the consequent—that is, if proposition (A) is true—then proposition (B) will turn out to be a necessary truth after all, and proposition (C) will turn out to be a tautology. The truth table for (C) will have the truth value T in every row. In case there is only a contingent connection between the antecedent and the consequent, proposition (B) will turn out to be a contingent truth. The truth table for (C) will not have the truth value T in every row; the truth table will have the truth value F in at least one row.

Let us construct the truth table for proposition (C) as follows:

P	Q	P & Q	(P & Q) → Q
T	T	T	T
T	F	F	T
F	T	F	T
F	F	F	T

We arrive at a truth table which shows that proposition (B) is a tautology. So this conditional is not merely a contingent proposition or material conditional but is a necessary truth, a tautology, and so is a logical implication. For (as we saw in Chapter IV), if a conditional proposition is a tautology, then it is a logical implication. And since proposition (B) is necessarily true, then proposition (A) is true, and the premise of the original argument logically implies its conclusion. Since the premise of the argument logically implies its conclusion, the argument is valid.

Every argument can be expressed in the form of a conditional proposition, with the conjunction of the premises serving as the antecedent and the conclusion as the consequent of that conditional proposition. For a particular argument, we will call this conditional proposition the **associated conditional** for that argument. Any argument, then, can be rewritten as the claim that its premises logically imply its conclusion.

However, since many arguments have more than one premise, these cases claim that the premises *taken together* logically imply the conclusion. So, when an argument has more than one premise, we have to conjoin the premises in the antecedent of the conditional that expresses the claim that the premises taken together logically imply the conclusion. Consider the disjunctive form of argument, discussed in Chapter III.

Example 77: (1) The bill will pass the committee or the bill will be brought to a vote on the floor of the Senate.

(2) The bill will not pass the committee.

Therefore, (3) the bill will be brought to a vote on the floor of the Senate.

This argument has the form:

(1) **P v Q**

(2) **~ P**

∴ (3) **Q**

We saw, in Chapter III, that this form of argument was valid. Now let us demonstrate that it is valid by constructing the truth table for the associated conditional that if the premises are true, then the conclusion is true. If this proposition turns out to be a necessary truth, a tautology, then the premises will logically imply the conclusion and the argument form is valid. If this proposition turns out not to be a necessary truth, then the premises will not logically imply the conclusion and the argument form is invalid. The associated conditional we need to consider, then, is

[(**P v Q**) & (**~ P**)] → **Q**

The antecedent of the conditional contained in the square brackets is the conjunction of the two premises, and the consequent of the conditional is the conclusion of the argument. Let us construct the truth table for this sentence:

P	Q	~P	P v Q	(P v Q) & (~ P)	[(P v Q) & (~ P)] → Q
T	T	F	T	F	T
T	F	F	T	F	T
F	T	T	T	T	T
F	F	T	F	F	T

Again the conditional associated with the argument form turns out to be a tautology. So the conditional is not a merely contingent proposition; it is a necessary truth. The antecedent (which is the conjunction of the premises)

logically implies the consequent (which is the conclusion). So this argument form and all arguments of this form are valid.

Let us consider another argument form. Consider the following argument:

(1) If the bill will pass the committee, then the bill will be brought to a vote on the floor of the Senate.

(2) The bill will be brought to a vote on the floor of the Senate.

Therefore, (3) the bill will pass the committee.

Abstracting the form of this argument gives us the following:

(1) P → Q
(2) Q
∴ (3) P

The conditional associated with this argument is

[(P → Q) & Q] → P

and the truth table for this conditional is

P	Q	P → Q	(P → Q) & Q	[(P → Q) & Q] → P
T	T	T	T	T
T	F	F	F	T
F	T	T	T	F
F	F	T	F	T

In this case, the conditional associated with this argument is not a tautology. The conditional is contingent, since it can be false, as shown by the third row of the truth table. This means that the conditional associated with this argument is not a necessary truth, and its antecedent does not logically imply its consequent. So the argument form is not a valid argument form and all arguments of this form are invalid. Notice that the case where the associated conditional is false in the third row just in the case where the premises **P → Q** (in the third column) and **Q** (in the second column) are true and the conclusion **P** is false. Since the truth table gives all the possible ways that matters can be with respect to the two simple propositions **P** and **Q**, it is possible for the premises to be true and the conclusion false together. So the argument form is invalid.

Our procedure for constructing the associated conditional for an argument form, then, is as follows:

(1) Connect the premise together in a conjunction. For two premises P_1 and P_2, the conjunction would be $(P_1 \& P_2)$; for three premises P_1, P_2, and P_3, the conjunction would be $((P_1 \& P_2) \& P_3)$, and so on.

(2) Make this conjunction the antecedent of a conditional with the conclusion as the consequent of the conditional. So for two premises the associated conditional would be $(P_1 \& P_2) \to C$; for three premises the associated conditional would be $((P_1 \& P_2) \& P_3) \to C$, and so on.

We test the validity of the argument form by constructing the truth table for this associated conditional. If the associated conditional is a tautology, then the argument form is valid. If the associated conditional is a not a tautology, then the argument form is invalid.

(B) A SHORTER PROCEDURE FOR DETERMINING VALIDITY

In looking at the last truth table above, we noticed that the row of the truth table where the associated conditional turns out to be false is just the row in which the premises **P** $\to$ **Q** and **Q** are both true and the conclusion **P** is false. This is exactly what we should expect, since an argument is invalid if it is possible that the premises be true and the conclusion false, and since each row of the truth table displays a possibility. This means that if instead of trying to demonstrate that an argument is valid, we try to show that it is invalid, then all we have to do is find out if its truth table has a row in which the premises are all true and the conclusion is false. If there is even one row in the truth table where the premises are all true and the conclusion is false, then the argument is invalid.

NOTE:
At this point, you should review the rules for constructing truth tables for the logical operator ~ and connectives & v → ↔ given at the end of Chapter III! Knowing these rules is necessary for using the short-cut method.

This gives us a short-cut method for determining the validity of arguments. Instead of constructing the whole truth table, we try to find an assignment of truth values for the simple propositions (the variables symbolized by the letters P, Q, R, etc.) in the argument form that, in accord with the rules for the logical operator and connectives, will make the premises true and the conclusion false. If we can find such an assignment of truth values, then the argument is invalid. If there can be no such assignment, then the argument is valid. So the short-cut truth table method seeks to show that the argument form is invalid. Only if *every possible attempt*, within the rules, to show that the argument form is invalid fails is the argument form valid.

This will become clearer if we apply this method to an example. Consider the following argument:

> (1) If the bill will pass the committee, then the bill will be brought to a vote on the floor of the Senate.
> (2) The bill will not pass the committee.
> _____
> Therefore, (3) the bill will not be brought to a vote on the floor of the Senate.

Abstracting the form of this argument gives us the following:

> (1) P $\rightarrow$ Q
> (2) ~ P
> _____
> ∴ (3) ~ Q

Instead of constructing the whole truth table for this argument form, let us try to locate a row in the truth table where the premises are true and the conclusion false. We can do this without constructing the associated conditional for the argument. Instead, we proceed by the following steps:

(1) **Make the conclusion false.**
Since the conclusion is ~ **Q**, we make **Q** true. For according to our rule for logical negation, if **Q** is true, then ~ **Q** is false.

(2) **Assign the same truth value to the simple propositions contained in the premises as we assigned to them in the conclusion.**
Since, we assigned **Q** the value true in the conclusion, we assign the **Q** contained in the first premise the value true as well. (If **Q** appeared in any other premises, we would assign it the value true in those premises as well.)

(3) **Try to find an assignment of truth values to the other simple propositions contained in the premises that will make the premises all true.**
Since we assigned **Q** the value true, it does not matter whether

we assign **P** the value true or assign **P** the value false in the first premise. In either case, according to our rule for truth functional conditionals, the first premise will turn out to be true. However, in order to make the second premise true, we have to assign **P** the value false. For if **P** is false, then ~ **P** will be true, according to our rule for logical negation.

(4) **If we can find an assignment of truth values for which the premises turn out to be true and the conclusion false, then the argument form is invalid (otherwise it is valid).**
In our example, by assigning the truth values **P** = false and **Q** = true, we find a case where the premises turn out to be true and the conclusion false, so this argument form is *invalid*, and every argument with this form will also be invalid. If we were to construct the truth table for the associated conditional for this argument form, we would find that in the row where **P** = false and **Q** = true the associated conditional would be false.

Let us consider another example. Consider the following argument:

(1) If the bill will pass the committee, then the bill will be brought to a vote on the floor of the Senate.
(2) The bill will not be brought to a vote on the floor of the Senate.

Therefore, (3) the bill will not pass the committee.

Abstracting the form of this argument gives us the following:

(1) P → Q
(2) ~ Q
∴ (3) ~ P

This argument has the same form as both the argument (Example 74) we considered earlier that Tycho Brahe put forward against the Copernican system of astronomy and the argument about plagiarism given earlier. We said then that the argument was valid (although Tycho's argument was not sound). Let us demonstrate its validity by the short-cut truth table method.

(1) **Make the conclusion false.**
Since the conclusion is ~ **P**, we make **P** true. For according to our rule for logical negation, if **P** is true, then ~ **P** is false.

(2) **Assign the same truth value to the simple propositions contained in the premises as we assigned to them in the conclusion.**
Since, we assigned **P** the value true in the conclusion, we assign the **P** contained in the first premise the value true as well.

(3) **Try to find an assignment of truth values to the other simple propositions contained in the premises that will make the premises all true.**
We assigned **P** the value true, and **P** is the antecedent of the conditional in premise (1). If we made **Q** false, that would give us a true antecedent and a false consequent. According to our rule for truth functional conditionals, that would make premise (1) false. But we are trying to make the premises true and the conclusion false, so we cannot assign **Q** the value false, we must assign **Q** the value true to make premise (1) true. However, according to our rule for logical negation, if **Q** is true, then ~ **Q** is false. So if we assign **Q** the value true to make the first premise true, then the second premise will turn out to be false.

(4) **If we can find an assignment of truth values for which the premises turn out to be true and the conclusion false, then the argument form is invalid (otherwise it is valid).**
We had no choice except to assign **Q** the value true to make the first premise true, and this made the second premise false. The difficulty would still arise if we started with premise (2). To make premise (2) true, we would have to assign **Q** the value false. But if **Q** is false, then premise (1) has to be false, since it would have a true antecedent and a false consequent. Our result is that, having exhausted the possibilities, there is no way to assign truth values to the simple propositions contained in the premises that would make the premises true and the conclusion false. This means that the argument form cannot be invalid, so this argument form is *valid*. Were we to construct the truth table for the associated conditional for this argument form, it would turn out to be a tautology.

This short-cut truth table method relies on the fact that an argument is invalid if it is possible that the premises are true and the conclusion false. The short-cut method tries to find an assignment of truth values to the simple propositions contained in an argument that will make the premises true and the conclusion false. This method applies to any argument which can be put in truth functional form. However, this method is a specific application of a more general procedure. For any deductive argument, if we can show that it is possible for the premises to be true and the conclusion false, then that argument is **invalid**. We did this in Examples 10 and 11 in Chapter I by finding a counterexample in each case where the premises would be true while the conclusion false. With respect to Example 11, we also did this by finding an argument with the same form that actually had true premises and a false conclusion. We need to recognize this as a general principle for evaluating arguments, so it is worth highlighting.

> **For any deductive argument, if we can show that it is possible for the premises to be true and the conclusion false, then that argument is invalid.**

It is worth noting that this principle is so general that it can apply even to arguments that are not strictly deductively valid but in which we understand possibility in more restrictive ways (as in Chapter IV, Part II, in which systematic restrictions on the meaning of "possible" were discussed). In such cases, we can ask whether it is possible, given the relevant sense of possibility, for the premises to be true and the conclusion false, and thereby sort out whether the conclusion is supported by the premises within the restricted context of the laws and rules constraining the possibilities in question in the context in which the argument is given. So an argument may not be strictly deductively valid, but if over and above the laws of logic we consider also, for example, the laws of nature, it may still be that the premises of the argument support the conclusion insofar as the argument is understood to be restricted not only by the laws of logic but also by the laws of nature.

(C) SOME STANDARD ARGUMENT FORMS

We may now identify some standard simple valid argument forms. These argument forms occur so frequently in ordinary argumentation that they have been given special names for easy identification. In each case, we will consider an argument, in English, stated in premises and conclusion form, translate it into our notation, and show that its form is valid using the short-cut truth table method.

(1) *Valid Argument Forms*

(a) Modus Ponens

Example 78:   (1) If she was out of state when the crime was committed, then the defendant is innocent.

(2) She was out of state when the crime was committed.

Therefore, (3) the defendant is innocent.

This argument contains the following simple propositions:

P = The defendant was out of state when the crime was committed.
Q = The defendant is innocent.

And the argument translates into the following form:

(1) P → Q
(2) P
∴ (3) Q

We can now test the validity of this argument form by following the steps for the short-cut truth table test.

(1) **Make the conclusion false.**
Since the conclusion is **Q**, we make **Q** false. This is all we need to do to make the conclusion false.

(2) **Assign the same truth value to the simple propositions contained in the premises as we assigned to them in the conclusion.**
Since, we assigned **Q** the value false in the conclusion, we assign the **Q** contained in the first premise the value false as well.

(3) **Try to find an assignment of truth values to the other simple propositions contained in the premises that will make the premises all true.**
We assigned **Q** the value false and **Q** is the consequent of the conditional in premise (1). If we made **P** true, that would give us a true antecedent and a false consequent. According to our rule for truth functional conditionals, that would make premise (1) false. But we are trying to make the premises true and the conclusion false. So

we cannot assign **P** the value true; we must assign **P** the value false to make premise (1) true. However, if we assign **P** the value false, that makes the second premise false.

(4) **If we can find an assignment of truth values for which the premises turn out to be true and the conclusion false, then the argument form is invalid (otherwise it is valid).**

We had no choice except to assign both **P** and **Q** the value false. But this made premise (1) true and premise (2) false. The difficulty would still arise if we start with premise (2). To make premise (2) true, we would have to assign **P** the value true to make premise (2) true. But if **P** is true, then premise (1) has to be false, by the rule for the conditional, since the conditional would have a true antecedent and a false consequent. Our result is that there is no possible way to assign truth values to the simple propositions contained in the premises that would make the premises true and the conclusion false. This means that the argument form cannot be invalid, so this form of argument is *valid*.

(b) Modus Tollens

Example 79:   (1) If she was out of state when the crime was committed, then the defendant is innocent.

(2) The defendant is not innocent.

Therefore, (3) she was not out of state when the crime was committed.

This argument contains the following simple propositions:

P = The defendant was out of state when the crime was committed.
Q = The defendant is innocent.

And the argument translates into the following form:

(1) $P \rightarrow Q$
(2) $\sim Q$
$\therefore$ (3) $\sim P$

This argument has the same form as Tycho Brahe's argument, which we discussed above. We have already shown this form to be valid above when we considered the argument

(1) If the bill will pass the committee, then the bill will be brought to a vote on the floor of the Senate.

(2) The bill will not be brought to a vote on the floor of the Senate.

Therefore, (3) the bill will not pass the committee.

which has the same form. As in all cases, any argument with a valid argument form will be valid, and any argument with an invalid argument form will be invalid (at least insofar as its form can be symbolized). This, of course, is why it is important that we are able to abstract the forms of arguments. The validity of deductive arguments is determined by their form, not their content.

(c) Disjunctive Syllogism

Example 80:   (1) Either the government will capitulate to UN demands, or the bombing will continue.

(2) The government will not capitulate to UN demands.

Therefore, (3) the bombing will continue.

This argument contains the following simple propositions:

P = The government will capitulate to UN demands.
Q = The bombing will continue.

And the argument translates into the following form:

(1) **P v Q**
(2) **~ P**
∴ (3) **Q**

Earlier, in Example 77, we showed this argument form to be valid by constructing the truth table for its associated conditional. We can now test the validity of this argument form by following the steps for the short-cut truth table test.

(1) **Make the conclusion false.**
Since the conclusion is **Q**, we make **Q** false, and this is all we need to do to make the conclusion false.

(2) **Assign the same truth value to the simple propositions contained in the premises as we assigned to them in the conclusion.**

Since we assigned **Q** the value false in the conclusion, we assign the **Q** contained in the first premise the value false as well.

(3) **Try to find an assignment of truth values to the other simple propositions contained in the premises that will make the premises all true.**

We assigned **Q** the value false, and **Q** is one of the disjuncts of the disjunction in premise (1). If we made **P** false, that would give us a false disjunction. According to our rule for logical disjunction, that would make premise (1) false. But we are trying to make the premises true and the conclusion false. So we cannot assign **P** the value false; we must assign **P** the value true to make premise (1) true. However, according to our rule for logical negation, if **P** is true, then ~ **P** is false. So if we assign **P** the value true, then the second premise will turn out to be false.

(4) **If we can find an assignment of truth values for which the premises turn out to be true and the conclusion false, then the argument form is invalid (otherwise it is valid).**

We had no choice except to assign **Q** the value false. If we assign **P** the value true, then premise (1) will be true, but premise (2) will be false. If we assign **P** the value false, then premise (2) will be true, but premise (1) will be false. Our result is that there is no possible way to assign truth values to the simple propositions contained in the premises that would make the premises true and the conclusion false. This means that the argument form cannot be invalid, so this form of argument is *valid*.

(d) Hypothetical Syllogism

Example 81:   (1) If the product sells well, then the company makes a profit.
(2) If the company makes a profit, then I will get a bonus.

Therefore, (3) if the product sells well, then I will get a bonus.

This argument contains the following simple propositions:

P = **The product sells well.**
Q = **The company makes a profit.**
R = **I will get a bonus.**

And the argument translates into the following form:

(1) P → Q
(2) Q → R
∴ (3) P → R

We can now test the validity of this argument form by following the steps for the short-cut truth table test.

(1) **Make the conclusion false.**
Since the conclusion is the conditional **P → R**, we make **P → R** false. The only way to do this is to make **P** true and **R** false. This is because, according to our rule for the conditional, a conditional is only false if the antecedent is true and the consequent is false.

(2) **Assign the same truth value to the simple propositions contained in the premises as we assigned to them in the conclusion.**
Since we assigned **P** the value true in the conclusion, we assign the **P** contained in the first premise the value true as well. Since we assigned **R** the value false in the conclusion, we must also assign the **R** contained in the second premise the value false.

(3) **Try to find an assignment of truth values to the other simple propositions contained in the premises that will make the premises all true.**
We assigned **P** the value true in premise (1). Since we are trying to make the premises true while the conclusion is false, we will have to assign **Q** the value true in premise (1). This is because, again, according to our rule for the conditional, a conditional is false if the antecedent is true and the consequent is false. However, if we assign **Q** the value true in premise (1), then we will make premise (2) false, because, since we had to assign **R** the value false, assigning **Q** the value true would make the antecedent of premise (2) true and its consequent false. On the other hand, if we make premise (2) true by assigning **Q** the value false, that would make premise (1) false; since we had to assign **P** the value true, assigning **Q** the value false would make the antecedent of premise (1) true and its conclusion false.

(4) **If we can find an assignment of truth values for which the premises turn out to be true and the conclusion false, then the**

argument form is invalid (otherwise it is valid).
We had no choice except to assign **P** the value true and **R** the value false to make the conclusion false. But if we assigned **Q** the value true, that would make premise (2) false, and if we assigned **Q** the value false that would make premise (1) false. Our result is that there is no possible way to assign truth values to the simple propositions contained in the premises that would make the premises true and the conclusion false. This means that the argument form cannot be invalid, so this form of argument is *valid*.

(e) Simplification

Example 82:   (1) The litmus paper turned red and the solution is acid.

Therefore, (2) the litmus paper turned red.

This argument contains the following simple propositions:

P = The litmus paper turned red.
Q = The solution is acid.

And the argument translates into the following form:

(1) **P & Q**

∴ (2) **P**

We can now test the validity of this argument form by following the steps for the short-cut truth table test.

(1) **Make the conclusion false.**
Since the conclusion is **P** and this is a simple proposition, we can assign the value false to **P**.

(2) **Assign the same truth value to the simple propositions contained in the premises as we assigned to them in the conclusion.**
Since we assigned **P** the value false in the conclusion, we assign the **P** in the premise the value false as well.

(3) **Try to find an assignment of truth values to the other simple propositions contained in the premises that will make the premises all true.**

Since the premise is a conjunction and one of the conjuncts, **P**, is false, then by the rule for logical conjunction **P & Q** must be false. So there is no way to make the premise true while the conclusion is false.

(4) **If we can find an assignment of truth values for which the premises turn out to be true and the conclusion false, then the argument form is invalid (otherwise it is valid).**

Our result is that there is no way to assign truth values to the simple propositions contained in the premises that would make the premises true and the conclusion false. This means that the argument form cannot be invalid, so this form of argument is *valid*.

(f) Addition

Example 83: (1) The litmus paper turned red.

Therefore, (2) either the litmus paper turned red, or the litmus paper turned blue.

This argument contains the following simple propositions:

P = **The litmus paper turned red.**
Q = **The litmus paper turned blue.**

And the argument translates into the following form:

(1) **P**
∴ (2) **P v Q**

We can now test the validity of this argument form by following the steps for the short-cut truth table test.

(1) **Make the conclusion false.**
Since the conclusion is **P v Q**, by the rule for disjunction, we can make **P v Q** false only by assigning the value false to both **P** and **Q**.

(2) **Assign the same truth value to the simple propositions contained in the premises as we assigned to them in the conclusion.**

Since we assigned **P** the value false in the conclusion, we assign the **P** in the premise the value false as well.

(3) **Try to find an assignment of truth values to the other simple propositions contained in the premises that will make the premises all true.**

There are no other choices besides assigning the value false to both **P** and **Q**, and that makes **P** in the premise false.

(4) **If we can find an assignment of truth values for which the premises turn out to be true and the conclusion false, then the argument form is invalid (otherwise it is valid).**

Our result is that there is no way to assign truth values to the simple propositions contained in the premises that would make the premises true and the conclusion false. This means that the argument form cannot be invalid, so this form of argument is *valid*.

Summary of Valid Simple Argument Forms:

Modus Ponens
(1) $P \rightarrow Q$
(2) P
∴ (3) Q

Modus Tollens
(1) $P \rightarrow Q$
(2) $\sim Q$
∴ (3) $\sim P$

Disjunctive Syllogism
(1) $P \vee Q$
(2) $\sim P$
∴ (3) Q

Hypothetical Syllogism
(1) $P \rightarrow Q$
(2) $Q \rightarrow R$
∴ (3) $P \rightarrow R$

Addition
(1) P
∴ (2) $P \vee Q$

Simplification
(1) $P \& Q$
∴ (2) P

(2) *Invalid Argument Forms: Formal Fallacies*

Just as there are certain common argument forms that are valid, likewise there are certain common argument forms that are invalid. People too often use these invalid argument forms without noticing their invalidity. Since the errors committed in these argument forms concern their form or structure, we call these invalid forms **formal fallacies**. We will consider two such common invalid argument forms and then compare them with the valid argument forms that they resemble.

(a) Denying the Antecedent

Example 84: (1) If she was out of state when the crime was committed, then the defendant is innocent.

(2) She was not out of state when the crime was committed.

Therefore, (3) the defendant is not innocent.

This argument contains the following simple propositions:

P = The defendant was out of state when the crime was committed.

Q = The defendant is innocent.

And the argument translates into the following form:

(1) **P → Q**

(2) **~ P**

∴ (3) **~ Q**

This argument form is named for its second premise, which is the negation of the antecedent of the conditional in premise (1). We have already shown this form to be invalid above when we considered the argument

(1) If the bill will pass the committee, then the bill will be brought to a vote on the floor of the Senate.

(2) The bill will not pass the committee.

Therefore, (3) the bill will not be brought to a vote on the floor of the Senate.

which has the same form. As in all cases, any argument with an invalid argument form will be invalid, while any argument with a valid argument form will be valid. This, of course, is why it is important that we are able to abstract the forms of arguments. The validity of deductive arguments is determined by their form, not by their content.

(b) Affirming the Consequent

Example 85: (1) If she was out of state when the crime was committed, then the defendant is innocent.

(2) The defendant is innocent.

Therefore, (3) she was out of state when the crime was committed.

This argument contains the following simple propositions:

P = The defendant was out of state when the crime was committed.
Q = The defendant is innocent.

And the argument translates into the following form:

(1) P → Q
(2) Q
_____
∴ (3) P

This argument form is named for its second premise, which affirms the consequent of the conditional in premise (1). We can now test the validity of this argument form by following the steps for the short-cut truth table test.

(1) **Make the conclusion false.**
Since the conclusion is **P**, we make **P** false, and this is all we need to do to make the conclusion false.

(2) **Assign the same truth value to the simple propositions contained in the premises as we assigned to them in the conclusion.**
Since, we assigned **P** the value false in the conclusion, we assign the **P** contained in the first premise the value false as well.

(3) **Try to find an assignment of truth values to the other simple propositions contained in the premises that will make the premises all true.**
We assigned **P** the value false, and **P** is the antecedent of the conditional in premise (1). Since we assigned the value false to the antecedent of the conditional in premise (1), it does not matter what truth value we assign the consequent because, according to our rule for truth functional conditionals, when the antecedent of a conditional proposition is false, the whole conditional is true. So we can now assign **Q** the value true, which then makes premise (2) true.

(4) **If we can find an assignment of truth values for which the premises turn out to be true and the conclusion false, then the argument form is invalid (otherwise it is valid).**
By assigning the truth values **P** = false and **Q** = true, we find a case where the premises turn out to be true and the conclusion false, so

this argument form is *invalid*. Notice that the assignment of truth values **P** = false and **Q** = true picks out exactly the same row in the truth table where the associated conditional is false, and this is the row where the premises are true and the conclusion is false.

Now we should compare these two formal fallacies with the valid argument forms Modus Ponens and Modus Tollens. Affirming the Consequent has a form similar to Modus Ponens and Denying the Antecedent has a form similar to Modus Tollens, and these forms should not be confused, as they often are. Let us compare these forms side by side.

VALID ARGUMENT FORMS	INVALID ARGUMENT FORMS
Modus Ponens	**Affirming the Consequent**
(1) P → Q	(1) P → Q
(2) P	(2) Q
∴ (3) Q	∴ (3) P
Modus Tollens	**Denying the Antecedent**
(1) P → Q	(1) P → Q
(2) ~ Q	(2) ~ P
∴ (3) ~ P	∴ (3) ~ Q

Notice that the valid Modus Ponens form can be transformed into the invalid Affirming the Consequent form by substituting the converse of the conditional in the first premise for the conditional. Likewise, the valid Modus Tollens form can be transformed into the invalid Denying the Antecedent form by substituting the converse of the conditional in the first premise for the conditional. This can be seen more clearly if we write these argument forms as follows:

VALID ARGUMENT FORMS	INVALID ARGUMENT FORMS
Modus Ponens	**Affirming the Consequent**
(1) P → Q	(1) Q → P
(2) P	(2) P
∴ (3) Q	∴ (3) Q
Modus Tollens	**Denying the Antecedent**
(1) P → Q	(1) Q → P
(2) ~ Q	(2) ~ Q
∴ (3) ~ P	∴ (3) ~ P

In the two formal fallacies, the second premise and the conclusion are the same as in the corresponding valid argument forms, but the first premises substitute the converse for the conditional. This clarifies a point we empha-sized earlier: The most common formal mistake in reasoning occurs when we confuse a conditional with its converse. Here we can see why this is an error in reasoning, not merely an error in translation. Confusing a conditional with its converse can mislead us that a valid argument form is really an invalid argument form, or vice versa.

(D) TESTING THE VALIDITY OF MORE COMPLEX ARGUMENT FORMS

The simple argument forms we have been discussing are surprisingly common. Many real arguments have these forms, and people often commit the errors of confusing the invalid forms of Affirming the Consequent and Denying the Antecedent with the valid forms of Modus Ponens and Modus Tollens. However, there are also many arguments, which can be modeled in proposi-tional logic, that do not have these simple forms. In these more complicated cases, we can test their validity in several ways. We could, of course, construct the truth tables for the propositions in these more complicated arguments; then we could test to see if the conditionals associated with these arguments were tautologies. However, this procedure becomes more cumbersome and time consuming as the arguments get more complicated. Alternatively, we can test these arguments by the short-cut truth table method. This method works as well with more complicated arguments as with simple ones. Finally, many complicated argument forms can be analyzed into a series of simple argument forms. If we know that the simple argument forms are valid, and that the premises of the simple argument forms are either premises in the original complicated argument or can be derived by other simple argument forms from those original premises, then the series of simple argument forms will demonstrate the validity of the complicated argument. We will now look at these latter two procedures in turn.

(1) Testing the Validity of More Complex Argument Forms by the Short-cut Truth Table Method

Consider the following complicated argument form:

(1) $Q \rightarrow (R \,\&\, W)$
(2) $(\sim (Q \,\&\, W)) \rightarrow (\sim Z)$
(3) $(\sim W) \,\&\, R$
$\therefore$ (4) $R \rightarrow (Q \,\&\, Z)$

We can test this more complicated argument form with the short-cut truth table method in the same way as we did with the earlier simpler argument forms.

(1) **Make the conclusion false.**

Since the conclusion is a conditional, according to the rule for truth functional conditionals we can make it false only by making the antecedent true and the consequent false. To do this we must make **R** true and the conjunction (**Q & Z**) false. To make the conjunction false, we must make one or the other or both of the conjuncts false. This means we have to try three different assignments of truth values to the conjunction (**Q & Z**) to see if any of them give us true premises and a false conclusion. So we will try each of the following assignments of truth values one at a time:

1st **R** = True, **Q** = True, **Z** = False
2nd **R** = True, **Q** = False, **Z** = True
3rd **R** = True, **Q** = False, **Z** = False

(2) **Assign the same truth value to the simple propositions contained in the premises as we assigned to them in the conclusion.**

For all our attempts we will make **R** true in the first premise and again in the third premise. For our first try we will make **Q** true in premises (1) and (2), and **Z** false in premise (2). For our second try we will make **Q** false in premises (1) and (2), and **Z** true in premise (2). For our third try we will make **Q** false in premises (1) and (2), and **Z** false in premise (2). Given that three different assignments of truth values to the simple propositions in the conclusion would make it false, we must try all three of these assignments of truth values to the premises to determine if they also make the premises true. If none of these assignments of truth values makes the premises true while the conclusion is false, only then would we show the argument form to be valid; it is not enough to examine one of these assignments of truth values, since any one may fail to yield true premises and a false conclusion and the argument still be invalid because one of the other assignments of truth values may yield true premises and a false conclusion. However, if any one of these assignments of truth values makes the premises true while the conclusion is false, then that would be sufficient to show that the argument form is invalid.

(3) **Try to find an assignment of truth values to the other simple propositions contained in the premises that will make the premises all true.**

1st attempt: We first make **R = True, Q = True, Z = False.** Since **Q** is true in the first premise and the premise is a conditional, we must make the conjunction (**R & W**) false because the rule for the truth functional conditional tells us that the conditional would be false if the antecedent were true and the consequent were false. Since we are trying to make this conditional premise true and the antecedent is true, we have to make the conjunction (**R & W**) false. But **R** is true, so we have to make **W** false to falsify the conjunction (**R & W**) because the rule for conjunction says that a conjunction is true only when both conjuncts are true. So, since **R** is true and we want to make the conjunction (**R & W**) false, we have to make **W** false to make at least one conjunct false. Hence, since the truth values for **Q** and **R** are set by the assignments of truth values in the conclusion, the only way to make premise (1) true is to make **W** false. But this means that **W** also has to be false in premise (3). If **W** is false, then by the rule for logical negation ~ **W** will be true, since the negation of any proposition assigns it the other truth value than that assigned to the proposition to be negated. But, since premise (3) is a conjunction and ~ **W** is one of the conjuncts, then by the rule for conjunction, which says that for a conjunction to be true both conjuncts must be true, premise (3) will have to be false. But that means that the assignment of truth values **R = True, Q = True, Z = False** in the conclusion cannot give us true premises and a false conclusion. However, that is not enough to show that the argument is valid, since there are two other assignments of truth values to **R, Q,** and **Z** that will make the conclusion false. We must try again.

2nd attempt: We now try the assignment of truth values **R = True, Q = False, Z = True.** Since **Z** is true in the second assignment of truth values that falsify the conclusion, we must make ~ **Z** true in the consequent of premise (2) because the rule for logical negation says that if a proposition is true its logical negation is false. If we are going to make premise (2) true, then since it is a conditional, we have to make its antecedent false because the rule for the truth functional conditional says that a conditional is false when the antecedent is true and the consequent is false. Since we now have a false consequent and we want a true conditional, we have to make the antecedent

false. But since we have assigned **Q** the value false, the conjunction
(**Q & W**) in the antecedent of the conditional in premise (2) will be
false no matter what truth value we assign to **W**, because the rule
for conjunction says that a conjunction is true only if both conjuncts
are true. That means that the negation of the conjunction ~ (**Q & W**)
will be true because the rule for logical negation says that the logical
negation of a proposition assigns it the other truth value than that
assigned to the proposition to be negated. Since the conjunction
(**Q & W**) is false, its logical negation is true, because of the rule for
logical negation. But that gives us a conditional with a true antecedent
~ (**Q & W**) and a false consequent ~ **Z**. This means that premise (2)
is false, because the rule for truth functional conditionals says that a
conditional is false when its antecedent is true and its consequent is
false. But that means that the assignment of truth values **R** = **True, Q**
= **False, Z** = **True** in the conclusion cannot give us true premises and
a false conclusion. However, that is not enough to show the argument
valid since there is still one more assignment of truth values to **R, Q**,
and **Z** that will make the conclusion false. We must try again.

3rd attempt: We now try the last assignment of truth values
R = **True, Q** = **False, Z** = **False**. Since **Q** is false, premise (1) will be
true. Premise (1) is a conditional and the rule for truth functional
conditionals says that a conditional is false only when it has a true
antecedent and a false consequent. But since **Q** is the antecedent
and is false, premise (1) will be true no matter what truth values
are assigned to **R** and **W**. We can make premise (3) true by
making **W** false. Premise (3) is a conjunction of **R** and ~ **W**. The
rule for conjunction says that a conjunction is true only when both
conjuncts are true. Our assignment of truth values to the conclusion
made **R** true and the rule for logical negation reverses the truth
value of **W**, so making **W** false will make ~ **W** true. This makes both
conjuncts true, making premise (3) true. But now the truth value
of premise (2) is fixed, since we have assigned truth values to all
its simple propositions. We have assigned **Q** = **False, R** = **True**, and
W = **False**. That makes the conjunction (**Q & W**) false, since both
of its conjuncts **Q** and **W** are false and the rule for conjunction
says that a conjunction is true only if both of its conjuncts are true.
Furthermore, the rule for logical negation assigns it the other truth
value than that assigned to the proposition to be negated, so since
(**Q & W**) is false, the negation ~ (**Q & W**) will be true. Since **Z** is

false and the rule for logical negation reverses the truth value of the proposition negated, ~ **Z** will be true. Premise (2) then is a conditional with a true antecedent and a true consequent, and the rule for truth functional conditionals says that a conditional is false only when it has a true antecedent and a false consequent. Since premise (2) has a true antecedent and a true consequent, premise (2) is true.

(4) **If we can find an assignment of truth values for which the premises turn out to be true and the conclusion false, then the argument form is invalid (otherwise it is valid).**
The argument, then, is *invalid* because it was possible to find an assignment of truth values to the simple propositions that makes the premises true and the conclusion false. The assignment **R = True, Q = False, W = False, Z = False** makes the premises true and the conclusion false. However, in this case we found an assignment of truth values to the simple propositions that makes the premises true and the conclusion false only by considering each way of making the conclusion false.

In using the short-cut truth table method of testing an argument form for invalidity, one can assign truth values only to the simple propositions, that is, to the single letters or variables. One cannot, for example, just assign a truth value to the logical negation of a proposition, since logical negations are compound propositions (see Chapter III, Part I). One must first assign a truth value to the simple proposition and then use the rule for logical negation to derive a truth value for the compound proposition, the logical negation. Likewise, for all compound propositions one must explicitly appeal to the rules for the various connectives to derive truth values for the compound propositions.

Finally, we are now in a position to demonstrate a point made in Chapter III, Part III regarding logical disjunctions. There it was pointed out that disjunctions should be translated as inclusive disjunctions unless stated explicitly as an exclusive disjunction and that an argument must be given to show that a disjunction is exclusive by showing why in any particular case both disjuncts are not true. Now it can be demonstrated that the formal fallacy affirming the disjunct is indeed a formally invalid argument. Consider the following two argument forms:

1) P v Q   1) (P v Q) & (~ (P & Q))
2) P   2) P
———————   ———————————————
∴ (3) ~ Q   ∴ (3) ~ Q

The difference between these two argument forms is that the first has an inclusive disjunction in premise (1) while the second has an explicitly stated exclusive disjunction for its premise (1); that is, the first premise of the second argument form says either **P** or **Q** but not both **P** and **Q**. The second of these argument forms should turn out to be valid, while the first of them should turn out to be invalid: the first argument form is a formal fallacy of affirming the disjunct, while the second is a valid argument with an exclusive disjunction for its first premise. Let us apply the short-cut truth table method of testing validity to both of these argument forms.

The formal fallacy of affirming the disjunct:

1) **P v Q**
2) **P**

∴ (3) ~ **Q**

(1) **Make the conclusion false.**
Since the conclusion is ~ **Q**, to make the conclusion false by the rule for logical negation we must assign **Q** the value true and derive the value false for ~ **Q**.

(2) **Assign the same truth value to the simple propositions contained in the premises as we assigned to them in the conclusion.**
Since we assigned **Q** the value true in the conclusion, we assign the **Q** in premise (1) the value true as well.

(3) **Try to find an assignment of truth values to the other simple propositions contained in the premises that will make the premises all true.**
In premise (1), since **Q** has already been assigned the value true, it does not matter whether **P** is true or false, since by the rule for disjunction if even one disjunct is true, then the whole disjunction is true. But since we are trying to make the premises true while the conclusion is false, and the only way to make premise (2) true is to assign **P** the value true, we must make **P** true.

(4) **If we can find an assignment of truth values for which the premises turn out to be true and the conclusion false, then the argument form is invalid (otherwise it is valid).**

However, since we had no choice except to make both **P** and **Q** true, that makes the premises true while the conclusion is false, and so this form of argument is *invalid*. Notice that the assignment of truth values that shows the argument form to be invalid is just the case where both of the disjuncts of the disjunction are true—that is, just in the case where the inclusive disjunction is true, because an inclusive disjunction is true when both disjuncts are true.

Now let us test for validity the similar argument with an explicitly stated exclusive disjunction for its first premise:

1) **(P v Q) & (~ (P & Q))**
2) **P**
_____

∴ (3) ~ **Q**

(1)   **Make the conclusion false.**
Since the conclusion is ~ **Q**, to make the conclusion false by the rule for logical negation we must assign **Q** the value true and derive the value false for ~ **Q**.

(2)   **Assign the same truth value to the simple propositions contained in the premises as we assigned to them in the conclusion.**
Since we assigned **Q** the value true in the conclusion, we assign both **Q**s in premise (1) the value true as well.

(3)   **Try to find an assignment of truth values to the other simple propositions contained in the premises that will make the premises all true.**
Since we are trying to make the premises true while the conclusion is false, and the only way to make premise (2) true is to assign **P** the value true, we must make **P** true. This means that in premise (1) both **P** and **Q** will have to be assigned the value true. By the rule for conjunction, premise (1) can be true only if both conjuncts **P v Q** and (~ (**P & Q**)) are true. Having assigned both **P** and **Q** the value true, then by the rule for disjunction **P v Q** will be true. However, the second conjunct will be false, since having assigned both **P** and **Q** the value true, **P & Q** will be true by the rule for conjunction and ~ (**P & Q**) will turn out to be false by the rule for logical negation. This makes premise (1) false by the rule for conjunction.

(4) **If we can find an assignment of truth values for which the premises turn out to be true and the conclusion false, then the argument form is invalid (otherwise it is valid).**

Since we had no choice except to make both **P** and **Q** true, and that makes premise (1) false, there is no way to assign truth values to the simple propositions contained in the premises that would make the premises true and the conclusion false. This means that the argument form cannot be invalid, so this form of argument is *valid*. Notice it was just by making ~ (**P & Q**) false that premise (1) was made false and the argument form shown to be valid, and it is ~ (**P & Q**) which denies that both disjuncts are true and which makes premise (1) an explicitly exclusive disjunction—thus making the argument form valid.

(2) Testing the Validity of Complex Arguments by Reducing Them to a Series of Simpler Arguments: Demonstrations

As we noted earlier, many complicated argument forms can be analyzed into a series of simple argument forms. When the simple arguments are valid, and the premises of these simple valid argument forms are either premises in the original complicated argument or can be derived from those original premises by other valid simple argument forms, then, since logical implication is transitive (see Chapter IV, Part I (C)), the series of valid simple argument forms will demonstrate the validity of the complicated argument. Consider the following complex argument.

(1) Either we negotiate, or if we bomb the military bases, then we commit to a long war.
(2) We will neither negotiate, nor will we commit to a long war.

Therefore, (3) we will not bomb the military bases.

This argument has the following form:

P = **We negotiate.**
Q = **We bomb the military bases.**
R = **We commit to a long war.**

(1) $P \lor (Q \rightarrow R)$
(2) $(\sim P) \, \& \, (\sim R)$

∴ (3) $\sim Q$

We can demonstrate the validity of this argument form by using a series of the simple argument forms we have already shown to be valid. We begin with the two premises we have been given. Then we derive intermediary conclusions from the given premises and previously derived intermediary conclusions. In each case, we must justify our derivation by citing the valid simple argument form we have used to derive that (intermediary) conclusion, and the premises and previously derived intermediary conclusions we have used as premises. Our example will make this clear.

DEMONSTRATION	JUSTIFICATION
(1) P v (Q → R)	given premise
(2) (~ P) & (~ R)	given premise
(3) ~ P	from (2) by Simplification
(4) Q → R	from (1) and (3) by Disjunctive Syllogism
(5) ~ R	from (2) by Simplification
(6) ~ Q	from (4) and (5) by Modus Tollens

The lines (3) – (6) are derived by applying the simple valid argument forms indicated in the justification to the each of the lines of the demonstration. For example, line (4) gives us the intermediary conclusion **Q → R** by applying the form of disjunctive syllogism to lines (1) and (3) as follows:

(1) **P v (Q → R)**
(3) **~ P**
─────────
∴ (4) **Q → R**

We can do this because the main connective in premise (1) is a disjunction and intermediary conclusion (3) is the negation of one of the disjuncts in premise (1). This means that lines (1) and (3) have the same form as the premises of a disjunctive syllogism, so we are justified in drawing the conclusion **Q → R**. We write **Q → R** because the disjunctive syllogism justifies us in arguing that since one disjunct of the disjunction in the first premise is negated in the second premise, we may conclude that the remaining disjunct, **Q → R**, is true.

The last line of the demonstration, line (6), is, of course, the conclusion of the original argument. Since we arrived at (6) through a series of steps, each step produced using a valid argument form, the series of steps demonstrates the validity of the original argument, that is ~ **Q** follows validly from premises (1) and (2). Our original argument in English, then, is valid.

Such demonstrations can become very complicated and coming up with them takes practice and creative thought (this procedure is not purely mechanical as are the various truth table methods). However, we should, at least, understand the principles that operate in demonstrations, and why demonstrations prove the validity of the original arguments. These points may be summarized as follows:

Given a valid deductive argument, we can demonstrate its validity by a series of steps in which

(a) Each step is justified because it has the same form as a simple valid argument form.

(b) The premises for each simple valid argument form used in each step either are one or more of the original premises of the argument or have already been derived from earlier steps in the demonstration by using valid argument forms.

(c) The last step of the demonstration is the conclusion of the original argument.

(d) Since each step is derived from previous lines in the demonstration using a valid argument form, and logical implication is transitive, the series of steps is valid. And since the last line derived by valid steps is the conclusion of the original argument, we can conclude that the series of steps demonstrates the validity of the original argument form.

Demonstrating why the law of non-contradiction is a law of logic:

As promised in Chapter III, we are now in a position to see why the law of non-contradiction is a law of logic. The law of non-contradiction states that

> **A proposition "P" and its negation "It is not the case that P" cannot both be true.**

For this proposition to be a law of logic, it must be true for any proposition whatsoever. This means that if the law of non-contradiction is not true, it would be impossible to separate true from false propositions, and the sentences purporting to express such propositions would be strictly nonsensical. Since the law of non-contradiction says that a proposition "P" and its logical negation "It is not the case that P" cannot both be true, were we to abandon the law of non-contradiction, then contradictory claims, such as **P** and ~ **P**, could both be true. If this were so, then it would become obscure whether the truth functional operator "not ..." has a meaning at all, since it would make no difference to the truth value of any proposition. This, then, would mean that if a description, theory, or set of beliefs contained a contradiction (or, which for our purposes amounts to the same thing, contained logically inconsistent propositions, since a conjunction of logically inconsistent propositions will be a contradiction), then every other contradiction would follow validly from that contradiction. If every contradiction followed validly from any contradiction, then every proposition and the negation of every proposition would both follow validly. It would then become impossible to separate true propositions from false propositions. The whole description, theory, or set of beliefs would collapse into incoherence and the sentences would, while appearing to have sense, be strictly nonsense.

To demonstrate this, all we need to do is show that by assuming a contradiction we can demonstrate that any proposition whatsoever follows validly. Consider the following argument, in which the premise is a contradiction and the conclusion is a proposition completely irrelevant to either the content or the form of the premise:

(1) We are holding class and we are not holding class.

Therefore, (2) the moon is made of green cheese.

We may symbolize this argument as follows:

P = We are holding class.
Q = The moon is made of green cheese.

(1) **P & (~ P)**

∴ (2) **Q**

DEMONSTRATION	JUSTIFICATION
(1) P & (~ P)	given premise (assumption)
(2) P	from (1) by Simplification
(3) P v Q	from (2) by Addition
(4) ~ P	from (1) by Simplification
(5) Q	from (3) and (4) by Disjunctive Syllogism

What this demonstration shows is that any proposition whatsoever follows validly from a contradiction. This means that we could have just as easily demonstrated that it is not the case that the moon is made of green cheese using the same contradiction as a premise and the same form of demonstration of validity. We would only have needed to add ~ **Q** rather than **Q** in step (3). This means that both **Q** and ~ **Q** follow validly from the contradiction **P** & (~ **P**). So the contradiction **Q** & (~ **Q**) follows validly from the contradiction **P** & (~ **P**). Since it is arbitrary what proposition **Q** stands for, any and every contradiction follows validly from a contradiction. But that says that if our description, theory, or set of beliefs includes a logical inconsistency, we can validly derive every proposition and its negation from that description, theory, or set of beliefs (this is what was meant in Chapter IV, Part I (B) when it was said, metaphorically, that contradictions are too full). If that is so, then we will be unable to separate true propositions from false propositions, and the entire description, theory, or set of beliefs becomes meaningless; it expresses no real propositions.

This is the primary reason that logically inconsistent propositions are undesirable: if we try to hold onto logically inconsistent propositions, then our whole description, theory, or set of beliefs is reduced to incoherence. That is also why the law of non-contradiction is a law of logic. If we allow propositions and their negations to both be true, then it becomes impossible to sort out true propositions from false ones and so it becomes impossible to express any propositions at all. Consequently, logically inconsistent propositions are undesirable because they are false, because they are necessarily false, and most importantly because they make it impossible to assign a truth value to any proposition whatsoever. This last point shows that we cannot allow contradictory propositions because they make it impossible for any proposition to have a truth value (i.e., to be meaningful). Hence, since a law of logic is a condition that must hold for any proposition to have a truth value, the law of non-contradiction is a law of logic.

Study Questions and Problems

Respond to each of the following questions and problems clearly and precisely.

1) What logical relation must hold between the set of premises of a valid argument, on the one hand, and the argument's conclusion, on the other hand? Why?

2) Using an example, explain how to construct the associated conditional for an argument.

3) Explain why the truth table for the associated conditional for an argument will show whether the argument is valid or invalid.

4) What are the steps in the short-cut truth table method of testing validity?

5) Using an example, explain how the short-cut truth table method tests the validity of argument forms.

6) For any deductive argument, what must we show in order to demonstrate that the argument is invalid?

7) List and give examples, in English, of each of our simple valid argument forms.

8) List and give examples, in English, of each of our simple formal fallacies.

9) What is the most common formal mistake made in reasoning? Why is it a mistake in reasoning and not merely an error of translation into our notation? Why is it so common?

10) What, in general, are the steps by which we can give a demonstration (using the simple valid argument forms) that the conclusion of an argument follows validly from its premises? Why do these steps justify the conclusion?

11) Explain as completely as possible why the law of non-contradiction is a law of logic, that is, why logically inconsistent propositions must be avoided.

Part III: From Validity to Soundness

We have been concerned primarily with the validity of arguments. This is because whether a deductive argument is valid or not determines the support relation between its premises and its conclusion. Understanding whether the premises of an argument support its conclusion is central to understanding, analyzing, and using arguments. However, a few remarks should be made about determining the soundness of deductive arguments as well. For an argument to be sound, it must both be valid and have all actually true premises. So, given that we have established the validity of an argument, to establish the argument's soundness requires that we determine whether its premises are all actually true.

There are three ways of proceeding in order to determine the truth of an argument's premises:

(1) we may give arguments to support the original argument's premises,

(2) we may assess the unsupported premises to see if it is reasonable to accept them without argument, or

(3) we may accept the original argument's premises provisionally as suppositions.

(A) PROVIDING ARGUMENTS THAT SUPPORT THE PREMISES OF AN ARGUMENT

Whenever a premise of an argument is dubious or a matter of controversy, that premise should be defended by giving good reasons in support of its truth. This means that we should give and assess additional arguments that have the same dubious or controversial premise for their conclusions. We have already seen a version of this sort of sequence of arguments when we discussed demonstrations of validity. There we connected arguments in a sequence, a chain of arguments, in which the conclusions of earlier arguments became the premises for later arguments.

The same proposition, then, can function as the premise of one argument and as the conclusion of another argument. Whether a proposition is a premise or a conclusion is a relative matter; no proposition is a premise or conclusion on its own. Whether a proposition is a premise or a conclusion depends on how that proposition functions in a particular argument, on whether the proposition is part of an argument, and on whether the proposition functions as a premise or as a conclusion in the specific argument of which it is a part. Any proposition may function as a premise in one argument and as the conclusion in another argument. What is not acceptable is for a proposition to function as both a premise and the conclusion of the same argument. When this occurs, we have committed the informal **fallacy of circular reasoning**.

Informal Fallacy: Circular Reasoning (also called Begging the Question[2])

Like the fallacies we discussed in Chapter III, circular reasoning has the form of a valid argument. We reason fallaciously, however, when we merely assume that such arguments are sound. In circular reasoning, the same proposition functions both as a premise and as the conclusion of the same argument. So, circular reasoning, in its simplest form, will apply to fallacious uses of arguments as follows:

1) **P**

∴ (2) **P**

This is, of course, a valid argument form. Since every proposition logically implies itself (logical implication is reflexive), the premise **P** will logically imply the conclusion **P**, so the argument will be valid. However, circular reasoning involves two problems. First, while circular arguments are necessarily valid, they need not be sound, for if **P** is false, then the argument is unsound. Second, and more important, circular arguments do not lend any *independent* support to their conclusions over and above the mere dogmatic assertion of their conclusions. That is to say, circular arguments are not really arguments. The premises of a legitimate argument must, at least, claim to lend independent support to its conclusion. Support for a conclusion is independent when assigning a truth value to the conclusion will not by itself fix the truth values of the premises. Since one of the premises of a circular argument is the same as its conclusion, the argument gives no more independent support to its conclusion than if we had just insisted on the truth of the conclusion without any support at all. A circular argument, then, is really just a form of dogmatic insistence on the truth of a proposition disguised as if there were an argument given in support of the truth of that proposition.

It is uncommon to find anyone seriously presenting an argument with a single premise identical to its conclusion. If this happens, the person is usually aware that they are merely dogmatically insisting that the proposition is true without support. However, people do commit circular reasoning fallacies when either (i) they claim to support a conclusion with a premise that expresses what amounts to the same proposition as the conclusion, or (ii) they lose track

---

2 Over the last couple of decades, the phrase "begging the question" has, in much discourse, come to be used with a different meaning than it has had since the sixteenth century. It is now too often used to mean simply eliciting or suggesting a question. The phrase arose in the sixteenth century as a mistranslation of the Latin phrase "petitio principii," which literally means assumed from the beginning, and was used to refer to circular reasoning.

of their conclusion in the complexity of the discussion or the complexity of the argument.

> **Example 86:** The belief in God is universal. After all, everyone believes in God.

In this example, what the conclusion that "everyone believes in God" says amounts to saying the same thing as said by the premise that "the belief in God is universal"; "universal" here means that the belief is held by everyone.

> **Example 87:** Sarah: Everything the Bible says is true.
>
> Mick: How do you know that?
>
> Sarah: Because the Bible was written by God, and what God has written must be true.
>
> Mick: And how do you know that what God has written must be true?
>
> Sarah: Because the Bible says so, and everything the Bible says is true.

In this discussion, Sarah has lost track of what was at issue. She defends the truth of the proposition that "what God has written must be true" by appealing to the truth of the proposition that "everything the Bible says is true." But the discussion began when Mick asked Sarah to defend that very proposition. So the proposition that "everything the Bible says is true" serves as both a conclusion and a premise in the same chain of arguments. Sarah has therefore committed a fallacy of circular reasoning, since she assumes as a premise the very conclusion that is at issue. To argue against this fallacy, we should note when and how a premise is the same as, or amounts to the same as, the conclusion, and then explain why such a premise gives no independent support for the conclusion.

(B) ASSESSING UNSUPPORTED PREMISES

When the premises of an argument are dubious or contentious, we require that they be supported by further arguments. However, this process cannot go on indefinitely. At some point we must accept some unsupported propositions as premises, even though we may often do so only provisionally (see below). This, however, does not mean that it is arbitrary which propositions we should accept. We should accept unsupported premises only when they

(a) state observation claims or do not conflict with reliable observations, and

(b) do not conflict with background knowledge, or other credible propositions, or

(c) come from a credible and unbiased source.

Let us deal with each of these provisions in turn.

(a) For the most part, when we directly observe some state of affairs, we should accept as true the proposition that describes that state of affairs. We say "for the most part" because there are circumstances when even our direct observations are unreliable, for example, when they are made in poor conditions, made without appropriate observational skills, made under the influence of misleading expectations or biases, and when our memory is not reliable, all of which are discussed in detail below. Moreover, we should rely less on our observations the more that is at stake in the argument.

(1) **To be reliable, observations must be made under condition favorable for observing the state of affairs in question.** Conditions will be poor when the circumstances involve poor lighting, noise, distractions, or faulty or imprecise measuring instruments, etc. When we cannot see or hear well because of external conditions, we cannot expect to observe accurately. So, for example, if we are looking at an object in the distance at twilight, we cannot reliably observe what sort of object it is. Sometimes we must make our observations using instruments that aid our senses. In these cases, our observations cannot be any more accurate than our instruments. For example, a magnifying glass will allow us to see some things smaller than we can see with the naked eye. However, the magnifying glass will be limited in its power to show us things smaller still, such as different sorts of bacteria. Moreover, observations made through instruments are not simple and require not only the observation itself but also arguments for the reliability of observations through the particular instrument in question. For example, when Galileo first observed the craters on the moon, the predominant understanding of time denied that there could be such irregularities in celestial objects, so many critics claimed that what Galileo had observed were faults in the telescope. It was not until the study of optics had advanced sufficiently to explain (i.e., give good arguments for) how the telescope worked that observations through telescopes could be accepted as reliable.

Conditions for observation will also be poor if we are not at our best. Psychological conditions such as fatigue, impaired senses, and emotional turmoil are likely to impair our ability to observe states of affairs accurately. For example, when we are very tired, our ability to keep track of complex traffic situations may be impaired. It is dangerous to drive when very tired because our judgment tends to be impaired and we do not observe our situation very well. The same applies to observational judgments we make when we are emotionally upset, or when our senses are not functioning properly (for example, when someone who needs corrective lenses tries to see things without those lenses).

(2) **To be reliable, observations must be made with appropriate observational skills.** People vary with respect to their observational powers. We do not all observe all sorts of things with the same degree of skill. Observation is a skill and it must be learned and practiced; it is not something we can do just because our senses are functioning properly. Moreover, different sorts of states of affairs require different sorts of training and practice in order to reliably observe them. For example, someone who plays chess well will be better able to observe and remember the positions of chess pieces on a chess board than someone who does not play chess. However, this is true only if the positions of the pieces on the board are what might be expected in normal play. If pieces are placed on the board at random, even master chess players are little better than anyone else at observing and remembering their positions. For another example, someone who has studied birds will be able to distinguish birds of different species better than someone who knows little about birds. A bird watcher cultivates and develops powers of observation that can pick out certain sorts of details of birds even when they are in motion and can be observed only briefly. Such observational skills include being able to notice details, being able to take in many features at once, and being able to focus on the sort of features that matter for distinguishing different birds.

(3) **To be reliable, observations must be made with a minimum of influence from our expectations and biases.** Our observations can be biased by our hopes, fears, and prejudices. We tend to see what we expect to see. For example, if we place unusual cards (like a red two of spades) in a pack of cards and show people each card

in the pack for a short time, people will tend to misperceive the unusual card. They will, for instance, tend to see a red two of spades as a two of hearts.[3] Our expectations affect what we will observe. Notoriously, this applies to our prejudices as well. Prejudiced witnesses to crimes tend to think they see the culprit as belonging to a group they are biased against, even when the actual culprit does not belong to that group.

(4) **Our observations are only as reliable as our memory.** We usually report our observations after we have made them. What matters for our understanding of the observed states of affairs is how they may be described by propositions that report what was observed; it is only these propositions that figure into our reasoning and understanding of the observed states of affairs. So we must depend on our memory when reporting what we observe. The time period between observation and report can be very short; for example, our bird watcher may see a bird only flash by and yet still be able to make a reliable identification. Such an identification depends on the bird watcher accurately remembering what was seen. We even test our observational skills by determining what we can remember from what we have observed. This, for instance, was the test we applied to our chess players, namely whether they could remember and reconstruct the position after observing it.

(5) **We should rely on observations less when the stakes are high.** Some issues and the arguments that concern those issues are more important than others. For example, an argument about who is the best pitcher in the current baseball season is not as important as an argument in a trial for murder about whether to impose the death penalty. In general, the more important the issues and arguments are, the less we should rely simply on observations. Hence, in the law courts, we tend to require physical evidence and are more reluctant to convict a defendant on eye-witness testimony alone.

(**b**) We should not accept unsupported premises when those premises conflict with background knowledge or other credible propositions. A proposition

---

3 This experiment is reported in Thomas S. Kuhn, *The Structure of Scientific Revolutions*, 2nd ed., U of Chicago P, 1970, pp. 62–64.

tends to be, at the very least, implausible when it conflicts with propositions that we already know to be true.

Here we must carefully distinguish between background *knowledge* and mere background or other beliefs. The test for accepting unsupported premises, which we are examining here, requires that unsupported premises be consistent with other propositions that we know to be true, or that at least have sufficient credibility for our purposes. One of the main reasons for subjecting propositions to critical thought is to determine whether the contents of our beliefs are true or not. Since contents of our beliefs are in question, we cannot depend on those beliefs' contents to help us determine which unsupported premises to accept. If we did rely on those belief contents, we would be likely to fall into circular reasoning. The contents of some of our beliefs are likely to be false, but we do not know which ones. Some background propositions are more credible than others. We require that such propositions be, at least, likely to be true (more likely to be true than to be false). The degree of credibility that background propositions need to have increases with the importance of the issue and argument in question. The more that is at stake, the greater the degree of credibility we should require of the background proposition to which we compare our premises. Moreover, the degree of credibility that background propositions need to have will differ with respect to different subject matters. In mathematics, for example, we should expect the highest degree of credibility, while in ethics we must be satisfied with background propositions that are likely to be true.

Notice that the requirement that unsupported premises not conflict with background knowledge (as well as the previous requirement that unsupported premises not conflict with reliable observations) means that logical consistency is a constraint on the acceptability of unsupported premises. That we must examine whether unsupported premises conflict with background knowledge means that we must have some knowledge of the subject matter we are concerned with in order to sort out which background propositions should be consistent with our unsupported premises. There are no neat formulas for assessing background knowledge. We have to acquire as much background knowledge as possible and evaluate it carefully using the techniques of critical thought we have been studying. It is, therefore, important to read widely and critically. It is important to actively inquire and to be prepared to question and investigate the truth of any particular proposition we encounter.

However, we cannot question all background propositions at once. We are like sailors who have to repair our boats while still at sea. We cannot take the boat completely apart and rebuild it from scratch, since we would have no place to stand to do the rebuilding, so what we do is replace one plank at a time, standing on the other planks while we do so.[4] This is analogous to how we use our background knowledge: We assess unsupported premises by checking that they are logically consistent with our background knowledge, and further check our background knowledge by checking that it is consistent with new knowledge. In this way we improve our knowledge by using the results of our arguments. We cannot operate in a vacuum; we cannot assess unsupported premises as if we knew nothing else at all. It would be unreasonable to pretend that propositions are unacceptable unless we could demonstrate them without knowing anything else. (This is yet another way of pointing out that a proposition's truth value cannot be isolated from the truth values of other propositions; see Chapter IV.)

(c) We should accept unsupported premises that come from a credible and unbiased source.

The source of unsupported premises, of course, concerns who expresses the proposition rather than its content—in other words, what it states. We have already discussed assessing credibility when we discussed appeals to authority in Chapter II. When accepting unsupported premises as coming from a credible and unbiased source, we apply the six standards for accepting an authority as legitimate. We must remember, in that case, that the appeal to authority is a very weak form of argument. Should the matter be sufficiently important, we should not rely on authorities but rather examine the arguments themselves—that is, we should seek reasons and additional arguments in support of our premises (as in (a) above).

---

4 This analogy was developed by the Austrian philosopher and sociologist Otto Neurath and exposited by W.V.O. Quine in his book *Word and Object*, new ed., with a foreword by Patricia Churchland, MIT P, 2015, p. 31.

(c) ACCEPTING AN ARGUMENT'S PREMISES PROVISIONALLY AS SUPPOSITIONS

Some arguments do not actually claim that their premises are true. We often suppose that certain premises are true, as we say, "for the sake of argument." We may do this merely to see what follows from certain suppositions, we may discover truths about relationships, as in Example 88 below, or we may be trying to show that certain propositions are false using a type of argument called ***reductio ad absurdum*** (reduction to absurdity). If we do not know whether certain propositions are true or if we know a proposition to be false, we may still come to know the truth of a conclusion or find it useful or interesting to see what conclusions follow from such propositions. We then suppose that such propositions are true and use them as premises in arguments. For example, we might be interested in what would happen under various economic conditions. We might begin with a supposition and see what would follow. Consider an argument like the following:

Example 88: Suppose that inflation increased rapidly so that prices doubled in a period of a few months. Since wages would not also increase at such a rate, many people would in effect lose their savings and be plunged into poverty.

This argument can be put in premises and conclusion form as follows:

(1) Inflation increases rapidly so that prices double in a period of a few months.

(2) Wages do not increase at such a rate.

(3) If inflation increases rapidly so that prices doubled in a period of a few months and wages do not increase at such a rate, then many people would in effect lose their savings and be plunged into poverty.

Therefore, (4) many people would in effect lose their savings and be plunged into poverty.

The argument actually stated in the example does not claim that premise (1) is true. It only *supposes* that it is true and then goes on to consider what would happen if it *were* true. So in assessing the soundness of this argument, it is inappropriate to reject it because premise (1) is false. The argument can acknowledge that premise (1) is false and still claim to be a good argument. And because the argument only supposes that premise (1) is true, it is not committed to the truth of that premise. However, the argument does give us a better understanding of the relationships between the subject matter of the premises and that of the conclusion.

Reductio ad Absurdum (*reduction to absurdity*) Arguments

One important type of argument that operates using suppositional reasoning is the *reductio ad absurdum* style of argument. *Reductio ad absurdum* arguments try to show that certain propositions are true by supposing that those propositions are false and then demonstrating that a contradiction follows validly from that supposition. *Reductio ad absurdum* arguments, then, begin by supposing the truth of the contradictory of the proposition we wish to demonstrate is true. If the argument can show that a contradiction follows validly from that supposition, then that supposition has been shown to logically imply an absurdity. If the supposition implies this sort of absurdity, then it must be false. Because the law of excluded middle demands that either a proposition or its logical negation be true, its contradictory—the proposition we originally wished to demonstrate—must be true.

We saw an example of this type of argument when we demonstrated that any proposition whatsoever follows validly from a contradiction (see pp. 268–69). We began by supposing a contradiction for our premise. We supposed that a contradiction was true, even though we knew that contradictions cannot possibly be true. Then we demonstrated that an arbitrarily chosen proposition followed validly from that supposition. This showed the absurdity of supposing a contradiction to be true. Another example of the *reductio ad absurdum* style of argument follows.

> **Example 89:**   We wish to show that the proposition "There is no largest number" is true. We then suppose that its contradictory "There is a largest number" is true. Even though we believe this proposition to be false, we suppose that it is true for the sake of the argument, as a hypothesis for the *reductio ad absurdum* argument. We can then show that a contradiction follows from this supposition by the following argument.

Suppose that (1) there is a largest number (call it N).

(2) We can always add 1 to any number. Adding 1 to N gives us the number N + 1. (For any number k, k + 1 is larger than k.)

Therefore, (3) N + 1 is larger than N.

(4) If N + 1 is larger than N, then N is not the largest number.
(3) N + 1 is larger than N.

Therefore, (5) N is not the largest number.

(1) N is the largest number.

(5) N is not the largest number.

Therefore, (6) N is the largest number and N is not the largest number.

(7) (6) is a contradiction.

(8) Contradictions cannot possibly be true.

(9) If a contradiction follows validly from a supposition, then the supposition must be false.

(10) (6) followed validly from our supposition (1).

Therefore, (1) must be false: there is no largest number.

In this example, we were able to show that the supposition along with some other premises together implied its own negation. This reduced the supposition to absurdity, so the supposition must be false; therefore, the contradictory of the supposition must be true. This example shows that it is true that there is no largest number, thus illustrating the *reductio ad absurdum* form of suppositional reasoning.

Notice that by using this form of argument we are able to demonstrate that its conclusion is actually true even though we began with a premise which we believed to be, and which turned out to be, false (and in the earlier argument that any proposition whatsoever follows validly from a contradiction, the supposition was necessarily false). Also, notice that we cannot easily determine the truth of our conclusion that there is no largest number by directly examining all numbers, while the *reductio ad absurdum* form of argument can demonstrate the conclusion's truth. This means that, with respect to our two considerations for determining whether an argument is good or bad, the actual truth of the premises of an argument is not as important as the consideration whether the premises of the argument support its conclusion. For we can justify the actual truth of these argument's conclusions without needing to have actually true premises.

Arguments by the Elimination of Cases

Another important type of argument that operates using a form of suppositional reasoning is called an **argument by elimination of cases**. These arguments arise when there are only a limited number of cases to be considered, that is, where there are a limited number of alternative situations that matter for the issue under consideration. For instance, there may only be four cases that matter for the issue under consideration, call them A, B, C, and D. Then, if we can give four arguments supposing, in turn, that one of these four cases holds and from each of these four arguments the same conclusion follows, then the conclusion must be true since no matter which case actually holds, that conclusion follows. The following is an example taken from Plato's dialogue *Meno*.

In the dialogue, the character Meno gives a definition of the ancient Greek notion of *areté*, or human excellence. Meno's attempt at a definition states that the excellence of a human being is both (a) to desire good things and (b) to be able to get them. Here the notion of a good thing is restricted to things that are good for the person who gets them. So Meno's definition of human excellence has the following structure, in which human excellence is in the intersection of the category of people desiring things that are good for the person who gets them and the category of persons who are able to get those good things.

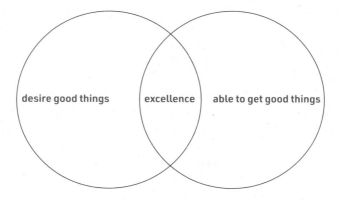

Socrates then argues that no one ever desires things that are bad for them, such that everyone desires only things that are good for them. Socrates' arguments here aim at eliminating Meno's first criterion that human excellence is defined by the desire to get things that are good for the person who gets them. If everyone desires only things that are good for them, then this cannot be a category that distinguishes excellent human beings from those that are not excellent, since the category would apply to everyone regardless of whether they are excellent or not. So, if successful, Socrates' argument will reduce Meno's definition to the claim that human excellence is the ability to get things that are good for the person who gets them; that is, it will reduce human excellence to power—the power to get things that are good for the person who gets them.

Socrates then makes the point that was made in Chapter II, namely that propositional attitudes such as desire are directed toward a proposition and its truth value, so that when some person P desires some object O, they have the attitude of desire directed to the proposition that they get O; that is, they desire that the proposition "I get O" be true. Socrates then makes a further distinction between the person knowing whether O is a good thing and the person not knowing that O is a good thing. The two distinctions—whether O is a good thing or a bad thing for the person who gets it and whether the person knows that O is a good thing for the person who gets it or knows that O is a bad thing for the person who gets it—yield only four possible cases:

	good things	bad things
knowing	a	d
not knowing	b	c

Socrates then considers each of these four cases. He argues that if we suppose that O is really a good thing for the person who gets O (cases (a) and (b) in the diagram), then it does not matter whether the person knows that O is good for that person or does not know that O is good for that person. For if O is really a good thing for that person, then that person desires a good thing. Now, if we suppose that O is a bad thing, then either P desires O knowing that O is a bad thing, or P desires O not knowing that O is a bad thing. If we suppose that case (c) holds and that O is really a bad thing for the person who gets O, and P desires O not knowing that O is a bad thing, then Socrates claims P thinks that O is a good thing and therefore P desires a good thing but is mistaken about which things are really good. Finally, if we suppose case (d) that O is a bad thing and P knows that O is a bad thing, then Socrates argues as follows:

(1) If desiring O means wanting to have it, and
(2) If bad things are bad for the person who has them, and
(3) Bad things make people miserable and unhappy, and
(4) No one wants to be miserable and unhappy.

Therefore, (5) no one wants O, if O is a bad thing and they know O is a bad thing.

Then if Socrates' arguments are good ones, the proposition "No one desires bad things" follows from each of the four cases, and Socrates concludes that everyone desires only things that are good for the person who gets them.

There are questions that can be raised about the legitimacy of the argument from (1), (2), (3), and (4) to the conclusion (5) regarding masochists who desire their own pain and humiliation, but these cases seem to be more like case (c), in which masochists do not know what is really good or bad for them. Also, there seem to be problems regarding cases of people whose will is too weak to resist temptations to get things that are bad for them such as alcohol or tobacco; however, perhaps such cases do not matter, because the more they are analyzed the more they seem like cases where the person does not have the ability or power to get good things and so fails to meet Meno's criterion (b) that human excellence requires the ability to get things that are good for them.

Regardless of these difficulties, the form of the argument is clear. Socrates confronts Meno with four possible cases and then gives arguments to eliminate each case as counting as an example in which a person desires something that is bad for that person. If the four cases exhaust the possibilities and the arguments regarding each case are good arguments, then it does not matter which case actually holds, since supposing each case to hold in turn supports the same conclusion for all possible cases, and that conclusion must be true.

Study Questions and Problems

Respond to each of the following questions and problems clearly and precisely.

1) What are the three ways of determining the truth value of the premises of an argument?

2) When is it legitimate for the same proposition to be both a premise and a conclusion? When is it illegitimate for the same proposition to be both a premise and a conclusion?

3) Explain why circular reasoning does not really provide an argument for its conclusion.

4) Under what conditions should we accept unsupported premises?

5) What are the five sorts of circumstances in which observations are reliable?

6) Explain what degree of credibility is necessary for us to determine whether conflict with background propositions should rule out accepting a premise without support.

7) Why is it that we cannot question all background propositions at once?

8) Explain why we may legitimately accept a premise as true, even though we know it is false.

9) Explain the strategy of *reductio ad absurdum* arguments.

10) Explain the strategy of argument by the elimination of cases.

Exercises: Tests of Validity

For each argument, determine whether it is valid or invalid using the short-cut truth table method. For numbers 13, 14 , 15, and 16, explain what you have done and what it shows.

1) P → Q
    (~ R) v (~ Q)
    (~ R) v (~ S)
    ∴ S v (~ P)

2) Z v (~ M)
    (~ K) & O
    ~ (Z & (~ O))
    ∴ (~ M) → K

3) (~ A)
    D → (A v R)
    ∴ R

4) P → (A & B)
    (A v B) → (~ Q)
    ∴ Q → (~ P)

5) (H & I) → J
    (~ K) → (I & (~ J))
    ∴ K v (~ H)

6) A → (U & W)
    ~ W
    T v A
    ∴ W → Q

7) (X v Y) → [~ (Z & (~ A))]
    Z & (~ A)
    ∴ ~ (X v Y)

8) L v (M → N)
    (~L) → (N → O)
    ~ L
    ∴ M → O

9) R
    (R & (~ P)) → U
    ∴ (~ U) → P

10) E → [(G & H) & (K & I)]
    ~ (G & H)
    ∴ (K & I) → (~ E)

11) ~ (P & (~ Q))
    (~ R) v P
    ∴ ~ (R → Q)

12) (W & S) → (M v B)
    ~ [(~ M) → (~ S)]
    ∴ ~ (W v B)

13) A → B
    C → B
    A v C
    ∴ B

14) P → A
    (~ A) v B
    (~ C) → B
    ∴ P → C

15) Q & (~ Q)
    ∴ R

16) R
    ∴ P v (~P)

Appendix: The Validity of the Argument Forms for Testing the Adequacy of Definitional Propositions

In Chapter III, we saw that we can test definitional propositions to see if they really give necessary and sufficient conditions for applying the term defined to its examples. The arguments we used there required that we find a counterexample to the claim that the definition gives a necessary condition, or that we find a counterexample to the claim that the definition gives a sufficient condition.

It is worth noting here that, in general, giving an example does not provide an argument for the truth of a general proposition (see Chapter VI, Part IV (B) on fallacies of hasty generalization). Examples typically illustrate and clarify the meanings that constitute general propositions; they do not establish the truth or falsity of general propositions that they illustrate. Counterexamples, however, can serve as premises in an argument that shows that a general proposition, like a definition, is false. In such cases, the proposition stating the counterexample serves as one premise which must be connected with other premises—in particular, at least one other premise making the general claim under consideration. Here the examples serve only to help construct an argument against the general proposition, and they can serve only to show the general proposition to be false; they cannot show the general proposition to be true. All it takes to show that a general proposition is false is to discover a single case that should, but does not, fit the general proposition. This is how counterexamples work in testing definitions (see the example of the definition of triangle given in Chapter III).

The use of counterexamples gives us a means of testing the adequacy of definitional propositions by testing whether it is true that the definition picks out both necessary and sufficient conditions for applying the general term, **W**, to the appropriate instances (things that are of the type **W**). This means that there will be two different sorts of test for the adequacy of a definitional proposition: a test to see if the definition gives necessary conditions for applying a term to its instances or examples, and a test to see if the definition gives sufficient conditions for applying a term to its instances or examples.

An adequate definition of a general term must give both necessary and sufficient conditions for applying that general term to its examples—that is, an adequate definition must pick out *all* and *only* examples of the general term it claims to define. We can express this in our notation in the following way:

Given a general term **W** and a set of defining conditions **C**, then

$$\textbf{W, if C}$$
symbolically: $\textbf{C} \to \textbf{W}$

expresses the claim that the set **C** states sufficient conditions for **W** to apply to its examples, and

W only if C

symbolically: **W → C**

expresses the proposition that the set of conditions **C** gives necessary conditions for applying **W** to its instances.

We can now express the proposed definition of **W** by the set of conditions **C** as follows:

W, if C, and W only if C

or

W if and only if C

(the standard biconditional form for expressing definitional propositions)

symbolically: **(W → C) & (C → W)**

or   **(W ↔ C)**

So a proposed definition **P** will state,

P = Something is a W if and only if that thing meets the defining conditions C.

where **W** is the general term to be defined and **C** states the conditions that the definition proposes are both necessary and sufficient for something to be an example of a **W**.

Suppose, to take another example from Plato's dialogue *Meno*,

W = human excellence

and the defining conditions **C** is

C = One rules over other people

(Here we have only one defining condition; other definitions may give several conditions that work together. Go back to Chapter III and look at the proposed definition for a triangle for such a case.) This gives us the proposed definition:

Someone has human excellence if and only if they rule over other people.

symbolically: **(W → C) & (C → W)**

or   **(W ↔ C)**

We can now consider separate arguments for each of the two conjuncts of this proposition; that the definition gives necessary conditions ($W \rightarrow C$), and that the definition gives sufficient conditions ($C \rightarrow W$).

(A) A CONDITION FOR APPLYING A GENERAL TERM IS A NECESSARY CONDITION IF AND ONLY IF THAT CONDITION MUST HOLD OF ALL INSTANCES OF THAT TERM

Hence, when arguing that a definition fails to give a necessary condition for the application of the term to be defined, we try to give a counterexample that presents an instance of the term to be defined which does not have the feature claimed to be necessary. The argument will include premises of the following sort:

(1) **A proposition stating the proposed definition.**
Suppose, for instance, that a proposed definition for a term **W** is given by a set of conditions **C**, so that the proposed definition states

P = Something is a W if and only if that thing meets the conditions C.

In our example:

P = Someone has human excellence if and only if they rule over other people.

(2) **A description of the counterexample showing that it is a thing of the sort to be defined.** (This may require more than one proposition, and so more than one premise.) Every counterexample to a proposed definition considers two claims:

(a) **The example proposed as a counterexample is an instance falling under the term W.**
(b) **The example proposed as a counterexample is an instance meeting the defining conditions C.**

If we call the proposed counterexample **E**, then we may symbolize these claims as follows:

(a) **Q = E is an instance of W.**
(b) **R = E is an instance of the conditions C.**

In the dialogue, Socrates considers the following example,

(a) **Q = A child's excellence is an instance of human excellence.**
(b) **R = A child's excellence is an instance of someone ruling over other people.**

(3) **An argument that the counterexample does not have the feature that the definition claimed was necessary.** (This may require more than one proposition, and so more than one premise.) The appropriate argument, in our example, will go as follows:

(1) If someone has human excellence if and only if they rule over other people, then a child's excellence is an instance of human excellence and a child's excellence is an instance of someone ruling over other people.
(2) A child's excellence is an instance of human excellence, but a child's excellence is not is an instance of someone ruling over other people.

Therefore, (3) it is not the case that someone has human excellence if and only if they rule over other people.

The argument can be put in symbolic form as follows:

(1) $P \rightarrow (Q \mathbin{\&} R)$
(2) $(Q \mathbin{\&} (\sim R))$
(3) $\therefore \sim P$

The conclusion states that the definition is inadequate. It is inadequate because the condition(s) it mentions (one rules over other people) is (are) not necessary.

(B) A CONDITION FOR APPLYING A GENERAL TERM IS A SUFFICIENT CONDITION IF AND ONLY IF WHEN THAT CONDITION HOLDS OF SOMETHING, THAT THING COUNTS AS AN INSTANCE OF THE GENERAL TERM TO BE DEFINED

Hence, when arguing that a definition fails to give a sufficient condition for the application of the term to be defined, we try to give a counterexample that presents an instance of the feature(s) claimed to be sufficient conditions which is (are) not an instance of the term to be defined.

The argument will include premises of the following sort:

(1) **A proposition stating the proposed definition.**
Suppose, for instance, that a proposed definition for a term **W** is given by a set of conditions **C**, so that the proposed definition states:

P = Something is a W if and only if that thing meets the conditions C.

In our example:

P = Someone has human excellence if and only if they rule over other people.

(2) **A description of the counterexample showing that it is a case of the feature claimed to be a sufficient condition.** (This may require more than one proposition, and so more than one premise.)
Every counterexample to a proposed definition considers two claims:

(a) **The example proposed as a counterexample is an instance falling under the term W.**
(b) **The example proposed as a counterexample is an instance meeting the defining conditions C.**

If we call the proposed counterexample **E**, then we may symbolize these claims as follows:

(a) **Q = E is an instance of W.**
(b) **R = E is an instance of the conditions C.**

In the dialogue, Socrates considers the following example,

(a) **Q = An unjust ruler is an instance of human excellence.**
(b) **R = An unjust ruler is an instance of the someone ruling over other people.**

(3) **A demonstration that the counterexample is not an instance of the term to be defined.** (This may require more than one proposition, and so more than one premise.) The appropriate argument, in our example, will go as follows:

(1) If someone has human excellence if and only if they rule over other people, then an unjust ruler is an instance of human excellence and an unjust ruler is an instance of the condition of ruling over other people.
(2) An unjust ruler is not an instance of human excellence, while an unjust ruler is an instance of the someone ruling over other people.

Therefore, (3) it is not the case that someone has human excellence if and only if they rule over other people.

The argument can be put in symbolic form as follows:

(1) **P → (Q & R)**
(2) **((~ Q) & R)**
—————————
∴ (3) **~ P**

The conclusion states that the definition is inadequate because the condition(s) it mentions is (are) not sufficient.

We have now abstracted the forms of these two sorts of arguments: arguments that a proposition (for example, a definition) does not give necessary conditions and arguments that a proposition (for example, a definition) does not give sufficient conditions. Now let us test these arguments for validity using the short-cut truth table method.

Let us begin with the argument form for testing whether a definition gives a necessary condition for applying a term to its instances. The argument has the following form:

(1) **P → (Q & R)**
(2) **(Q & (~ R))**
—————————
∴ (3) **~ P**

Now we test this argument for validity using the short-cut truth table method.

(1) **Make the conclusion false.**
Since the conclusion is ~ **P**, we make **P** true. For according to our rule for negation, if **P** is true, then ~ **P** is false.

(2) **Assign the same truth value to the simple propositions contained in the premises as we assigned to them in the conclusion.**
Since we assigned **P** the value true in the conclusion, we assign the **P** contained in the premise (1) the value true as well.

(3) **Try to find an assignment of truth values to the other simple propositions contained in the premises that will make the premises all true.**
According to the rule for conditionals, a conditional is false when the antecedent is true and the consequent is false. So, since we assigned **P** the value true in the conditional in premise (1), we must assign the value true to the conjunction (**Q & R**) to make premise

(1) true. Because the rule for conjunction states that a conjunction is true only when both conjuncts are true, we must assign the value true to both **Q** and **R** to make the conjunction (**Q & R**) true. So both **Q** and **R** have to be assigned the value true in premise (2). But if both **Q** and **R** are true, then premise (2) turns out to be false, because ~ **R** will be false and so the conjunction (**Q & (~ R)**) will be false. Again this is because, according to the rule for conjunction, a conjunction is true only when both conjuncts are true.

(4) **If we can find an assignment of truth values for which the premises turn out to be true and the conclusion false, then the argument form is invalid (otherwise it is valid).**
We had no choice except to assign the value true to **P** to make the conclusion false. This left us with no choice except to assign the value true to **Q** and **R** to make premise (1) true. But that made premise (2) false. Notice that if we make premise (2) true by assigning the value true to **Q** and false to **R**, that would make premise (1) false. Our result is that there is no way to assign truth values to the simple propositions contained in the premises that would make the premises true and the conclusion false. This means that the argument form cannot be invalid, and so the argument is *valid*.

We now turn to the argument form for testing whether a definition gives a sufficient condition for applying a term to its instances. The argument has the following form:

(1) P → (Q & R)
(2) ((~ Q) & R)
$$\overline{}$$
∴ (3) ~ P

Now we test this argument for validity using the short-cut truth table method.

(1) **Make the conclusion false.**
Since the conclusion is ~ **P**, we make **P** true. For according to our rule for logical negation, if **P** is true, then ~ **P** is false.

(2) **Assign the same truth value to the simple propositions contained in the premises as we assigned to them in the conclusion.**
Since we assigned **P** the value true in the conclusion, we assign the **P** contained in the premise (1) the value true as well.

(3) **Try to find an assignment of truth values to the other simple propositions contained in the premises that will make the premises all true.**

According to the rule for conditionals, a conditional is false when the antecedent is true and the consequent is false. So, since we assigned **P** the value true in the conditional in premise (1), we must assign the value true to the conjunction (**Q & R**) to make premise (1) true. Because the rule for conjunction states that a conjunction is true only when both conjuncts are true, we must assign the value true to both **Q** and **R** to make the conjunction (**Q & R**) true. So both **Q** and **R** have to be assigned the value true in premise (2). But if both **Q** and **R** are true, then premise (2) turns out to be false, because ~ **Q** will be false and so the conjunction ((~ **Q**) & **R**) will be false. Again this is because, according to the rule for conjunction, a conjunction is true only when both conjuncts are true.

(4) **If we can find an assignment of truth values for which the premises turn out to be true and the conclusion false, then the argument form is invalid (otherwise it is valid).**

We had no choice except to assign the value true to **P** to make the conclusion false. This left us with no choice except to assign the value true to **Q** and **R** to make premise (1) true. But that made premise (2) false. Notice that if we make premise (2) true by assigning the value false to **Q** and true to **R**, that would make premise (1) false. Our result is that there is no way to assign truth values to the simple propositions contained in the premises that would make the premises true and the conclusion false. This means that the argument form cannot be invalid, and so this form of argument is *valid*.

We have determined the validity of the complex arguments for testing whether a definition provides both necessary and sufficient conditions. The same short-cut truth table procedure can be used for any propositional arguments, no matter how complex.

Chapter VI

ARGUMENTS IN ORDINARY LANGUAGE

We have now completed our study of the elements of arguments: the nature of propositions, construction of compound propositions using truth functional operators and connectives, logical relations among sets of propositions, and assessing whether the premises of arguments support their conclusions. In doing this we have constructed a simplified model of propositions and arguments that has allowed us to rigorously test propositional arguments for validity. Finally, we made some remarks about determining the soundness of arguments. What remains is to turn to real arguments expressed in ordinary English and to develop some skills in reading and assessing them.

Arguments arising in everyday contexts are not expressed as clearly or neatly as the arguments we have been examining. First, ordinarily these arguments are not presented in premises and conclusion form. Second, the premises and conclusion may be presented in any order. For instance, the conclusions are often stated first, with the premises stated afterwards. There is nothing wrong with presenting arguments this way, and it can be rhetorically effective, but it can also be confusing and make it difficult to identify which propositions function as premises and which propositions function as conclusions. Moreover, third, when we present or find arguments in everyday contexts, we are usually concerned with other matters besides the argument. We present arguments in a wider context of background information that is not part of the arguments. Such additional information may include, but is not limited to the following:

(a) descriptions of states of affairs and details of circumstances or conditions that serve as a framework for our discussion but that do not help support any conclusions—these include, for instance, reports of arguments given in support of other viewpoints, and specifications of the kinds of cases to which an argument's conclusions may apply;

(b) explanations of the meanings of key terms or claims, and (causal) explanations for why some events occurred;

(c) propositions that explain the problems or interests we are addressing, or that give other versions of the position defended, or attempts to convince the reader that an argument is worth considering;

(d) illustrations, examples, analogies, editorial comments, and anecdotes that clarify the context, and other information that may be of interest to the text's readers (for example, propositions that identify sources); and

(e) summaries, appearing either at the beginning or the end of the argument, that restate the argument or its conclusion.

When we find an argument embedded in such contexts, the argument's premises and conclusion are often interspersed among these additional claims.

We are also usually concerned with presenting arguments and their context in an appropriate style. Our purposes and interests determine the style in which we present arguments. For example, in an informal attempt to persuade our audience, we may try to achieve the desired rhetorical effect by presenting our arguments in a manner we hope will be pleasing to our audience. To do this, we may include personal anecdotes, humorous elements, or language designed to make our audience feel included. We may also present arguments in a rhetorical context of debate and controversy, using a more polemical (i.e., adversarial) style. In contrast, presentation of arguments in an academic essay or in reporting the results of a scientific investigation usually incline toward a more formal, neutral, and impersonal style.

So real arguments may appear in a context of other activities and interests, we present them in various styles, and their premises and conclusions may appear in any order. All this means that extracting arguments presented in ordinary language and everyday circumstances requires careful reading and analysis of the texts. Such an analysis must, then, be reconstructed and reorganized to display the argument in premises and conclusion form. Once we have an argument displayed in premises and conclusion form, we can extract its form and test it for validity using the techniques we have already developed (or similar techniques for arguments that are not propositional arguments).

Part I: Identifying Arguments

When reading a text, we must first recognize whether the text contains an argument. Texts often consist of many propositions making assertions, but with few arguments. We must avoid confusing arguments with various propositions that may appear to be arguments but are not actually arguments.

It is a common error to confuse contingent conditional propositions with arguments. As we have seen, deductive arguments suppose that their premises together logically imply their conclusions. We have also seen that not every conditional proposition is a logical implication. Only conditional propositions that are necessarily true are logical implications. Contingent conditionals do not suppose that their antecedents logically imply their consequents. So it is a mistake to read ordinary contingent conditional propositions as if they expressed arguments. A conditional proposition such as

> If the price of stocks continues to rise, then wealth will become concentrated in fewer hands.

does not state an argument; it is merely a contingent conditional proposition. Its antecedent is not the premise of an argument nor is its consequent the conclusion of an argument. This conditional proposition might be used as a premise or used as the conclusion of an argument, but it does not express an argument by itself.

Our definition of argument tells us that an argument is a set of propositions such that the truth of one, its conclusion, is supposed to be supported by the truth of the others, its premises. When a text makes the claim that some propositions are supposed to support another, it contains an argument. This means that to find an argument in a text, we need to look for indicators that some of the propositions in the text are supposed to support one proposition as a conclusion. Thus, when reading a text, we must look for the supposition that a support relation holds between some claims made in the text.

To discover whether the supposition is made that the premises support the conclusion, we must identify the premises and conclusion of that argument and extract them from the rest of the text. The supposition that some propositions support another may be overtly indicated by certain words or phrases that mark a proposition as a conclusion or mark a proposition as a premise. These indicators help us to identify the premises and conclusion of arguments by claiming, in one way or another, that there is supposed to be a support relation holding between some of the propositions in the text.

When trying to discover whether a text contains an argument, it is usually best to try to identify the conclusion first. We count how many arguments are in a text by counting how many conclusions it contains. Each argument will have exactly one conclusion, while it may have many premises. Therefore, it will be easier to identify an argument by identifying its conclusion first and then looking for the premises that are supposed to support it.

In many arguments, the conclusion is indicated by words or phrases that precede that conclusion and identify it as the conclusion. Here is a list of some common English expressions which often indicate that the proposition following them is a conclusion:

Conclusion Indicators

therefore	justifies the claim that	which shows that
hence	ergo	which means that
so	in conclusion	demonstrates that
thus	in consequence	for this reason
shows that	proves that	for these reasons
accordingly	implies that	as a result
consequently	entails that	allows us to infer that
it follows that	establishes the fact that	we can conclude that

While these words and phrases often indicate that what follows them is a conclusion (and so indicate that the text contains an argument), they do not always do so. Sometimes these same words and phrases serve other functions. For example, in the following paragraph, the word "so" indicates that the proposition "Rising wages do not always give people more buying power" is the conclusion of the argument.

> **Example 90:**   It is clear that rising wages fuel inflation, and that if inflation rises above a certain amount, people's salaries will not go as far as they did before, and people will not be able to buy as much as they used to. **So** rising wages do not always give people more buying power.

However, in the following example, the word "so" does not indicate that "we can go out" is the conclusion of an argument.

Example 91:   Has it stopped raining? If **so**, we can go out.

The phrase "if so" means "if it has stopped raining." Hence the word "so" functions as a place holder: it holds the place of the proposition "It has stopped raining"; it does not function as a conclusion indicator, and the sentence does not contain an argument.

The phrase "as a result" may be used to indicate the conclusion of an argument, but it may also be used to indicate a causal relation. When "as a result" indicates a causal relation, the phrase does not act as a conclusion indicator. In the following example, the phrase "as a result" does not indicate that the proposition "the car won't start" is the conclusion of an argument.

Example 92:   The battery is dead. **As a result**, the car won't start.

In this example, the phrase "as a result" alleges that the dead battery is the cause of the car failing to start. The phrase "as a result" here refers to the result, the effect, of the state of affairs of the battery being dead. The phrase does not indicate a conclusion, and there is no argument present in this example.

Example 93:   Either the governor will appoint more parents to the board of education or he will appoint members of his own party. But, in the present political climate, he will not appoint members of his own party. **As a result**, he will appoint more parents to the board of education.

In this example, however, the phrase "as a result" does act as a conclusion indicator. The paragraph clearly contains an argument (in the form of a disjunctive syllogism) and is not merely describing a causal relation. The two propositions (the premises)—"Either the governor will appoint more parents to the board of education, or he will appoint members of his own party" and "In the present political climate, he will not appoint members of his own party"—together give reasons that are supposed to *support* the truth of the conclusion "he will appoint more parents to the board of education." It is not at all plausible that the two premises describe causes of the conclusion as their effect. Moreover, the paragraph has the form of a disjunctive syllogism, and this strongly suggests that there is an argument present (see below).

Once we have identified the conclusion of an argument, we then need to find the premises. Often the remaining propositions in the paragraph either will be premises or will contribute to the context or presentational style of the argument. As with the conclusion, there are certain common words and phrases that identify the proposition that follows them as a premise. Here is a list of some common English expressions which often indicate that the proposition following them is a premise:

Premise Indicators

since	is proved by	inasmuch as
for	as proved by	is deduced from
because	is shown by	follows from the fact that
follows from	can be shown by	in view of the fact that
is implied by	the reason is that	can be concluded from
is entailed by	for the reason that	may be inferred from the fact that

While these words and phrases often indicate that what follows them is a premise (and so indicate that the text contains an argument), they do not always do so. Sometimes these same words and phrases serve other functions. For example, in the following sentence, the word "because" indicates that the proposition "One will be better prepared to ask questions and to benefit from the teacher's knowledge and experience" is a premise in an argument for the conclusion "It is best to read the assigned material before class."

> **Example 94:** It is best to read the assigned material before class, **because** one will be better prepared to ask questions and to benefit from the teacher's knowledge and experience.

In this example, the word "because" indicates that the proposition that follows it gives a reason that is supposed to support the truth of the conclusion. However, in the following example, the word "because" does not indicate that "Its foundation was constructed from inferior building material" is a premise of an argument for "The building did not survive the earthquake" as a conclusion.

> **Example 95:** The building did not survive the earthquake **because** its foundation was constructed from inferior building material.

In this example, the proposition "The building did not survive the earthquake" is not a conclusion. Instead, it describes a state of affairs that has already occurred. We are expected to take this proposition as true. Rather than supporting the truth of this proposition, the proposition about the foundation is meant to explain the state of affairs of the building's destruction by giving its cause. In this case, the word "because" alleges that the inferior building materials in the foundation caused the state of affairs that the building did not survive. Here the word "because" does not indicate a premise, nor does it show that an argument is present. The word "because" does not indicate a relationship between the truth values of propositions; it indicates a causal relation between events.

The premise and conclusion indicators on our two lists are neither the only indicators, nor are they always used in texts that present arguments. When a text contains indicator words or phrases, it will very seldom contain indicators of both the argument's conclusion and its premises. So Example 90 above contains only a conclusion indicator and Example 94 contains only a premise indicator. We must identify the premises from a careful reading of the text. We must make reasonable judgments about which propositions are premises, using the indicated conclusion as a guide. In Part III below, we will consider some rules of thumb to aid us in making these sorts of judgments.

When there are no premise or conclusion indicators, we must consider the possibility that there is no argument present. However, since arguments may well be presented without indicator words, we should look for the proposition that best expresses the main point and consider whether the text supposes that it gives reasons in support of this point. This, again, takes good judgment, which is best acquired through practice and careful reading. The following example contains no indicator words, but it does contain an argument.

Example 96: The nomination is far from settled. The election is a long way off, and a lot can happen before the national convention. If the election is a long way off, and a lot can happen before the national convention, then the nomination is far from settled.

The proposition "The nomination is far from settled" is the conclusion, and the other two propositions form the premises of a Modus Ponens argument form. Since there is a valid argument form present in the text, there is reason (see Part III below regarding the Principle of Charity) to read this paragraph as presenting an argument, even though it contains no indicator words or phrases.

Throughout this chapter, we will find that ordinary English is complex and nuanced. There are no hard and fast rules for careful reading, nor can the rules of thumb given be followed mechanically. Reading a text in order to extract and assess the arguments it contains requires careful and considered judgments and much practice. However, understanding the nature and forms of simple arguments we have already acquired gives us an advantage, because we know what an argument is and what some simple common argument forms look like. This understanding helps us because it tells us to look for the support relation, and to look for familiar forms of arguments. When we look for the form of an argument, we will try to discover connections between propositions, seeking connectives and the repetition of simple propositions. Of course, as we have seen, the connectives are not always expressed in the same way. Likewise, simple propositions may be expressed in various forms, forcing us to make judgments about when two sentences say the same thing and when they differ.

Study Questions and Problems

Respond to each of the following questions and problems clearly and precisely.

1) What sorts of additional information besides the premises and conclusion may be found in presentations of arguments in everyday contexts?

2) Using examples, explain why contingent conditional propositions should not be confused with arguments.

3) What should we look for to determine whether a text contains an argument?

4) Explain the function of premise and conclusion indicator words and phrases. Explain why such indicators do not always serve to indicate premises or conclusions.

Part II: Diagramming the Flow of Premises and Conclusions

In identifying arguments, it is useful to diagram the flow from premises to conclusions in a text. Such diagrams give us a visual representation of how the arguments in a text are structured, thus enabling us to assess the arguments more easily. We will use a method of diagramming arguments developed by the philosopher Monroe Beardsley,[1] so the diagrams produced by this method are called **Beardsley diagrams**. We begin by representing the flow from the premises to the conclusion of arguments embedded in texts. Consider the following simple argument:

> **Example 97a:** The social security fund needs to be restructured because there will not be enough contributors in the future to pay for all the fund's commitments after the next twenty years.

We begin by circling the indicator words. In this case, the word "because" indicates that the proposition that follows it is a premise. Next, we bracket the separate propositions in the argument and number them consecutively. Our marked text, then, looks like this:

---

1   See Monroe C. Beardsley, *Practical Logic*, Prentice-Hall, 1950.

Example 97b: (1) {The social security fund needs to be restructured} (because) (2) {there will not be enough contributors in the future to pay for all the fund's commitments after the next twenty years.}

This gives us the following propositions:

(1) **The social security fund needs to be restructured.**

(2) **There will not be enough contributors in the future to pay for all the fund's commitments after the next twenty years.**

Notice that we have separated the sentence into two propositions, since the indicator word separates the sentence into two parts, each of which expresses a separate proposition (see Chapter II on the difference between sentences and propositions). Proposition (2) is a premise, since it is preceded by the premise indicator "because." Even though we do not have a conclusion indicator, it is clear on close reading that (2) is supposed to support (1), so (1) is the conclusion. We can now diagram the flow from premise to conclusion by drawing a vertical arrow from the premise to the conclusion as follows.

This argument has only one premise, which is supposed to support a single conclusion. However, most arguments have more than one premise. When an argument has more than one premise, the premises that are supposed to support its conclusion may function together or they may function independently of one another.

DEFINITION OF DEPENDENT PREMISES (DEPENDENT REASONS):

The premises of an argument are dependent premises if and only if they are supposed to be taken together in support of the conclusion.

For example, an argument with the Modus Ponens form has two premises. Its two premises function together to support its conclusion. Neither premise, by itself, is enough to logically imply the conclusion. Consider the following argument:

Example 98a: If the amount of dust in the atmosphere has increased, then the sunsets will become more spectacular. The amount of dust in the atmosphere has increased. Therefore, the sunsets will become more spectacular.

We begin by circling the indicator words. In this case, the word "therefore" indicates that the proposition that follows it is a conclusion, and we draw a circle around the word. Next we bracket the separate propositions in the argument and number them consecutively. We can, then, mark the text and put it in Modus Ponens form as follows:

Example 98b: (1) {If the amount of dust in the atmosphere has increased, then the sunsets will become more spectacular.}

(2) {The amount of dust in the atmosphere has increased.}

(Therefore), (3) {The sunsets will become more spectacular.}

We may diagram the flow from premises to conclusion by connecting the two premises with a line underlining the two premises and then drawing a vertical arrow from the premise to the conclusion as follows.

Here is a more difficult example, in ordinary English, of an argument with two premises that function together to support a conclusion:

Example 99a: A tremendous amount of money changes hands in disaster cleanups, so ecological disasters are among the greatest contributors to economic growth, since growth means only that money has changed hands.

We begin by circling the indicator words. In this case, the word "so" indicates that the proposition that follows it is a conclusion, so we draw a circle around the word. Also, the word "since" indicates that the proposition that follows it is a premise, and we draw a circle around that word too. Next, we bracket the separate propositions in the argument and number them consecutively. Our marked text, then, looks like this:

Example 99b: (1) {A tremendous amount of money changes hands in disaster cleanups},(so)(2) {ecological disasters are among the greatest contributors to economic growth},(since) (3) {growth means only that money has changed hands.}

This gives us the following propositions:

(1) A tremendous amount of money changes hands in disaster cleanups.

(2) Ecological disasters are among the greatest contributors to economic growth.

(3) Growth means only that money has changed hands.

The indicator word "so" tells us that proposition (2) is the conclusion and is supposed to be supported by (3). But (3) does not function alone. We can see this by noticing that were (3) the only premise, the argument would not be a good one (see the discussion of the Principle of Charity below). If no money changed hands during ecological disasters, it would be possible for (3) to be true and (2) false. However, we see that (1) remedies this deficiency. So (1) and (3) function together to support (2), and the argument will be represented by the following diagram.

While in some arguments premises function together, sometimes we find premises that do not function together to support a conclusion. Each of the premises is, by itself, supposed to support the conclusion. So, were one of the premises to turn out false or be withdrawn, the other would be sufficient to support the conclusion.

DEFINITION OF INDEPENDENT PREMISES (INDEPENDENT REASONS):
The premises of an argument are independent premises if and only if each premise (or set of premises) is supposed to support the conclusion regardless of whether the other premise (or other set of premises) is supposed to support the conclusion.

Consider the following argument:

Example 100a: The plan is bound to fail, since no one is motivated to carry it out. It also must fail because there are not enough resources available to carry it out.

We begin by circling the indicator words. In this case, we would circle the words "since" and "because" to indicate that the proposition that follows each of these words is a premise. Next, we bracket the separate propositions in the argument and number them consecutively. Notice that in this example the propositions "The plan is bound to fail" and "It ... must fail" say the same thing and function as a single conclusion. Hence, we give the two propositions the same number. Finally the word "also" here serves as a structuring term, that is, as a word that tells us that (2) and (3) are independent reasons. We will underline such structuring terms. Our marked text, then, looks like this:

> **Example 100b:** (1) {The plan is bound to fail}, (since) (2) {no one is motivated to carry it out.} (1) {It <u>also</u> must fail} (because) (3) {there are not enough resources available to carry it out.}

This gives us the following propositions:

> (1) **The plan is bound to fail.**
> (2) **No one is motivated to carry it out.**
> (3) **There are not enough resources available to carry it out.**

The indicator words tell us that (2) and (3) are premises, and they both obviously are supposed to support (1). However, as we have noted in this example, (2) is supposed to support (1) independently of whether (3) supports (1), and (3) is supposed to support (1) independently of whether (2) supports (1). So (2) and (3) function independently to support (1), and we represent this independent support by drawing separate arrows from the independent premises to their common conclusion. Hence, the argument will be represented by the following diagram.

More complicated arguments will have some premises that function together and some that function independently. We can combine the elements of the preceding diagrams to represent such arguments. Consider the following argument:

> **Example 101a:** The United States cannot succeed in censoring the Internet, since it is an international system. Any international system is beyond the control of the laws of a single nation. Besides, the net treats any attempt at censorship as a bug. If the system finds a bug, it finds a route around it.

We begin by circling the indicator words. In this case, the word "since" indicates that the proposition that follows it is a premise. The word "besides" is not an indicator of either a premise or a conclusion; it is a structuring term separating two independent parts of the argument. It tells us that the propositions that follow it offer independent reasons. Hence, we do not circle "besides" but instead underline it as a structuring term. Next, we bracket the separate propositions in the argument and number them consecutively. Our marked text, then, looks like this:

Example 101b: (1) {The United States cannot succeed in censoring the Internet}, (since) (2) {it is an international system.} (3) {Any international system is beyond the control of the laws of a single nation.} Besides, (4) {the net treats any attempt at censorship as a bug.} (5) {If the system finds a bug, it finds a route around it.}

This gives us the following propositions:

(1) **The United States cannot succeed in censoring the Internet.**
(2) **It is an international system.**
(3) **Any international system is beyond the control of the laws of a single nation.**
(4) **The net treats any attempt at censorship as a bug.**
(5) **If the system finds a bug, it finds a route around it.**

In this example, the indicator "since" clearly separates propositions (1) and (2), so we are justified in dividing the sentence into separate propositions. In general, **the only cases where we are justified in dividing sentences into separate propositions and numbering them differently is when one part of the sentence functions as a conclusion and the other part functions as a premise.** The indicator word also suggests that (1) is the conclusion. However, as we already noticed, the word "besides" is a **structuring term** which tells us that (2) and (3) function independently from (4) and (5). Premises (2) and (3) function together, since it is not plausible that either could support (1) by itself. Likewise, (4) and (5) function together, since it is not plausible that either could support (1) by itself. This analysis gives us the following diagram.

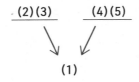

Often a text will contain more than one argument. We have seen that whether a proposition is a premise or a conclusion is relative to its function in an argument. The conclusion of one argument may serve as a premise in another. It is quite common for a conclusion to function in this way as an **intermediate conclusion.**

DEFINITION OF INTERMEDIATE CONCLUSION:
A proposition is an intermediate conclusion if and only if it functions both as the conclusion of one argument and the premise of another argument.

We count arguments by counting conclusions. So when we find an intermediate conclusion serving as a premise in an argument for another conclusion, we have two arguments that are linked together. We can diagram this situation by drawing an arrow from the intermediate conclusion to the main conclusion and a separate arrow to the intermediate conclusion from the premises that support it. Consider the following argument:

> **Example 102a:** Since whoever murdered the victim had to be shorter than six feet tall, we can be sure that the butler was not the murderer, for the butler is six feet five inches tall. And so we are forced to conclude that the murder was the victim's sister, since the murderer was either the butler or the victim's sister.

We begin by circling the indicator words. In this case, the words "since" and "for" indicate that the propositions that follows them are premises. The indicator "since" appears twice and so picks out two separate premises. Also the phrases "we can be sure that" and "And so we are forced to conclude that" both function as conclusion indicators. Next, we bracket the separate propositions in the argument and number them consecutively. Our marked text, then, looks like this:

> **Example 102b:** (Since)(1) {whoever murdered the victim had to be shorter than six feet tall}, (we can be sure that)(2) {the butler was not the murderer,} (for)(3) {the butler is six feet five inches tall.} (And so we are forced to conclude that)(4) {the murderer was the victim's sister}, (since)(5) {the murderer was either the butler or the victim's sister.}

This gives us the following propositions:

(1) **Whoever murdered the victim had to be shorter than six feet tall.**
(2) **The butler was not the murderer.**
(3) **The butler is six feet five inches tall.**
(4) **The murderer was the victim's sister.**
(5) **The murderer was either the butler or the victim's sister.**

In this example, the phrase "we can be sure that" separates the first sentence into two propositions (1) and (2), and along with the word "since" indicates that (2) is a conclusion and (1) a premise that is supposed to support (2). The word "for" indicates that (3) is also a premise that is supposed to support (2). The phrase "so we are forced to conclude that" indicates that (4) is also a conclusion, while the word "since" indicates that (5) is a premise that is supposed to support (4). The question remains whether the two conclusions (2) and (4) are connected to each other. We can see that they are because (5) does not, by itself, give adequate support for (4). For (4) to follow validly from (5), the disjunction in (5) would have to be one premise in a disjunctive syllogism form of argument. To have the second premise in that disjunctive syllogism, it would also have to be true that the butler was not the murderer, and that is just what (2) says. Hence, while (2) is a conclusion from (1) and (3), it is also a premise that functions together with (5) and is supposed to support (4). Therefore, (2) is an intermediate conclusion. This analysis gives us the following diagram.

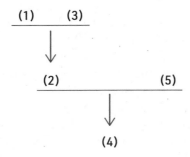

So this example contains an intermediate conclusion linking two arguments together in a chain. Premises (1) and (3) are supposed to support (2), which then serves as a premise that, together with (5), is supposed to support (4).

Study Questions and Problems

Respond to each of the following questions and problems clearly and precisely.

1) How do we tell how many arguments appear in a text?

2) Using examples, explain the difference between dependent and independent premises.

3) What is an intermediate conclusion?

Part III: Principles of Interpretation: Enthymemes[2]

As we have said, arguments arising in everyday contexts seldom get expressed neatly in premises and conclusion form. Arguments may not be presented in order, and they are usually embedded in more complicated contexts. In addition, many arguments are not made completely explicit. It is often the case that one or more of the premises is not stated. The writer may think the premise is too obvious to state, or common knowledge, or may not notice that the premise is missing. Sometimes the conclusion is not stated, and the reader is expected to supply it. Incompletely presented arguments are common enough to have a special name: **enthymemes**. Enthymemes are common because they save needlessly belaboring the trivial or obvious. Enthymemes are also common because people get so habituated to simple argument forms that they fail to notice they have not explicitly stated all the premises. But enthymemes can also be misleading or deceptive; in particular, the unstated premises may be left unstated so as to keep them from being critically examined. For this reason, they can also have strong rhetorical force. As a rhetorical device, for example, the conclusion may not be stated in order to get the audience to draw the conclusion themselves, which may have a persuasive psychological effect. In any case, when analyzing arguments in texts, we need to recognize enthymemes and supply their missing premises (or conclusions).

---

2 This section has benefited greatly from Alec Fisher's *The Logic of Real Arguments* (see Introduction for Students, above), which is highly recommended for more extensive study of the issues herein.

DEFINITION OF ENTHYMEME:
An argument is an enthymeme if and only if it is an argument that leaves either the conclusion or one or more of the premises unstated.

Recognizing enthymemes requires that we correctly interpret the meaning of the text and understand the arguments it presents. The fundamental principle that we use to interpret texts is the principle of charitable interpretation, the **Principle of Charity** (sometimes called the principle of the benefit of the doubt). This principle says that when interpreting, evaluating, reconstructing, or criticizing a text, we interpret it as presenting the best arguments for its conclusions which are compatible with what the text explicitly states.

PRINCIPLE OF CHARITY:
When analyzing and evaluating an argument, one should interpret, reconstruct, and criticize the argument in its strongest form (compatible with the explicit content of the text).

Thus the Principle of Charity says that when alternative interpretations and reconstructions of an argument are possible, we should select the interpretation or reconstruction in which the premises give the strongest support for the conclusion. The restriction that our interpretation or reconstruction be compatible with the explicit content of the text cautions us against reading assumptions into the text that the text does not intend. It warns us against what are usually called straw man fallacies (see below).

The point of the Principle of Charity is to help us to get at the truth. As critical thinkers, we seek the truth. We are not interested in winning a fight but rather in finding the best arguments: those arguments that will lead us to true conclusions by providing adequate support. The Principle of Charity helps us pursue this goal by requiring that, in interpreting texts and in reconstructing and criticizing arguments from those texts, we avoid easily corrected weaknesses. Some (but not all) of the consequences of the Principle of Charity are that it requires that we do the following:

(a) avoid dwelling on trivial matters,
(b) avoid nit-picking over unclarities that can easily be cleared up in the context of the argument (for example, some vague or ambiguous language),
(c) avoid attributing assumptions to the text that are stronger than needed for the argument,

(**d**) avoid dwelling on or exploiting weaknesses that can be easily corrected, and

(**e**) avoid claiming that we have disproven a proposition just because we have shown that one argument for it has failed (there may be other, good arguments for the truth of the proposition).

Moreover, the Principle of Charity tells us that when reading a text, if we can recover only clearly bad arguments from that text, we should suspect that the text does not really present arguments at all. We attribute bad arguments to a text when those arguments are clearly and explicitly presented as arguments. Otherwise, the charitable interpretation is that the text has not presented arguments for its claims at all. In the absence of clear reasons for attributing a bad argument to a text, we should interpret the text as giving good arguments or no arguments at all.

The Principle of Charity, then, is both a matter of respectful and courteous treatment of others' arguments and views and a way of learning and benefiting from those arguments and views. We benefit, because by interpreting arguments in their strongest form, we must then confront the best reasoning the text has to offer. This sort of interpretation is more likely to get us to the truth, because if the argument is a good one, then we have good reason to expect that we have got to the truth of the matter. On the other hand, if we refute the argument in its strongest form, we have good reason to think we have actually refuted the best argument the text can give us. In other words, the Principle of Charity is designed to help us avoid the **straw man fallacy**.

INFORMAL FALLACY: THE STRAW MAN FALLACY

When someone distorts, exaggerates, or misrepresents the actual position someone puts forward and the reasoning they use, then they have committed a straw man fallacy or have given a straw man argument. The fallacy is given this name because by attacking a misrepresentation of a person's actual position, it is as if they set up a straw copy of the person, knock it down, and then pretend to have knocked the real person down. Straw man arguments exhibit the following pattern:

(1) One person presents an argument (or simply expresses a claim or position).

(2) Another person gives a misrepresentation or distorted version of the first person's argument (claim or position).

(3) The person giving the misrepresented or distorted version then criticizes or attacks that distorted version.

(4) The person giving the misrepresented or distorted version then claims to have refuted[3] the original argument.

Straw man arguments are fallacious because even a genuine refutation of a distorted version or misrepresentation of an argument (claim or position) does not undermine the actual argument. To show that an argument is fallacious, we must deal with the actual argument itself, not with some other, weaker argument that may seem similar.

> **Example 103:** Senator Smith: "We should not fund continuing oil exploration, since the oil yet to be discovered is widely distributed and in small pockets. So it would cost more to get this oil out of those areas, than could be recovered in the value of the oil."
>
> Senator Jones: "Senator Smith tells us that we should not fund oil exploration because there is almost no oil left to be found. But studies tell us that there are millions of barrels of oil still in the ground."

In this example, Senator Jones has misrepresented Senator Smith's argument and commits a straw man fallacy. Senator Smith has not argued that there is almost no oil left to be found. She has said that whatever oil there is to be found is not to be found in large enough deposits to make its extraction economically viable. A charitable interpretation of Senator Smith's argument would assume that she would be willing to acknowledge that there may well still be millions of barrels of oil in the ground. For even were that true, it would not refute the argument Smith actually gave.

The Principle of Charity helps us reconstruct missing premises in enthymemes. When an argument neglects to make its premises explicit, then its stated form is usually invalid. In accordance with the Principle of Charity, we should, at the very least, assume that the arguments presented in a text have valid forms. Hence the Principle of Charity suggests the following rule of interpretation; such "rules" are, of course, only guidelines, and as usual there is no substitute for close careful reading of the text and making good judgments.

---

3 All too often the term "refute" is used when all that is warranted is that a claim or position has been denied. To refute a claim is to demonstrate, by using a good argument, that the claim is false, while to deny a claim is merely to say that it is false without having given an argument.

RULE OF INTERPRETATION (1):
When the form of an argument in a text is invalid, try to add one premise that will make its form into a valid argument form.

Here, knowing the simple argument forms described in Chapter V will be invaluable, because we can sometimes reconstruct the missing premises of an enthymeme by completing one of these simple valid forms. Consider the following example:

> **Example 104:** Since Natasha rollerblades every day, it follows that she must be in good shape.

This argument has the form

P = **Natasha rollerblades everyday.**
Q = **Natasha is in good shape.**

(1) P
_____
∴ (2) Q

This, of course, is not a valid argument form. However, it can easily be transformed into a valid argument form by adding the premise "If Natasha rollerblades every day, then she is in good shape." This conditional premise completes the valid argument form of Modus Ponens. The argument now says,

> [If Natasha rollerblades everyday, then she is in good shape.] Since Natasha rollerblades everyday, it follows that she must be in good shape.

Where the conditional (in the brackets and small type) supplies the unstated premise.

This example illustrates a technique for reconstructing enthymemes called **conditionalizing the argument**. Whenever we are confronted with a conclusion that is not connected with its premises, we can add an appropriate conditional as a missing premise and produce a valid argument. The technique of conditionalizing the argument should be used only when there is no other clear and direct way of reconstructing a valid argument. This technique can easily be overused. In arguments with many premises, the technique of conditionalizing the argument can lead to awkward and overly complicated premises that are difficult to understand and whose truth value is difficult to assess. Conditionalizing arguments is a common technique because people often leave out conditional premises, and we have seen how important conditional propositions are. Leaving conditional propositions out tends to make us think claims are unconditional or merely lists of unconnected "opinions" when the arguments given are really enthymemes.

In the following example, conditionalizing the argument is clearly not the best way to reconstruct the missing premises, since there is a much simpler way of providing the enthymeme with a valid form.

Example 105: If Natasha is in good shape, then she exercises regularly. It follows that she must not be in good shape.

This argument has the invalid form

P = Natasha is in good shape.
Q = Natasha exercises regularly.

(1) P → Q
―――――――
∴ (2) ~ P

It is much too complicated and also unnecessary to reconstruct a valid form for this argument by conditionalizing the argument. That would lead us to add the unnecessarily complicated premise "If if Natasha is in good shape, then she exercises regularly, then Natasha is not in good shape." Instead, we should add the much simpler premise "Natasha does not exercise regularly." Adding this premise completes the valid argument form of Modus Tollens. The premise is easier to understand and, because of its simplicity, it is easier to assess its truth value. So while many arguments can be given a valid argument form by adding a conditional as a premise of a certain form, this method of supplying missing premises should be used only as a last resort.

When drawing the diagram of an argument with an unstated premise, we use capital letters to mark the unstated premises. So the diagram for this example will look as follows.

(1)   (A)
―――――――――――
         │
         ↓
        (2)

Where (A) stands for the unstated premise "Natasha does not exercise regularly."

These examples also demonstrate two other rules for interpreting and reconstructing the missing premises of enthymemes:

RULE OF INTERPRETATION (2):
State the missing premises as simply and clearly as possible, so that it is as easy as possible to determine their truth values.

RULE OF INTERPRETATION (3):
When reconstructing enthymemes, use only the minimum information required to provide the argument with a valid form.

In accordance with rule (2), we should not make the missing premises any more complicated than necessary, because the more complicated a proposition is, the harder it is to make good judgments about its truth value. So in the previous example, it is difficult to judge the truth value of the complicated premise "If if Natasha is in good shape, then she exercises regularly, then Natasha is not in good shape." This gives another reason to treat conditionalizing an argument as a last resort, since determining the truth value of the appropriate conditional to add to an argument is nearly as difficult as determining the validity of the argument. (Determining the actual truth value of the added conditional is not the same as determining the validity of the argument, because, even if the conditional is actually true, that does not mean that it states a logical implication.)

In accordance with rule (3), we should not interpret a text as stating any premise stronger than is strictly necessary to make its form valid. If we fail to follow this rule, we are likely to produce a straw man argument and treat the text unfairly. Consider the following example.

Example 106: Whales must be warm blooded, because they are mammals.

In this example, the argument is an enthymeme whose form can be completed by adding the premise "If something is an animal, then it is warm blooded." Adding this premise would, of course, make the argument valid because whales are animals. However, this premise is a far stronger claim than is necessary to give the argument a valid form. We could, instead, add the premise "If something is a mammal, then it is warm blooded." This would also make the argument valid. Moreover, since this premise is true, adding it also makes the argument sound, where the former premise is false and would have made the argument unsound. Were we to add the stronger premise, we would commit a straw man fallacy and violate the Principle of Charity.

Finally, in accordance with both rules (2) and (3), we should add only premises that are both relevant and make a significant difference to the argument. We are, after all, trying to understand what the text says, and the Principle of Charity tells us that we should try to read the text as making the best argument possible compatible with what the text explicitly states. We should, then, read the text carefully and only add premises that give a valid form to the argument the text actually gives. We should not add premises, even if they give good reasons, unless they are directly relevant to what the text actually says. We may think that there are better reasons in support of a conclusion than those given by the text, but that does not justify us in assuming that the text gives those reasons.

> **Example 107:** The government of Turkey restricts the activities of its Kurdish minority, because the Turkish government does not allow the Kurds to travel freely within the borders of Turkey.

It is legitimate to treat this as an enthymeme and add the premise "Either the Turkish government allows the Kurds to travel freely within the borders of Turkey, or it restricts the activities of its Kurdish minority." It would not, however, be legitimate to add the premise "When any government does not allow its citizens to travel freely within its own borders, it restricts their activities, is morally wrong, and violates the citizens' rights." This proposition is more general than warranted by the text (it speaks of "any government," not just the Turkish government) and it brings in matters (issues about rights and morality) beyond anything mentioned in the text. While we may feel that these issues are important and should be raised when considering the treatment of the Kurds in Turkey, these issues are not raised in the text. The text does not make these claims, and we should not assume that it does.

STEPS FOR ARGUMENT ANALYSIS

The procedure for analyzing arguments we have been developing can be summarized in the following steps.

(1) Carefully read the passage as a whole.

(2) Circle any indicator words, noting whether they indicate premises or conclusions, and underline structuring terms and note how they structure the flow of argument into dependent or independent reasons.

(3) Bracket the sentences in the passage.
   (a) In general, bracket sentences before the initial word and after the final period.
   (b) Place brackets at the ends of sentences before indicator words and at the beginnings of sentences after indicator words. Do *not* include indicator words or structuring terms within the brackets.
     One should only break up sentences into more than one part, when one part of the sentence functions as a premise and another part functions as a conclusion. In other words:
   (c) Break up sentences when indicator words appear in sentences where one of the parts separated by the indicators functions as a premise and another part functions as a conclusion.
   (d) One may also break up sentences into separate sentences when doing so is necessary to make sense of the argument.
   (e) Do *not* break up conditional sentences (those connected by "If..., then...."), nor disjunctive sentences (those connected by "Either..., or...").
   (f) Since conjunctions are true only when both conjuncts are true, a conjunction can either be left whole or divided into separate propositions. However, this is possible only when the conjunction is the main connective in the proposition.

(4) Number the bracketed sentences consecutively.

(5) Locate and identify the main conclusion (paraphrasing when necessary).

(6) Locate and identify premises purporting to support the main conclusion (paraphrasing when necessary).

(7) Determine if any of the premises are intermediary conclusions relative to the main conclusion, and if so which premises are supposed to support these intermediary conclusions.

(8) Determine whether premises provide dependent or independent reasons for the conclusions they are supposed to support.

(9) Identify any unstated premises or unstated conclusions when necessary.

(10) Draw a diagram of the flow of premises and conclusions (using the numbers of the bracketed sentences) which shows the flow of the argument or arguments embedded in the passage.

Consider the following example of the analysis of a complex argument using some of the basic argument forms. We will analyze this argument step by step using the above procedure and then symbolize the results in our notation and evaluate the arguments.

Example 108a: Values are not merely matters of opinion. If values were merely matters of opinion, then value judgments would be arbitrary. But value judgments are not arbitrary. For if value judgments were arbitrary, then there would not be any wrong answers to questions of value. But there are wrong answers to questions of value. Shooting my friend is the wrong way to solve her dating problems. If shooting my friend is the wrong way to solve her dating problems, then there is a wrong answer to a question of value.

After reading this paragraph over several times (step (1)), we can see that it contains more than one argument. For one thing, the subject matter shifts from the general consideration of value judgments to the specific case of solving the friend's dating problem. We can perform steps (2), (3), and (4) immediately, as follows.

Example 108b: (1) {Values are not merely matters of opinion.} (2) {If values were merely matters of opinion, then value judgments would be arbitrary.} But (3) {value judgments are not arbitrary.} (For) (4) {if value judgments were arbitrary, then there would not be any wrong answers to questions of value.} But (5) {there are wrong answers to questions of value.} (6) {Shooting my friend is the wrong way to solve her dating problems.} (7) {If Shooting my friend is the wrong way to solve her dating problems, then there is a wrong answer to a question of value.}

We now proceed to identify premises and conclusions and any intermediate conclusions, following steps (5), (6), and (7). We can see that our suspicion that there are several arguments present is well founded, because some propositions seem to act as intermediate conclusions. Proposition (5) functions as a conclusion with respect to propositions (6) and (7), for propositions (6) and (7) have the form of a Modus Ponens argument. Yet proposition (5) also functions as a premise with respect to proposition (3), since proposition (5) along with proposition (4) have the form of a Modus Tollens argument. Also, proposition (3) functions as a conclusion with respect to propositions (4) and

(5), and proposition (3) also functions as a premise with respect to proposition (1) because proposition (3) along with proposition (2) also have the form of a Modus Tollens argument.

The premises in the argument forms of Modus Ponens and Modus Tollens are dependent premises (step (8)), and there do not seem to be any unstated premises (step (9)). So we can now draw the diagram of the flow of premises and conclusions (step (10)) as follows.

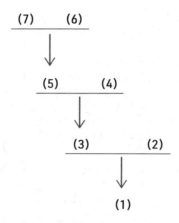

These separate arguments can be summarized as follows.

Arg 1:   (7) If shooting my friend is the wrong way to solve her dating problems, then there are wrong answers to questions of value.
(6) Shooting my friend is the wrong way to solve her dating problems.

Therefore, (5) there are wrong answers to questions of value.

Arg 2:   (4) If value judgments are arbitrary, then it is not the case that there are wrong answers to questions of value.
(5) There are wrong answers to questions of value.

Therefore, (3) it is not the case that value judgments are arbitrary.

Arg 3:   (2) If values are merely matters of opinion, then value judgments are arbitrary.
(3) It is not the case that value judgments are arbitrary.

Therefore, (1) it is not the case that values are merely matters of opinion.

Let the following letters stand for the indicated propositions:

> **P = Values are merely matters of opinion.**
> **Q = Value judgments are arbitrary.**
> **R = There are wrong answers to questions of value.**
> **U = Shooting my friend is the wrong way to solve her dating problems.**

We can represent the three arguments as follows:

Arg 1:	Arg 2:	Arg 3:
(7) U → R	(4) Q → (~ R)	(2) P → Q
(6) U	(5) R	(3) ~ Q
∴ (5) R	∴ (3) ~ Q	∴ (1) ~ P

Since each of these is a valid argument form, the sequence of arguments is valid. Notice that to see if these arguments are sound, we have only to assess the truth values of premises (7), (6), (4), and (2). Premises (3) and (5) are supported by valid arguments and so must be true if their premises are true.

In steps (5) and (6), we have added that in identifying the premises and conclusion, we should paraphrase the propositions when necessary. Sentences are often phrased in different ways and yet still express the same proposition (see Example 100a). Writers may use complicated language, repeat propositions, and add supplementary or unnecessary material. In extracting the arguments from a text, we must simplify and paraphrase these sentences, so that we can display the meaning of the text more clearly.

Consider the following example:

> **Example 109a:** Without a doubt, it is abundantly clear that our water resources are in dire need of protection and the guardianship of the concerned citizens of Colorado. The citizens of this state cannot sit idly by and allow irresponsible corporations and other uncaring polluters license to destroy our beloved lakes and rivers. We all know this. There is little room for doubt. Therefore, there can be no retreat in face of the fact that citizens of Colorado must band together and act in unison to stop the unscrupulous and senseless destruction of our precious waters by voting for referendum 42.

This paragraph is long-winded and filled with phrases designed to flatter the reader and revile its adversaries. Phrases like "without a doubt" and "it is abundantly clear that" are merely meant to coax the reader into being well disposed toward the text's position. The sentences "We all know this" and "There is little room for doubt" are either superfluous or question begging. Adjectives like "unscrupulous and senseless" and "precious" have rhetorical force as dysphemisms and euphemisms, but they add nothing to the content of the argument. All of these phrases and sentences are extraneous to the argument, which can be paraphrased simply without losing any of its meaning. The argument can be paraphrased by eliminating the superfluous material, identifying what is essential to the argument, and paraphrasing it into straightforward, simple prose. We begin by underlining the essential phrases and striking out superfluous ones:

> Example 109b: ~~Without a doubt, it is abundantly clear that~~ <u>our water resources</u> ~~are in dire~~ <u>need</u> ~~of~~ <u>protection</u> ~~and the guardianship of the concerned citizens of Colorado.~~ <u>The citizens of this state cannot</u> ~~sit idly by and~~ <u>allow</u> ~~irresponsible~~ <u>corporations and other</u> ~~uncaring~~ <u>polluters</u> ~~license~~ <u>to destroy our</u> ~~beloved~~ <u>lakes and rivers</u>. ~~We all know this. There is little room for doubt.~~ <u>Therefore,</u> ~~there can be no retreat in face of the fact that~~ <u>citizens of Colorado, must</u> ~~band together and act in unison to~~ <u>stop the</u> ~~unscrupulous and senseless~~ <u>destruction of our</u> ~~precious~~ <u>waters by voting for referendum 42.</u>

Now we can paraphrase the second sentence as "Citizens of Colorado should prevent corporations and other polluters from destroying our water resources." We also paraphrase the reference to "lakes and rivers" with the term "water resources," since the two phrases amount to the same thing for the purposes of this argument. We also need to add the unstated premise "If referendum 42 passes, then it will prevent corporations and other polluters from destroying our water resources," since the text clearly assumes that the passage of this referendum will stop the destruction of water resources. So the actual argument now reads as follows:

> Example 109c: Our water resources need protection. Citizens of Colorado should prevent corporations and other polluters from destroying our water resources. If referendum 42 passes, then it will prevent corporations and other polluters from destroying our water resources. Therefore, citizens of Colorado should vote for referendum 42.

By eliminating superfluous material and by using careful paraphrases that pay attention to the meaning of the text, we are able to extract the argument from the text.

Paraphrasing requires careful attention to the meaning of the text. We need to be able to distill the core of what the text says without distorting its meaning. Assessing the meaning of a text requires careful attention to the details of the text and may require several careful readings. Attention to those aspects of the text that are not part of the argument (see the beginning of this chapter) often helps to clarify the meaning of the argument. Considering these other aspects of the text will give us some understanding of the author's attitudes and purposes and will help us identify the conclusions of the arguments by directing our attention to the point of the text. These aspects of the text also help us to recognize rhetorical questions, ironic and satirical comments, and other figures of speech and not mistake them for literal claims.

How do we decide what a sentence means? Of course, to do this, we must depend on our intuitive understanding of English, along with hints we can derive from context. However, in addition, discovering the meaning of a sentence that is part of an argument demands that we sort out how the proposition it expresses fits into the argument in which it functions. We have said that to count as a proposition a sentence expressing it must be able to be either true or false. Hence, to understand what a sentence means, it is a necessary condition (although not a sufficient condition) that we be able to give some sort of account of what argument would show whether the sentence was true or false. If we can give no account of how we would decide whether a sentence was true or false, then we do not understand the sentence.

THE MEANING PRINCIPLE:
Understanding the meaning of a sentence requires that we at least be able to give an account of what would make that sentence true and what would make that sentence false.

As a necessary condition for assessing the meaning of a sentence, this suggests a close connection between meaning and argument. It suggests that we can use this connection to help us identify the premises of an argument once we have identified its conclusion, for by assessing the meaning of the conclusion, we will be able to suggest what a good argument in support of that conclusion would look like, and we may be able to construct an argument that would support the conclusion. Since we grasp the meaning of the conclusion partly from the text and context in which it is embedded, we will be able to construct an argument that could, plausibly, be the one given in the text. This means that by asking how the conclusion could be justified, we can find premises that the text is likely to give in support of this conclusion. Then we need to read through the text to see if it states those premises we think it is likely to give. If the text asserts these propositions, then those propositions are probably the premises the text uses to support its conclusion. The text may, of course, not state these premises in the way we have but may instead contain claims that amount to the same thing as the premises we have suggested. As always, there is no substitute for close careful reading.

We may call the principle we are using here the **justification principle**. We may state it as follows:

THE JUSTIFICATION PRINCIPLE:
When reading a text, one way to discover the premises of an argument is to ask what good argument, consistent with the text, would justify this conclusion.

We can state the question the justification principle asks as follows:

What good argument would justify this conclusion as true?

This question asks what we would have to know, what premises would have to be true, for us to be justified in accepting the conclusion given in the text. Then, in accordance with the justification principle, we look to see if the text contains those premises. Consider the following example taken from "Psychiatry for Everyday Needs" by William C. Menninger:[4]

> **Example 110a:** First the personality and character—which are really synonymous—take their form during the first six or eight years of life. During this period of infancy and childhood, we select and develop the techniques which gain us satisfaction, defend us against threats, and become the tools in coping with the endless variety of problem situations that will be encountered later in life. It is during this time that we develop our methods of relating ourselves to other people and undergo the experiences which determine the strengths and weaknesses within our personality. As adults we are not able to remember the details of these formative years. Therefore, we cannot understand our own behavior fully.

Let us circle the indicator words, and number and bracket the propositions in this paragraph.

---

4 This argument is taken from www.bonevac.info/deduction/Deduction1answers.pdf, which is reproduced from chapter 1 in Daniel Bonevac, *Deduction: Introductory Symbolic Logic*, 2nd ed., Wiley-Blackwell, 2002.

Example 110b: (1) {First the personality and character—which are really synonymous—take their form during the first six or eight years of life.} (2) {During this period of infancy and childhood, we select and develop the techniques which gain us satisfaction, defend us against threats, and become the tools in coping with the endless variety of problem situations that will be encountered later in life.} (3) {It is during this time that we develop our methods of relating ourselves to other people and undergo the experiences which determine the strengths and weaknesses within our personality.} (4) {As adults we are not able to remember the details of these formative years.} (Therefore) (5) {we cannot understand our own behavior fully.}

The conclusion—"We cannot understand our own behavior fully"—is indicated by the word "therefore" in the last sentence, (5). Now let us ask what would have to be true to justify this proposition. Clearly, if there were some piece of our behavior that we could not understand, then this conclusion would be true. However, perhaps this is too strong. As stated, the conclusion does not say that there is a particular piece of our behavior that we can never understand; all it says is that some piece or other of our behavior will always escape our understanding. So all we would really need to know to justify this conclusion is that no matter how much of our behavior we come to understand, there would always be some remaining piece of our behavior that escapes our understanding. This means that the premises that would support this conclusion would have to give us some reason for thinking that not all of our behavior is accessible to us.

When we go back and read the paragraph again, this is just what we find. Proposition (4) says that we cannot remember the details of our formative years. Proposition (3) says that it is in our formative years that our personality is determined. Finally, if we interpret proposition (2) as saying that our personality determines our behavior later in life, (2) states that our later behavior is determined by the formation of our personality. This gives us much of what we were seeking. However, the conclusion is about understanding our behavior, and none of the other propositions in the paragraph mentions understanding behavior. But (2), (3), and (4) together say that we cannot remember what formed our personality and that our personality is responsible for determining whether we will behave one way or another. All we need to add is that understanding our behavior requires that we understand what determines whether we will behave one way or another. Once we have added this unstated premise, we have found an argument in the form that our answer to the justification question led us to expect.

This analysis was made easier by applying the justification principle. Notice that we did not have to use sentence (1). The reason for this is that (2) gives us all we need from (1). What (1) does is tell us that "personality" and "character" count as synonymous for the purposes of this discussion and that the personality is formed in our infancy and early childhood. But the former was not something that we needed to justify the conclusion, and the latter is already part of what (2) says. So (1) is not part of the argument.

We can use the justification principle to find the premises of arguments in longer texts by using the same procedures. The justification principle helps us separate the premises from the other claims in the text.

Study Questions and Problems

Respond to each of the following questions and problems clearly and precisely.

1) What is an enthymeme?

2) Explain the Principle of Charity, what it is, and why it is important.

3) Explain what has gone wrong when someone commits a straw man fallacy.

4) What rule of interpretation is suggested by the Principle of Charity? Why?

5) What is meant by conditionalizing the argument? Why should it not be overused in reconstructing arguments?

6) Using examples, explain the point of the second and third rules of interpretation.

7) List and explain the steps for analyzing arguments in texts.

8) How do we decide what a sentence (that is part of an argument) means?

9) State and explain the point of the justification principle.

Part IV: Argument Assessment Strategies

To conclude, we will consider some ways in which we may assess arguments expressed in ordinary English. We begin by recalling (from Chapter I, Part II) that there are two separate questions that must be answered in assessing any argument:

> **(1) Do the premises support the conclusion?**
> **(2) Are the premises all true?**

The answers to these questions, as noted earlier, are independent of each other. Furthermore (as discussed in Chapter V, Part III), there are three ways to answer question (2):

> (1) we may give arguments to support the original argument's premises,
>
> (2) we may assess the unsupported premises to see if it is reasonable to accept them without argument, or
>
> (3) we may accept the original argument's premises provisionally as suppositions.

In case (3), there is no need to answer question (2). In case (1), if a premise **P** is supported by another argument, then we have to assess that other argument. We do not need to consider anything more than this other argument to assess the truth of the premise **P**. This is one of the great benefits of critical reasoning. We need not consider the truth value of every proposition separately or on its own. When we give or find arguments, the truth values of some propositions depend on the truth values of other propositions, so we need assess only the truth values of the unsupported premises, as in case (2). The assessment of the arguments provides all the assessment we need of the truth values of the intermediate and final conclusions. We have discussed above (Chapter V, Part III) how to assess the truth values of unsupported claims. Nothing of this changes when we confront arguments expressed in ordinary English.

(A) ASSESSING THE VALIDITY OF ARGUMENTS IN ORDINARY ENGLISH

The only other difficulties we need to consider concern our answer to question (1): Do the premises support the conclusion? Even here we can go a long way with the techniques we have learned up to this point. We can use the techniques we have developed to translate an argument from ordinary English into our notation and then use one of the techniques for testing validity to determine whether the premises support the conclusion.

However, if we cannot translate the argument into our notation, we have to find other ways of using what we have learned about arguments to assess whether the premises support the conclusion. In such cases, we can use our understanding of validity to adapt the procedures analogous to those we used in the short-cut truth table method of assessing validity, so that we may assess whether the premises of an argument give deductive support to its conclusion. We recall that the definition of validity states that a deductive argument is valid if and only if it is impossible for the premises to be true and the conclusion false together. The short-cut truth table method exploits this definition. In each case, we attempt to find an assignment of truth values to the simple propositions such that it would make the premises true and the conclusion false together. If we find such an assignment of truth values, it demonstrates that the argument is invalid.

Similarly, we may ask of any deductive argument whether it is possible to conceive of a case in which the premises are all true and the conclusion false. If such a case is even conceivable, then the argument is invalid. After all, deductive arguments suppose that it is *impossible* for the premises to be true and the conclusion false. So if we can tell a logically consistent story in which the premises of an argument would be true and the conclusion false, then it is at least possible for the premises to be true and the conclusion false, in which case the argument is invalid. This is a method of counterexample, similar to the method we used to test the adequacy of definitional propositions (Chapter V, Part II (D) and Appendix), only here we are searching for counterexamples to the claim that the premises of an argument support its conclusion.

We can invent counterexamples of this sort by constructing an appropriate story building on the content of the argument in question. Telling such stories requires that we read the argument carefully and that we imagine alternative possibilities. Remember that the story need not be true; it need only be conceivable, that is, possibly true. Here we see that good critical thinking calls for us to exercise our imaginations. We must be able to imagine logically possible circumstances, regardless of whether what we imagine actually occurs.

Here is a very simple example:

Example 111:   If it is raining, then the streets are wet. The streets are wet, so it
is raining.

Now, we could use our techniques of analysis and translate this argument into our notation and then test it for validity using the methods we developed earlier.

(In fact, this turns out to be an instance of the formal fallacy of affirming the consequent.) But we can also approach this argument directly. Can we imagine a case where the premises "If it is raining, then the streets are wet" and "The streets are wet" are true and the conclusion "it is raining" false? The answer is yes. We can easily imagine that it is a sunny, rainless day and that the streets are wet, since the streets could get wet some other way. For instance, a fire hydrant could break, or the city might clean the streets with a machine that wets them down. In either case, we have imagined a possible story in which the premises would be true and the conclusion false. This shows that the argument is invalid.

Let us consider a slightly more complicated example.

> **Example 112:** Vagabond Travel Company is unable to pay the interest on its debts. All bankrupt companies are companies unable to pay the interest on their debts. Consequently, Vagabond Travel Company is bankrupt.

This example is not easily translated into our notation. However, we can still test it for validity by asking whether we can think of a possible case where the premises "Vagabond Travel Company is unable to pay the interest on its debts" and "All bankrupt companies are companies unable to pay the interest on their debts" are both true and yet it is false that "Vagabond Travel Company is bankrupt." Again the answer is yes, we can imagine such a case: the premise "All bankrupt companies are companies unable to pay the interest on their debts" does not say that all companies unable to pay the interest on their debts are bankrupt (this difference arises from the difference between necessary conditions and sufficient conditions; see Chapter III, Part IV). It is possible that there are companies unable to pay the interest on their debts that are not bankrupt, so we may imagine that Vagabond Travel is not one of the bankrupt companies, even though it cannot pay the interest on its debts. If this were the case, then the premises of the argument would be true and the conclusion false. Since it is possible that the premises be true and the conclusion false, the argument is invalid.

(B) ASSESSING INDUCTIVE ARGUMENTS

We have been concerned mainly with deductive arguments. We have done this because the principles that govern deductive arguments most clearly exhibit the central features of good critical thinking. However, something more should be said about inductive arguments. Many arguments we encounter in ordinary situations are inductive arguments. The methods for assessing such arguments are complicated, involving the techniques of experimental science, the theory of probability, and techniques of statistical analysis. These topics are best studied in courses that deal with such topics; however, even without exploring these complicated methods of assessing inductive arguments, we should still take note of a simple informal fallacy commonly committed when confronted with inductive reasoning. One form (although not the only form) of inductive reasoning consists in reasoning from the properties of an observed sample taken from a large population to conclude that the whole population has the same properties as the observed sample. This can be a legitimate form of reasoning, so long as the sample is truly representative of the population. There are several features that samples may have or lack that are relevant to determining whether they are representative. For one, the sample must be typical of the population it is supposed to represent. In general, when we cannot show that the sample is typical of the population, we choose a random sample. In addition, the larger the sample size, the better the inductive argument will be. When this last feature is ignored, we may fall prey to the **fallacy of hasty generalization.**

Informal Fallacy: Hasty Generalization

A fallacy of hasty generalization occurs when the size of the sample is too small, or not sufficiently representative of the population, to support the conclusion.

> **Example 113:** Three players in the National Football League tested positive for performance-enhancing drugs last week. It is likely that most athletes use such drugs to give them an edge in the competition.

Here the sample consists of the three National Football League (NFL) players who tested positive for performance-enhancing drugs last week, and the population is most athletes. There are several points to note about this argument. First of all, it commits a fallacy of hasty generalization because the sample is far too small in relation to the size of the population. The population consisting of most athletes is very large; a sample of three of these is far too small to be representative. In addition to the fallacy of hasty generalization, the sample fails to be representative in other ways. What applies to participants in one sport may not apply to participants in other sports. There is little reason to think that what goes on in the NFL is representative of what happens in other sports. Moreover, nothing is mentioned about differences between professional and amateur sports. "Most athletes" includes a great deal of diversity, for example, players of little league baseball, weekend tennis players in local tennis clubs, and professional curlers. The interests and practices of these and other athletes will likely differ so much from the three NFL players that the sample will not represent the population. Finally, the sample was selected with an already built-in bias; instead of selecting players at random, the argument selects examples that have already been found to use performance-enhancing drugs. Any focus on this sample will significantly bias and undermine the legitimacy of the argument; instead, the sample should be drawn at least from all players in the league (or given the conclusion, from all athletes) and then determine how many of all the players are using such drugs. When confronted with an inductive argument of this sort, we should, therefore, identify the size of the sample and the size of the population and then see if the sample size is too small or, because of its specific features, unrepresentative of the population.

Study Questions and Problems

Respond to each of the following questions and problems clearly and precisely.

1) Explain how critical thinking eliminates the need to determine the truth value of every proposition on its own.

2) How does the short-cut truth table method of testing validity serve as a model for testing the validity of arguments that cannot be translated into our symbolism?

3) What is the role of imagination in determining the validity of deductive arguments?

4) What features must a sample have so that the sample can be used in good inductive arguments?

5) Explain what has gone wrong when someone commits the fallacy of hasty generalization.

Exercises: Complete Argument Analyses

For each of the following arguments:
(a) Circle the indicator words and say what they indicate.
(b) Place each of the propositions relevant to the arguments in brackets and number them consecutively.
(c) Draw the Beardsley diagram mapping the flow of premises and conclusions.
(d) Abstract its propositional form.
(e) Test it for validity.

1) The litmus paper turns red only if the solution is acid. Hence, if the litmus paper turns red, then either the solution is acid or something is wrong in the experiment.

2) If the victim had money in his pockets, then robbery was not the motive for the crime. But robbery or vengeance was the motive for the crime. The victim did not have money in his pockets. Therefore, vengeance was the motive for the crime.

3) If the laws are good and their enforcement is strict, then crime will diminish. If strict enforcement of laws will make crime diminish, then our problem is a practical one. The laws are good. Therefore, our problem is a practical one.

4) If the first disjunct of a disjunction is true, the disjunction as a whole is true. So, if both the first and second disjuncts of the disjunction are true, then the disjunction as a whole is true. We may also argue that if the second disjunct of a disjunction is true, the disjunction as a whole is true. So, again, if both the first and second disjuncts of the disjunction are true, then the disjunction as a whole is true.

5) One of the servants is implicated. Because, either the robber came in the door, or else the crime was an inside job and one of the servants is implicated. And because the robber could come in the door only if the latch had been raised from the inside; however, if one of the servants is surely implicated, then the latch had been raised from the inside.

6) The man knew (because of the special circumstances of the incident) that publicity about the matter would wreck his career.

If so, then he wouldn't have telephoned the police unless he had actually been blackmailed. Since he did not call the police, he must have been blackmailed.

7) The speed of an object varies in inverse proportion to the resistance provided by the medium in which the object is moving. Assuming this is so, then if there exists a perfect vacuum, any body moving through it would have an infinite speed. However, no body could have an infinite speed—even in a vacuum. This means there is no perfect vacuum. If there is no perfect vacuum, then there must always be resistance to motion. Hence, there is always resistance to any motion.

8) Lung cancer is more common among male smokers than it is among female smokers. If smoking were the cause of lung cancer, this would not be true. The fact that lung cancer is more common among male smokers means that it is caused by something in the male make-up. It follows that lung cancer is not caused by smoking but by something in the male make-up.

9) If you have free will, then the consequences of your actions cannot be predicted. For if you have free will, then your actions are not determined by any antecedent events. And if you have free will, then if your actions are not determined by any antecedent events, then your actions cannot be predicted. But your actions cannot be predicted if the consequences of your actions cannot be predicted.

10) Either the new courthouse will have an inconvenient location or it will be inadequate to its functions. For, if the new courthouse is to be conveniently located, it will have to be situated in the heart of the city; and if it is to be adequate to its function, it will have to be built large enough to house all the city offices. If the new courthouse is situated in the heart of the city and is built large enough to house all the city offices, then its cost will run to over a million dollars. But, its costs cannot exceed a million dollars.

From the Publisher

A name never says it all, but the word "Broadview" expresses a good deal
of the philosophy behind our company. We are open to a broad range of
academic approaches and political viewpoints. We pay attention to the
broad impact book publishing and book printing has in the wider world;
for some years now we have used 100% recycled paper for most titles.
Our publishing program is internationally oriented and broad-ranging.
Our individual titles often appeal to a broad readership too; many are
of interest as much to general readers as to academics and students.

Founded in 1985, Broadview remains a fully independent
company owned by its shareholders—not an imprint
or subsidiary of a larger multinational.

For the most accurate information on our books (including
information on pricing, editions, and formats) please
visit our website at www.broadviewpress.com. Our print
books and ebooks are available for sale on our site.

broadview press

www.broadviewpress.com

The interior of this book is printed on 100% recycled paper.

100%

TCF

PERMANENT